I0427681

PREFACE

1. Scope

This publication provides joint doctrine for the conduct of amphibious operations.

2. Purpose

This publication has been prepared under the direction of the Chairman of the Joint Chiefs of Staff. It sets forth joint doctrine to govern the activities and performance of the Armed Forces of the United States in joint operations and provides the doctrinal basis for interagency coordination and for US military involvement in multinational operations. It provides military guidance for the exercise of authority by combatant commanders and other joint force commanders (JFCs) and prescribes joint doctrine for operations, education, and training. It provides military guidance for use by the Armed Forces in preparing their appropriate plans. It is not the intent of this publication to restrict the authority of the JFC from organizing the force and executing the mission in a manner the JFC deems most appropriate to ensure unity of effort in the accomplishment of the overall objective.

3. Application

a. Joint doctrine established in this publication applies to the Joint Staff, commanders of combatant commands, subunified commands, joint task forces, subordinate components of these commands, and the Services.

b. The guidance in this publication is authoritative; as such, this doctrine will be followed except when, in the judgment of the commander, exceptional circumstances dictate otherwise. If conflicts arise between the contents of this publication and the contents of Service publications, this publication will take precedence unless the Chairman of the Joint Chiefs of Staff, normally in coordination with the other members of the Joint Chiefs of Staff, has provided more current and specific guidance. Commanders of forces operating as part of a multinational (alliance or coalition) military command should follow multinational doctrine and procedures ratified by the United States. For doctrine and procedures not ratified by the United States, commanders should evaluate and follow the multinational command's doctrine and procedures, where applicable and consistent with US law, regulations, and doctrine.

For the Chairman of the Joint Chiefs of Staff:

B.E. Grooms
Rear Admiral, USN
Vice Director, Joint Staff

i

Intentionally Blank

- **Updates and harmonizes discussion of amphibious operations with the constructs and context of the keystone and capstone joint publications.**

- **Simplifies and reorganizes organization of text to facilitate comprehension and remove redundancy.**

- **Reclassifies the five types of amphibious operations by replacing "other amphibious operations" with "amphibious support to other operations." The five types of amphibious operations are: amphibious assault, amphibious raid, amphibious demonstration, amphibious withdrawal, and amphibious support to other operations**

- **Updates discussion of the landing force to address the Marine Special Operations Company.**

- **Realigns Chapter III, Conduct of Amphibious Operations, by removing dated constructs, organizations, capabilities, and terminology and improving the flow of the material presented.**

- **Updates Chapter V to more accurately reflect extant capabilities, procedures, and processes.**

- **Adds an appendix on Landing Force Logistics Planning.**

- **Glossary has been significantly revised by deleting outdated terms, modifying and adding a number of definitions, and properly sourcing all terms.**

- **Modifies the definitions of the terms "action phase," "advance force," "afloat pre-positioning force", "amphibious assault ship (multipurpose)", "amphibious construction battalion", " amphibious objective area", "approach schedule", "assault phase", "assault schedule", "attack group", "beach party", "boat lane", "carrier strike group", "causeway launching area", "command element", "commander, amphibious task force", "commander. landing force", "composite warfare commander", "covering fire", "dock landing ship", "follow-up shipping", "hydrographic reconnaissance", "landing area", "landing area diagram", "line of departure", "naval beach group", "planning directive", "planning phase", "preassault operations", "regimental landing team", "seabasing", "ship-to-shore movement", "target information center", "times", "transport group", and "wave".**

- **Removes the terms "amphibious assault area," "amphibious assault landing," "amphibious chart", "amphibious command ship", "amphibious control group", "amphibious group", "amphibious objective study", "amphibious reconnaissance", "amphibious reconnaissance unit", "amphibious striking forces", "assault area", "assault area diagram", "beach minefield", "beach organization", "beach reserves", "boat diagram", "consecutive voyage charter", "deployment diagram", "distant support area", "floating reserve", "horizon", "initial reserves", "joint amphibious operation", "joint amphibious task force," "landing attack", "landing force supplies", "landing schedule", "marker ship", "military sealift Command-controlled ships", "naval support area", "other landing ship areas", "prelanding operations", "salvage group", "screening group", "supporting aircraft", "survey, liaison, and reconnaissance party", "tactical air commander (ashore)", "tactical air groups (shore-based)" "tactical air operation", "tactical deception group", "target classification", and "vertical takeoff and landing aircraft transport area" from Joint Publication 1-02, *Department of Defense Dictionary of Military and Associated Terms***

- **Adds a definition for the terms "air support coordination section", "air traffic control section", "amphibious breaching", "amphibious defense zone", "assault breaching", "establishing directive", "helicopter coordination section", and "tactical air direction center."**

TABLE OF CONTENTS

Intentionally Blank

EXECUTIVE SUMMARY

COMMANDER'S OVERVIEW

- **Provide an Overview of Amphibious Operations**

- **Discuss Command and Control of Amphibious Operations**

- **Discuss the Conduct of Amphibious Operations**

- **Discuss Amphibious Operations Against Coastal Defenses**

- **Discuss Support to Amphibious Operations**

- **Provide Reference for Landing Force Logistics Planning**

Overview

The primary purpose of an amphibious operation is introducing a landing force (LF) ashore.

This publication provides fundamental principles and guidance to assist joint force commanders (JFCs), their staffs, and supporting and subordinate commanders in the planning, execution, and assessment of amphibious operations. An amphibious operation is a military operation launched from the sea by an amphibious force (AF), embarked in ships or craft with the primary purpose of introducing a landing force (LF) ashore to accomplish the assigned mission. An AF is an amphibious task force (ATF) and an LF together with other forces that are trained, organized, and equipped for amphibious operations.

Amphibious operations seek to exploit the element of surprise and capitalize on enemy weakness by projecting and applying combat power precisely at the most advantageous location and time.

Amphibious operations apply maneuver principles to maritime power projection in joint and multinational operations.

Amphibious operations can be designed to achieve operation or campaign objectives in one swift stroke; comprise the initial phase of a campaign or major operation to establish a military lodgment; serve as a supporting operation to deny the use of an area or facilities; to fix enemy forces and attention; to outflank an enemy; or to support military engagement, security cooperation, deterrence, humanitarian assistance, and civic assistance.

AFs provide the JFC with a tailored, mobile force that is flexible enough to facilitate the entry of follow-on forces, be the main or supporting effort, or accomplish a coup-de-main.

Amphibious operations take place across the range of military operations and are categorized into five types: assaults, raids, demonstrations, withdrawals, and amphibious support to other operations.

An amphibious assault involves the establishment of an LF on a hostile or potentially hostile shore.

An amphibious raid is a type of amphibious operation involving swift incursion into or temporary occupation of an objective followed by a planned withdrawal.

An amphibious demonstration is a show of force conducted to deceive with the expectation of deluding the enemy into a course of action (COA) unfavorable to it.

An amphibious withdrawal is the extraction of forces by sea in ships or craft from a hostile or potentially hostile shore.

Amphibious support is a type of amphibious operation which contributes to conflict prevention or crisis mitigation.

Amphibious operations may be used to support a wide variety of objectives, including:

- Attacking enemy critical vulnerabilities or decisive points
- Seizing a lodgment, to include ports and airfields
- Seizing areas for the development of advanced bases
- Destroying, neutralizing, or seizing enemy advanced bases and support facilities
- Seizing or conducting a preemptive occupation of areas
- Providing an afloat-strategic, operational, or tactical reserve
- Providing strategic, operational, or tactical

- Evacuating US citizens, selected host nation citizens, or third country
- Providing a secure environment until follow-on forces arrive

An amphibious operation is ordinarily joint in nature and may require extensive air, land, maritime, space, and special operations forces participation. The key characteristic of an amphibious operation are close coordination and cooperation.

To achieve success, an AF should be assured of local maritime and air superiority and a substantial superiority over enemy forces ashore.

Amphibious operations and can be tailored and scaled to support a specific mission or situation.

Amphibious forces (AFs) are task-organized based on the mission.

Amphibious operations commence with the initiating directive to the AF commanders to conduct military operations issued by the unified commander, subunified commander, Service component commander, or JFC delegated overall responsibility for the operation.

Amphibious operations generally follow distinct phases; planning, embarkation, rehearsal, movement, and action.

Command and Control of Amphibious Operations

Following the principles for joint operations provides for unity of effort through unity of command; centralized planning and direction; and decentralized execution.

Amphibious operations follow the principles for joint operations. A JFC has the authority to organize forces to best accomplish the assigned mission based on the concept of operations (CONOPS). Sound organization provides for unity of effort through unity of command; centralized planning and direction; and decentralized execution.

The JFC has full authority to assign missions, redirect efforts, and direct coordination among subordinate commanders. The JFC should allow Service tactical and operational assets and groupings to function generally as they were designed.

Joint force commanders (JFCs) may establish functional component commands or subordinate joint task forces.

JFCs may decide to establish a functional component command. A JFC may also establish a subordinate joint task force (JTF) on a geographical area or functional basis. A JTF is dissolved when the purpose for which it was created has been achieved or when it is no longer required.

Commander, amphibious task force (CATF) is the Navy officer designated in the initiating directive as the commander of the ATF. Commander, landing force (CLF) is the officer designated in the initiating directive as the commander of the LF for an amphibious operation.

The JFC achieves unity of effort in pursuit of amphibious objectives by establishing unity of command over AFs.

The JFC will organize the AF in such a way as to best accomplish the mission based on the CONOPS. In amphibious operations, Service component commanders normally retain operational control of their respective forces.

Planning decisions must be reached on a basis of common understanding of the mission; objectives; tactics, techniques, and procedures; and on a free exchange of information. An establishing directive is normally issued to specify the purpose of support relationships, the effects desired, and the scope of the action to be taken.

The supporting commander determines the forces, tactics, methods, procedures, and communications to be employed in providing this support.

Support is a command authority. Unless limited by the establishing directive or the initiating directive, the supported commander has the authority to exercise general direction of the supporting effort.

Except in emergencies, no significant decision contemplated by a commander in the chain of command that affects the plans, disposition, or intentions of a corresponding commander in another chain of command will be made without consultation with the commander concerned.

There is no standard organization applicable to all situations encountered in amphibious operations.

No standard organization is applicable to all situations that may be encountered in an amphibious operation. Each task group may be organized separately, or several may be combined based upon operational requirements. Flexibility is essential.

JFCs may use boundaries to define areas of operations for land and maritime forces.

Amphibious operations normally require a three-dimensional geographic area, within which is located the AF's objective(s). The operational area must be of sufficient size to conduct sea, land, and air operations to execute the mission of the AF. In addition, JFCs employ various maneuver and movement control and fire support coordination measures.

The amphibious operation requires that the LF be organized at various times in one of three functional forms: the *organization for embarkation*, a temporary administrative task organization of forces established to simplify planning and facilitate execution of embarkation at all levels of command; the *organization for landing*, a specific tactical grouping of forces that facilitates landing and actions to accomplish the assigned mission; and the *organization of LF units for accomplishment of missions ashore*, employed as soon as possible following the landing of various assault elements of the LF.

Joint air operations in support of the AF, are performed with air capabilities and forces made available by components in support of the JFC's or AF's objectives. The JFC normally designates a joint force air component commander, area air defense commander (AADC), and airspace control authority for the joint operations area (JOA).

The AADC bears overall responsibility for air defense activities of the joint force. A coherent air defense plan requires the designated commander to conduct coordinated planning with all supporting and adjacent commanders and the JFC to establish a robust command and control (C2) arrangement.

Conduct of Amphibious Operations

Amphibious operations apply maneuver and rapid, focused operations at a tempo greater than the enemy can withstand.

An amphibious operation applies maneuver principles to expeditionary power projection by establishing a LF ashore. The AF executes rapid, focused operations to accomplish the JFC's objectives. All actions focus on achieving the commander's objectives. Operations should create freedom of action for the AF, while creating a tempo greater than the enemy can withstand.

The key to successful LF operations is the rapid build up of combat power ashore.

The preferred tactic for AFs operating against coastal defenses is to avoid or bypass the strong points if unable to exploit gaps in these defenses. The AF realizes maximum effectiveness by using all available capabilities.

The phases of an amphibious operation are: planning, embarkation, rehearsals, movement, and action. The action phase has been further divided into the four types of amphibious operations: assaults, raids, demonstrations, and withdrawals.

Successful amphibious planning requires commanders' involvement and guidance, unity of effort, and an integrated planning effort.

Planning for an amphibious operation is continuous, from the receipt of the initiating directive through the termination of the operation. The tenets of successful amphibious planning are commanders' involvement and guidance, unity of effort, and an integrated planning effort.

The cornerstone of amphibious operations execution is the six-step planning process: mission analysis; COA development; COA wargame; COA comparison and decision; orders development; and transition.

AF commanders make certain primary decisions during the planning process before further planning for an amphibious operation can proceed.

Assessment is a process that measures progress of the AF toward mission accomplishment and occurs at all levels. Assessment actions and measures help commanders adjust operations and resources as required, determine when to execute branches and sequels, and make other critical decisions.

The CATF is responsible for preparing a movement plan. Subordinate force and group commanders will prepare their own detailed movement plans.

Postponement may be necessary because of weather conditions, unexpected movement of major enemy forces, or failure to meet go/no-go criteria after the AF has started its movement from final staging areas toward the operational area. The postponement plan will be prepared by the CATF and is usually promulgated as part of the OPLAN.

Movement plans must be flexible enough for execution of alternate plans at any point between the final staging area and the operational area.

Sea routes and route points to the operational area and in the operational area will normally be planned by the CATF. Sea routes in the operational area should be selected that: ensure a minimum of interference among ships and formations; are clear of mines and navigational hazards; provide sufficient dispersion to prevent concentrations that would make the AF a desirable target for attack; and provide for economy of screening forces.

A complete system of geographic reference should be formulated to minimize the possibility of interference between various elements of the AF and other supporting forces.

Plans will be made by the CATF, in consultation with the CLF, to use staging areas while en route to the operational area.

To minimize the possibility of interference between various elements of the AF and other supporting forces, sea areas in the vicinity of the landing area will be selected, designated, and divided into operating areas.

The AF's intelligence center is responsible for timely dissemination of pertinent intelligence information to the CATF and CLF. ATF ships receiving such information are responsible for passing it to the embarked landing forces.

Forces not a part of the AF that are supporting the AF must coordinate their movement within the amphibious objective area with the ATF. Individual commanders must remain aware of the need for maintaining the schedule and proceeding along prescribed routes.

Proper coordination and timing is of utmost importance in the final stages of the approach.

Approach to the operational area includes the arrival of various task groups in the vicinity of the operational area.

The plan for ship-to-shore movement is developed by the CATF and CLF to ensure that troops, equipment, and supplies are landed at the prescribed times, places, and in the formation required to support the LF scheme of maneuver.

Detailed planning for the ship-to-shore movement can begin only after the LF scheme of maneuver ashore is determined. The landing and fire support plans must be carefully integrated.

The CATF, in close coordination with the CLF, is responsible for the preparation of the overall ship-to-shore movement and landing plan. Commanders of other forces assigned to the AF are responsible for determining and presenting their requirements to the CATF. Ship-to-shore movement planning for the LF is given final form and expression in the landing plan. All landing plan documents are the responsibility of either the CATF or CLF. CATF develops the naval landing plan documents required to conduct ship-to shore movement.

Over-the-horizon operations hide intentions and capabilities, exploit the element of tactical surprise and expand the shoreline the enemy must defend.

An over-the-horizon (OTH) amphibious operation is an amphibious operation initiated from beyond visual and radar range of the enemy shore. An OTH operation is a tactical option to hide intentions and capabilities and to exploit the element of tactical surprise. It provides greater protection to the AF from near-shore threats, and provides escort ships a greater opportunity to detect, classify, track, and engage incoming hostile aircraft and coastal defense missiles while expanding the shoreline the enemy must be prepared to defend.

The second phase, embarkation, is the period during which the forces, with their equipment and supplies, are embarked in assigned shipping. The primary goal is the orderly assembly of personnel and materiel and their embarkation in assigned shipping in a sequence designed to meet the requirements of the LF CONOPS ashore. Critical to embarkation planning is an understanding of the required amphibious lift.

Rehearsal tests adequacy of plans, timing of detailed operations, communications information systems, combat readiness, and ensures all echelons are familiar with the plan.

Rehearsal is the period during which the prospective operation is practiced to test adequacy of plans, timing of detailed operations, and combat readiness of participating forces; ensure that all echelons are familiar with the plan; and test communications-information systems. During this period the AF, or elements of, conduct one or more rehearsal exercise(s), ideally under conditions approximating those encountered in the littorals and expected landing area. The objective during this phase will be to exercise as much of the force and the OPLAN as the situation permits, with operational security and time being limiting factors.

The movement phase commences upon departure of ships from loading points in the embarkation areas, and concludes when ships arrive at assigned stations in the operational area. During this phase, the AF is organized into movement groups, which execute movement in accordance with the movement plan on prescribed routes. Based on the landing plan, AF assets are organized for embarkation and deployment to support the amphibious operation.

The action phase is the period of time between the arrival of the LF of the AF in the operational area and the accomplishment of their mission.

In an amphibious operation, the action phase is the period of time between the arrival of the LF of the AF in the operational area and the accomplishment of their mission. The LF is organized to execute the landing and to conduct initial operations ashore in accordance with the commander's CONOPS. The action phase is characterized by decentralized execution of the plan by subordinate commanders.

AF commanders may seek to shape their operational environment through three complementary operations: supporting operations, advance force operations, and pre-assault operations.

The CATF is responsible for overall control of both surface and air ship-to shore movement. Control and coordination measures necessary for employment of airborne elements of the LF will be established by the CATF in conjunction with the CLF and other concerned commanders specified in the initiating directive or establishing directive, if appropriate. Prior to the execution of the decisive action phase of an amphibious operation, the AF commanders may seek to shape their operational environment through three complementary operations: supporting operations, advance force operations, and pre-assault operations.

The mission developed by the commander, and as amplified by the CONOPS ashore, is the principal means by which the commander ensures that his intent is understood and accomplished in detailed planning and execution of the operation.

An amphibious assault begins on order, after sufficient elements of the main body of the AF arrive in the operational area. In the amphibious assault, combat power is progressively phased ashore.

In the concept for phasing ashore, the LF combat power should plan for the reestablishment of centralized control of the LF.

An amphibious raid is a swift incursion or occupation followed by a planned withdrawal.

An amphibious raid is an operation involving a swift incursion into or the temporary occupation of an objective to accomplish an assigned mission followed by a planned withdrawal. Surprise is an essential ingredient in the success of an amphibious raid. Withdrawal must be planned in detail, including provisions as to time and place for re-embarkation.

The amphibious demonstration is intended to confuse the enemy as to time, place, or strength of the main operation.

The amphibious demonstration is intended to confuse the enemy as to time, place, or strength of the main operation. Effectiveness increases in direct proportion to the degree of realism involved in execution. The timing must be coordinated to achieve the maximum desired level of reaction from the enemy force. The demonstration must occur over a long enough period to allow the enemy to react.

Amphibious withdrawals are operations conducted to extract forces by sea in ships or craft from a hostile or potentially hostile shore. Withdrawal begins with establishment of defensive measures in the embarkation area and ends when all elements of the force have been extracted and embarked on designated shipping.

AFs must be prepared for involvement in a wide range of operations. In general, these additional operations focus on deterring war, resolving conflict, promoting peace, and supporting civil authorities in response to domestic crises.

Amphibious Operations Against Coastal Defenses

The preferred tactic against coastal defenses is to avoid, bypass, or exploit gaps whenever possible.

The preferred tactic for AFs operating against countries or organizations employing coastal defenses is to avoid, bypass, or exploit gaps in these defenses whenever possible. Operational limitations may preclude this tactic and a breach of these defenses may be required.

Coastal defenses depend on the hydrography, terrain, resources, development time available, and ingenuity of the antagonists. Antilanding doctrine usually focuses on the development of four layered barriers within the littorals. The four barriers from the littorals to land are perimeter, main, engineer, and beach.

AFs should request national and theater collection assets to conduct reconnaissance and surveillance of the defended coastal area to determine the best landing area to conduct the breach. Water depth and beach characteristics are key factors.

If rules of engagement permit, mine-countermeasures are best accomplished by destruction of mines prior to their deployment.

Two primary mine-countermeasures (MCM) techniques are mine hunting and minesweeping. Local air and maritime superiority in the operational area is required in order for MCM forces to commence operations.

Suppression, obscuration, security, reduction, and deception are fundamentals that must be applied to amphibious breaching operations to ensure success.

Commanders must maintain a clear understanding of potential chemical, biological, radiological, and nuclear (CBRN) threats, and planning must include measures to minimize associated AF vulnerabilities.

The principles of chemical, biological, radiological, and nuclear defense are: avoidance, protection, and decontamination.

The principles of CBRN defense are: avoidance of CBRN and toxic industrial materials (TIM) hazards, particularly contamination; protection of individuals and units from unavoidable CBRN and TIM hazards; and required decontamination in order to restore operational capability.

Support to Amphibious Operations

Support for amphibious operations can be broken down into intelligence, fire support, communications, logistics, protection, and seabasing.

Supporting operations may set the conditions for the advance force to move into the operational area and are enablers that support the execution of the amphibious operation. These operations are conducted by forces other than the AF and need to be thoroughly coordinated.

Amphibious operations involve extensive planning in all functional areas to ensure that ships, aircraft, landing craft, and supporting fires are synchronized to arrive at specific points at specific times to take advantage of enemy critical vulnerabilities and expedite combat power build-up and sustainment ashore. This requires comprehensive joint intelligence preparation of the operational environment, including harmonization of intelligence and operational planners to ensure that COAs are feasible and that enemy capabilities, vulnerabilities, and centers of gravity are identified and taken into consideration.

Properly planned and executed supporting fires are critical to the success of an amphibious operation. Fires in support of amphibious operations are the synergistic product of three subsystems: target acquisition (TA), C2, and attack resources. TA systems and equipment perform the key tasks of target detection, location, tracking, identification, and classification in sufficient detail to permit the effective attack of the target. C2 systems bring all information together for collation and decision making. Attack systems include fires delivered from air, surface, land, and subsurface attack systems.

Fire support plans optimize the employment of fire support to achieve the designated commander's intent.

Fire support planning is the continuous and concurrent process of analyzing, allocating, and scheduling of fire support to integrate it with the forces to maximize combat power. The purpose is to optimize the employment of fire support to achieve the designated commander's intent by shaping the operational area and providing support to maneuver forces.

The CATF is responsible for preparation of the overall naval surface fire support (NSFS) plan, based on the CLF and Navy requirements. The plan includes allocation of gunfire support ships and facilities. The CATF is also responsible for the general policy on targeting priorities.

The CLF is responsible for determination of LF requirements for NSFS, including selection of targets to be attacked in preassault operations, those to be fired on in support of the LF assault, and the timing of these fires in relation to the LF scheme of maneuver.

Command and control systems must be robust, flexible, sustainable, survivable, and as expeditionary as the AF.

Amphibious operations require a flexible C2 system capable of supporting rapid decision making and execution to maintain a high tempo of operations. These systems must be robust, flexible, sustainable, survivable, and as expeditionary as the AF. CATF and CLF are responsible for communications system support planning, with the designated commander consolidating the requirements.

The CATF is normally responsible for determining overall logistic requirements for the AF. Like all logistic systems, the AF logistic systems must be responsive, simple, flexible, economical, attainable, sustainable, and survivable.

Protection of the AF is essential for all operations, but especially during ship-to-shore movement. Maritime superiority permits the conduct of amphibious operations without prohibitive interference by the opposing force.

In formulating plans for movement to the operational area, sea routes and rendezvous points must be carefully selected. Sea routes through mineable waters, or close to enemy shore installations from which the enemy can carry out air, surface, or subsurface attacks, are to be avoided if possible. To minimize probability of detection, routes will be planned to avoid known or probable areas of enemy surveillance. Communications security is essential and must be maintained throughout planning.

Seabasing provides options for closing, assembling, employing, sustaining, and reconstituting forces for amphibious operations.

Seabasing is the deployment, assembly, command, projection, reconstitution, and reemployment of joint combat power from the sea without reliance on land bases within the JOA. Employing the seabasing construct provides a JFC with options for closing, assembling, employing, sustaining, and reconstituting forces for amphibious operations. Seabasing provides operational maneuver for ship-to-shore movement and assured access to the joint force during the action phase of amphibious operations while significantly reducing the footprint ashore, and minimizing the permissions required to operate from host nations. Seabasing also increases the maneuver options for LF ashore by reducing the need to protect elements such as C2 and logistic supplies.

CONCLUSION

This publication establishes joint doctrine for amphibious operations.

Intentionally blank

CHAPTER I
OVERVIEW

> *"A landing on a foreign coast in the face of hostile troops has always been one of the most difficult operations of war."*
>
> **Captain Sir Basil H. Liddell Hart (1895-1970)**

1. General

a. This publication provides fundamental principles and guidance to assist joint force commanders (JFCs), their staffs, and supporting and subordinate commanders in the planning, execution, and assessment of amphibious operations. An amphibious operation is a military operation launched from the sea by an amphibious force (AF), embarked in ships or craft with the primary purpose of introducing a landing force ashore to accomplish the assigned mission.

b. This publication specifically addresses the five types of amphibious operations, command relationships, particular planning responsibilities and processes, command and control (C2) during execution, and various support considerations. An understanding of the information provided herein provides a basis for mission analysis, course of action (COA) development, and development of a commander's intent with associated planning guidance and assessment criteria considerations.

2. Applications

a. Amphibious operations apply maneuver principles to maritime power projection in joint and multinational operations. Maneuver, in conjunction with fires, is used to achieve a position of advantage in order to destroy or seriously disrupt the enemy's cohesion through a variety of rapid, focused, and unexpected actions that create a turbulent and rapidly deteriorating situation with which the enemy cannot cope. Amphibious operations seek to **exploit the element of surprise and capitalize on enemy weakness** by projecting and applying combat power precisely at the most advantageous location and time. Conducted alone, or in conjunction with other military operations, they can be designed to:

(1) Achieve operation or campaign objectives in one swift stroke by capitalizing on surprise and simultaneous execution of supporting operations to strike directly at enemy critical vulnerabilities and decisive points in order to defeat strategic or operational centers of gravity (COGs).

(2) Comprise the initial phase of a campaign or major operation where the objective is to establish a military lodgment to support subsequent phases.

(3) Serve as a supporting operation in a campaign in order to deny the use of an area or facilities to the enemy, or to fix enemy forces and attention in support of other combat operations.

(4) Outflank an enemy.

(5) Support military engagement, security cooperation, deterrence, and humanitarian and civic assistance.

b. An AF is an amphibious task force (ATF) and a landing force (LF) together with other forces that are trained, organized, and equipped for amphibious operations. An ATF is defined as a Navy task organization formed to conduct amphibious operations. An LF is defined as a Marine Corps or Army task organization formed to conduct amphibious operations. AFs provide the JFC with a tailored, mobile force that is flexible enough to facilitate the entry of follow-on forces, be the main or supporting effort, or accomplish a coup-de-main. The ability to conduct and sustain scalable operations from over the horizon (OTH), without the requirement for diplomatic clearance or host-nation support, provides the JFC with additional options for the use of the military instrument of national power in supporting US security objectives.

3. Types of Amphibious Operations

a. Amphibious operations take place across the range of military operations and are categorized into five types: assaults, raids, demonstrations, withdrawals, and amphibious support to other operations.

(1) **Amphibious Assault**. An amphibious assault involves the establishment of an LF on a hostile or potentially hostile shore. The organic capabilities of AFs, including air and fire support, logistics, and mobility, allow them to gain access to an area by forcible entry. The salient requirement of an amphibious assault is the necessity for swift buildup of sufficient combat power ashore, from an initial zero capability to full coordinated striking power, as the attack progresses toward AF objectives. Other types of **forcible entry operations** are addressed in Joint Publication (JP) 3-18, *Joint Forcible Entry Operations*.

(2) **Amphibious Raid.** An amphibious raid is a type of amphibious operation involving swift incursion into or temporary occupation of an objective followed by a planned withdrawal.

(3) **Amphibious Demonstration.** An amphibious demonstration is a show of force conducted to deceive with the expectation of deluding the enemy into a COA unfavorable to it.

(4) **Amphibious Withdrawal.** An amphibious withdrawal is the extraction of forces by sea in ships or craft from a hostile or potentially hostile shore.

(5) **Amphibious Support to Other Operations**. A type of amphibious operation which contributes to conflict prevention or crisis mitigation. AFs routinely conduct amphibious support to other operations such as: security cooperation, foreign humanitarian

assistance (FHA), civil support, noncombatant evacuation operations (NEOs), peace operations, recovery operations, or disaster relief, etc.

b. Amphibious operations may be used to support a wide variety of objectives, including:

(1) Attack enemy critical vulnerabilities or decisive points that lead to the defeat of strategic or operational COGs.

(2) Seize a lodgment, to include ports and airfields, for the introduction of follow-on forces.

(3) Seize areas for the development of advanced bases.

(4) Destroy, neutralize, or seize enemy advanced bases and support facilities.

(5) Seize or conduct a preemptive occupation of areas that either enable friendly freedom of movement or deny freedom of movement by adversaries.

(6) Provide an afloat strategic, operational, or tactical reserve to exploit opportunities and counter threats.

(7) Provide strategic, operational, or tactical deception to force the enemy to defend along littoral areas.

(8) When directed, evacuate US citizens, selected citizens from the host nation, or third country nationals whose lives are in danger.

(9) Provide a secure environment until follow-on forces arrive on-scene to allow humanitarian relief efforts to progress and facilitate the movement of food and medical care to relieve suffering and prevent the loss of life.

4. **Characteristics**

a. **Integration of Navy and Landing Forces.** The key characteristic of an amphibious operation is close coordination and cooperation between the ATF, LF, and other designated forces. **An amphibious operation is ordinarily joint in nature** and may require extensive air, land, maritime, space, and special operations forces participation. It is typified by close integration of forces trained, organized, and equipped for different combat functions.

b. **Rapid Buildup of Combat Power from the Sea to Shore.** The salient requirement of an amphibious assault is the necessity for swift, uninterrupted buildup of sufficient combat power ashore, from an initial zero capability to full coordinated striking power, as the attack progresses toward AF objectives. **To achieve success, an AF should be assured of local maritime and air superiority and a substantial superiority over**

enemy forces ashore. In the face of compelling necessity, commanders may undertake an amphibious operation on the basis of a reasonable superiority of the entire force. For example, maritime and air superiority may justify a landing even though the LF does not possess the desired numerical superiority in ground forces, if friendly surface and air units can be used effectively to negate the enemy's advantage. In addition to reasonable superiority within the landing area, an AF should have the ability to provide continuous support for forces ashore.

c. **Task-organized forces** are capable of multiple missions across the full range of military operations to enable joint and multinational operations. **AFs are task-organized based on the mission.** While forward-deployed AFs routinely deploy with a similar task organization, they can be quickly reinforced or augmented with other assets in theater, from adjacent theaters, from the continental United States, or with multinational forces. The C2 capabilities of the ATF and LF facilitate the accomplishment of multiple and diverse missions and the integration of joint and multinational forces.

d. **Unity of Effort.** Amphibious operations require an exceptional degree of unity of effort. **The inherent complexity of amphibious operations normally requires the JFC's personal attention and timely decisions for numerous planning, integration, and support activities.**

5. Capabilities

a. Amphibious operations can be tailored and scaled to support a specific mission or situation, allowing the commander to increase or decrease the level of intensity to reflect a changing situation. The adaptability and versatility of AFs provide unique capabilities to the JFC.

b. The conduct of an amphibious operation is possible under a wide variety of weather conditions and various types of emission control (EMCON).

c. AFs have the capability to conduct amphibious operations from OTH, beyond visual and radar range of the shoreline. Diplomatic concerns may require keeping ATF ships out of view of a foreign shore, while retaining the capability to insert an LF ashore via air and landing craft assets.

d. Routinely forward-deployed AFs, comprised of an ATF and an LF, provide the JFC with a force proficient in time-sensitive planning and capable of rapid response in crisis situations. These AFs operate without the requirement for bases, ports, and airfields, and often experience fewer overflight restrictions. They can perform a wide range of mission-essential tasks to facilitate the accomplishment of the joint force mission.

e. When any special operations forces (SOF) element is part of the AF, the AF becomes special operations capable.

6. Initiating an Amphibious Operation

Amphibious operations commence with the initiating directive, issued by the commander with establishing authority, to the AF commanders. The initiating directive is an order to subordinate commanders to conduct military operations. It is issued by the unified commander, subunified commander, Service component commander, or JFC delegated overall responsibility for the operation. **The initiating directive may come in the form of a warning order, an alert order, a planning order, or an operation order (OPORD).** The complete information required to conduct an amphibious operation may come from a combination of these orders (e.g., a warning order followed by an alert order or OPORD). The initiating directive normally provides the following information:

a. The establishing authority's mission, intent, and concept of operations (CONOPS).

b. Designation of required commanders, establishment of their command relationships, and provision of special instructions (SPINS) as required to support the AF organization and mission. SPINS may include an establishing directive when a support relationship is established among designated commanders of the AF. The establishing directive is discussed in detail in Chapter II, "Command and Control."

c. Designation of the AF's assigned, attached, and supporting forces.

d. Assignment of an operational area as appropriate.

e. Assignment of tasks.

f. Assignment of responsibility and provision of necessary coordinating instructions for the conduct of supporting operations.

g. Target dates for execution of the operation.

h. Additional coordinating instructions, as required.

7. Phases of an Amphibious Operation

Amphibious operations generally follow distinct phases, though the sequence may vary. The phases are planning, embarkation, rehearsal, movement, and action (see Figure I-1).

a. While planning occurs throughout the entire operation, it is normally dominant prior to embarkation. Successive phases bear the title of the dominant activity taking place within the phase.

b. When AFs are forward deployed, or when subsequent tasks are assigned, the sequence of phases may differ. **Generally, forward-deployed AFs use the sequence "embarkation," "planning," "rehearsal" (to include potential reconfiguration of**

PHASES OF AN AMPHIBIOUS OPERATION

PLANNING

The planning phase normally denotes the period extending from the issuance of an initiating directive that triggers planning for a specific operation and ends with the embarkation of landing forces. However, planning is continuous throughout the operation. Although planning never ends, it is useful to distinguish between the planning phase and subsequent phases because of the change that may occur in the relationship between amphibious force commanders at the time the planning phase terminates and the next phase begins.

EMBARKATION

The embarkation phase is the period during which the landing force with its equipment and supplies, embark in assigned shipping. The landing plan and the scheme of maneuver ashore will influence which staffs and units are embarked on which ships, the number and type of landing craft that will be embarked, and how the units will be phased ashore. The organization for embarkation needs to provide for flexibility to support changes to the original plan. The extent to which changes in the landing plan can be accomplished may depend on the ability to reconfigure embarked forces.

REHEARSAL

The rehearsal phase is the period during which the prospective operation is rehearsed for the purpose of:
- Testing the adequacy of plans, timing of detailed operations, and combat readiness of participating forces
- Ensuring that all echelons are familiar with plans
- Testing communications and information systems

Rehearsal may consist of an actual landing or may be conducted as a command post exercise.

MOVEMENT

The movement phase is the period during which various elements of the amphibious force move from points of embarkation or from a forward-deployed position to the operational area. This move may be via rehearsal, staging, or rendezvous areas. The movement phase is completed when the various elements of the amphibious force arrive at their assigned positions in the operational area.

ACTION

The action phase is the period from the arrival of the amphibious force in the operational area, through the accomplishment of the mission and the termination of the amphibious operation.

Figure I-1. Phases of an Amphibious Operation

embarked forces), "movement to the operational area," and "action." However, significant planning is conducted prior to embarkation to anticipate the most likely missions and to load assigned shipping accordingly.

Note: The reader should not confuse the phasing model for amphibious operations with that addressed in JP 3-0, *Joint Operations,* and JP 5-0, *Joint Operation Planning.* An amphibious operation could be planned or executed within any of the six phases of that major operation/campaign phasing model.

8. Terminating an Amphibious Operation

The ability to know how and when to terminate amphibious operations is part of operational design. The termination of the amphibious operation is predicated on the accomplishment of the amphibious mission per the specific conditions contained in the initiating directive. **Upon completion of the amphibious operation, the establishing authority will provide direction as required for command arrangements and assignment of AFs.** Some type of military operation may be required and will normally continue after the conclusion of the amphibious operation. Commanders and their staffs should continually assess the ongoing operation in light of assigned objectives and in consideration of the transition to other operations, anticipated or not.

Intentionally Blank

CHAPTER II
COMMAND AND CONTROL

"Amphibious warfare requires the closest practicable cooperation by all the combatant services, both in planning and execution, and a command organization which definitely assigns responsibility for major decisions throughout all stages of the operation, embarkation, overseas movement, beach assault, and subsequent support of forces ashore."

Admiral Henry K. Hewitt, US Navy (1887-1972)

1. General

a. Amphibious operations follow the principles for joint operations as delineated in JP 1, *Doctrine for the Armed Forces of the United States.*

b. Command relationships during multinational operations are based on international standardization agreements or on bilateral agreements between nations. The command relationships for these operations will be defined in the initiating directive.

Refer to JP 3-16, Multinational Operations, *and Allied Tactical Publication-8(B),* Doctrine for Amphibious Operations, *for more information.*

c. "JFC" is a general term applied to a combatant commander, subunified commander, or joint task force (JTF) commander authorized to exercise combatant command (command authority) or operational control (OPCON) over a joint force. A JFC has the authority to organize forces to best accomplish the assigned mission based on the CONOPS. The organization should be sufficiently flexible to meet the planned phases of the contemplated operation and any development that may necessitate a change in plan. The JFC will establish subordinate commands, assign responsibilities, establish or delegate appropriate command relationships, and establish coordinating instructions as required. **Sound organization provides for unity of effort through unity of command, centralized planning and direction, and decentralized execution.**

Refer to JP 1, Doctrine for the Armed Forces of the United States, *for more details on joint force organization.*

d. All joint forces include Service component commands that provide administrative and logistic support. The JFC may conduct operations through the Service component commanders or, at lower echelons, Service force commanders. This relationship is appropriate when stability, continuity, economy, ease of long-range planning, and scope of operations dictate organizational integrity of Service forces for conducting operations. The JFC has full authority to assign missions, redirect efforts, and direct coordination among subordinate commanders. The JFC should allow Service tactical and operational assets and groupings to function generally as they were designed. The intent is to meet the requirements of the JFC while maintaining the tactical and operational integrity of the Service organizations.

e. JFCs may decide to establish a functional component command to integrate planning; reduce their span of control; and/or significantly improve combat efficiency, information flow, unity of effort, weapon systems management, component interaction, or control over the scheme of maneuver.

f. A JFC may also establish a subordinate JTF on a geographical area or functional basis when the mission has a specific, limited objective and does not require centralized control of logistics. The mission assigned to a JTF should require execution of responsibilities involving a joint force on a significant scale and close integration of effort, or should require coordination within a subordinate area. A JTF is dissolved by the JFC when the purpose for which it was created has been achieved or when it is no longer required.

g. The terms "commander, amphibious task force" (CATF) and "commander, landing force" (CLF) are used throughout this publication solely to clarify the doctrinal duties and responsibilities of these commanders. CATF is the Navy officer designated in the initiating directive as the commander of the ATF. CLF is the officer designated in the initiating directive as the commander of the LF for an amphibious operation. During operations, amphibious commanders may be referred to by either their operational command titles (e.g., amphibious squadron and Marine expeditionary unit [MEU] commanders) or assigned task force designators (e.g., Combined or Commander Task Force 62.1).

SECTION A. COMMAND AND CONTROL OF AMPHIBIOUS FORCES

> *"Command and control is just one element in the complex tapestry of warfare. A poor system well executed can beat a good system when that system's execution breaks down . . . any command and control system must be complemented by sound tactical doctrine, realistic training, and superbly motivated troops."*
>
> **Extract from Army Command and General Staff College FC 101-34**

2. Overview

The JFC achieves unity of effort in pursuit of amphibious objectives by establishing unity of command over AFs. The JFC may establish unity of command over AFs by retaining OPCON over the Service or functional component commands executing the amphibious operation, or by delegating OPCON or tactical control (TACON) of the AF. The JFC may remain the common superior to the CATF and CLF or delegate to a subordinate commander which may accelerate decision cycles. Forces, not command relationships, are transferred between commands. When forces are transferred, the command relationship the gaining commander will exercise (and the losing commander will relinquish) over those forces must be specified.

a. The JFC will organize the AF in such a way as to best accomplish the mission based on the CONOPS.

b. The command relationships established among the CATF, CLF, and other designated commanders of the AF are important decisions. The type of relationship chosen by the common superior commander, or establishing authority, should be based on mission, nature and duration of the operation, force capabilities, C2 capabilities, operational environment, and recommendations from subordinate commanders. While the full range of command relationship options as outlined in JP 1, *Doctrine for the Armed Forces of the United States*, are available, in amphibious operations, Service component commanders normally retain OPCON of their respective forces. If the JFC organizes along functional lines, functional component commanders will normally exercise OPCON over their parent Services' forces and TACON over other Services' forces attached or made available for tasking.

(1) **Typically a support relationship is established between the commanders and is based on the complementary rather than similar nature and capabilities of the ATF and LF. However, it is not the intent to limit the common superior's authority to establish either an OPCON or TACON command relationship as appropriate.**

(2) Regardless of the command relationships, when the initiating directive is received, unique relationships are observed during the planning phase. **The AF commanders, designated in the initiating directive, are coequal in planning matters.** Planning decisions must be reached on a basis of common understanding of the mission, objectives, and tactics, techniques, and procedures and on a free exchange of information. Any differences between commanders that cannot be resolved are referred to the establishing authority. If a change in the mission occurs after commencement of operations or if an amphibious operation is initiated from an afloat posture, coequal planning relationships (either as described above or as specified in the initiating directive) will apply to any subsequent planning. However, as the operational situation dictates, the commander delegated OPCON of the AF may specify planning relationships to coordinate planning efforts, especially during crisis action planning (CAP), under the provisions of the Chairman of the Joint Chiefs of Staff Manual (CJCSM) 3122.01A, *Joint Operation Planning and Execution System, Vol I: (Planning Policies and Procedures)*.

(3) An establishing directive is essential whenever the support command relationship will be used to ensure unity of effort within the AF. Normally, the commanders within the AF will develop a draft establishing directive during the planning phase to provide the specifics of the support relationship. The commanders within the AF submit the draft establishing directive to the establishing authority for approval. The establishing directive is normally issued to specify the purpose of the support relationship, the effect desired, and the scope of the action to be taken. It may also include, but is not necessarily limited to, the following:

(a) Forces and other resources allocated to the supporting effort.

(b) Time, place, level, and duration of the supporting effort.

(c) Relative priority of the supporting effort.

(d) Authority, if any, of the supporting commander(s) to modify the supporting effort in the event of an exceptional opportunity or an emergency.

(e) Degree of authority granted to the supported commander over the supporting effort.

(f) Force protection responsibilities afloat and ashore.

(4) Unless otherwise stated in the initiating or establishing directive, the CATF and CLF will identify the events and conditions for any shifts of the support relationship throughout the operation, ideally during the planning phase, and forward them to the establishing authority for approval.

(5) The establishing authority will resolve any differences among the commanders.

(6) Support is a command authority. This relationship is appropriate when one organization should aid, protect, complement, or sustain another force. The designation of the supporting relationships is important as it conveys priorities to the commanders and staffs who are planning or executing the operation. The support relationship is, by design, a somewhat vague and therefore very flexible arrangement.

(7) A supported commander may be designated for the entire operation, a particular phase or stage of the operation, a particular function, or a combination of phases, stages, events, and functions. Unless limited by the establishing directive or the initiating directive, **the supported commander has the authority to exercise general direction of the supporting effort**. General direction includes the designation and prioritization of targets or objectives, timing and duration of the supporting action, and other instructions necessary for coordination and efficiency. The establishing authority is responsible for ensuring that the supported and supporting commanders understand the degree of authority that the supported commander is granted.

(a) If not specified in the initiating directive, the CATF and CLF will determine who has primary responsibility for the essential tasks during the mission analysis in the planning process.

See Chapter III, "Conduct of Amphibious Operations," for mission analysis and the planning process.

(b) **In an operation of relatively short duration, the establishing authority will normally choose one commander as supported for the entire operation.** When there is no littoral threat to the AF the establishing authority may designate the CLF as the supported commander for the entire operation. During the movement or transit phase, the CATF may be designated the supported commander based on having responsibility for the major action or activity during that phase. The CATF may be designated the supported commander based on capabilities for airspace control and air defense for the entire operation if, for example, the LF does not intend to establish a tactical air command center ashore (see Figure II-1).

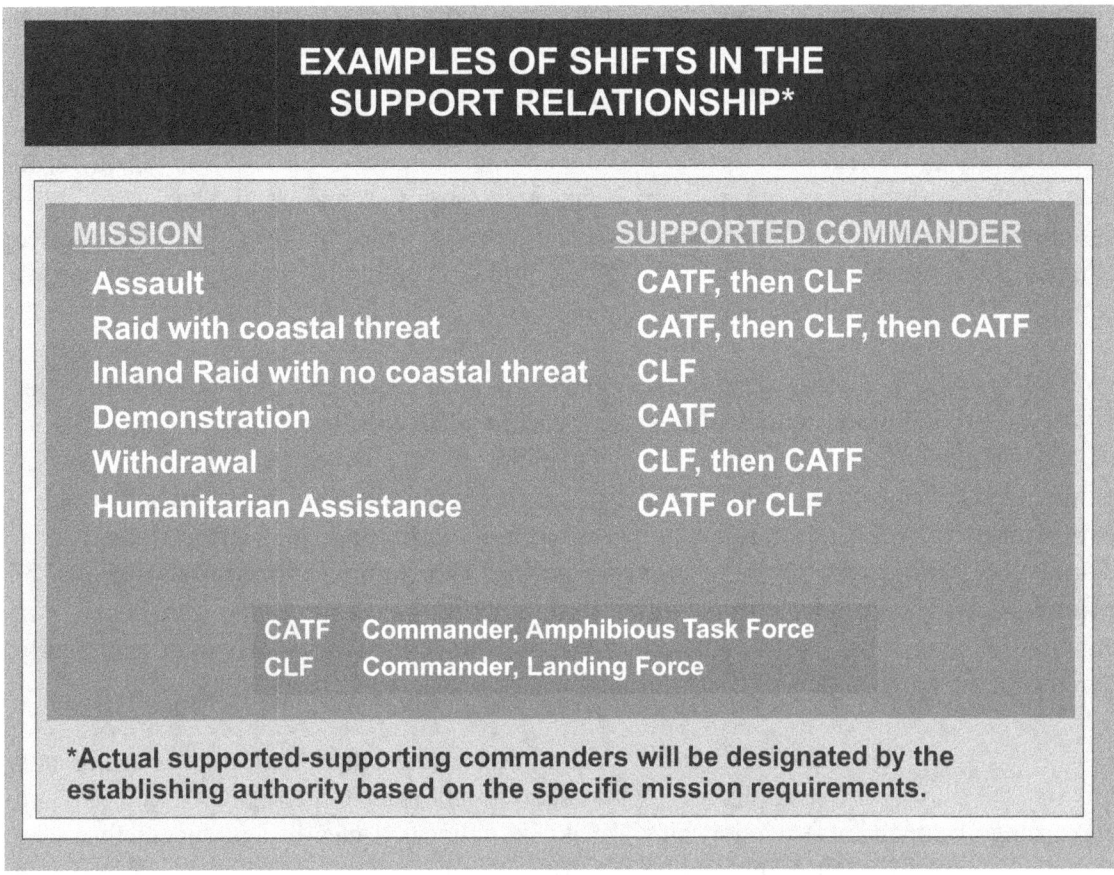

Figure II-1. Examples of Shifts in the Support Relationship

(c) Considerations for shifts in the support relationship include but are not limited to the following:

1. Responsibility for the preponderance of the mission.

2. Force capabilities.

3. Level of threat.

4. Type, phase, and duration of operation.

5. C2 capabilities.

6. Operational environment assigned.

7. Recommendations from subordinate commanders.

(d) The supporting commander determines the forces, tactics, methods, procedures, and communications to be employed in providing this support. The supporting commander will advise and coordinate with the supported commander on matters concerning the employment and limitations (e.g., logistics) of such support, assist in planning for the integration of such support into the supported commander's effort as a whole, and ensure that support requirements are appropriately communicated throughout the supporting commander's organization. The supporting commander has the responsibility to ascertain the needs of the supported force and take full action to fulfill them within existing capabilities, consistent with priorities and requirements of other assigned tasks. When the supporting commander cannot fulfill the needs of the supported commander, the establishing authority will be notified by either the supported or supporting commander. The establishing authority is responsible for resolving these issues.

(e) Elements of the AF (ATF, LF, and other forces) may be embarked for what could be extended periods of time on the same platforms, but responsible to different or parallel chains of command. Such parallel chains of command create special requirements for coordination. **Except in emergencies, no significant decision contemplated by a commander in the chain of command that affects the plans, disposition, or intentions of a corresponding commander in another chain of command will be made without consultation with the commander concerned.** In emergency situations, the commander making an emergency decision will notify corresponding commanders of his or her action at the earliest practicable time.

(f) Command relationships should be based on the nature of the mission and the objectives to be accomplished. Command relationships, including supported and supporting commander(s) relationships should be delineated clearly and succinctly. The specific command relationships will vary based on the mission assigned, environment within which operations must be conducted, and the makeup of existing and potential adversaries and the time available to achieve the end state.

3. **Amphibious Force Task Organization**

a. **Task Organization. AFs are task-organized based on the mission.** No standard organization is applicable to all situations that may be encountered in an amphibious operation. Each task group may be organized separately, or several may be combined based upon operational requirements. Flexibility is essential. The relationship of the commanders will be determined by the JFC based upon mission requirements and promulgated in appropriate orders (e.g., initiating directive, establishing directive, operation plan [OPLAN]).

b. **Task Designators.** Task designators are utilized by US and North Atlantic Treaty Organization naval forces that assign forces in a task force, task group, task unit, and task element hierarchical structure.

c. **Navy Forces.** At the CATF's discretion and as promulgated in the initiating directive and establishing directive, two or more of these groups may be combined and others added or deleted as dictated by operational requirements. For example, control groups may not be required when conducting OTH operations. The Navy forces of the AF, which may consist of US and multinational forces, is task-organized according to the separate tasks required to meet the operational requirements. CATF uses the Navy's composite warfare commander (CWC) construct to defend the ATF at sea. The CWC conducts operations to counter threats to the force and to maintain tactical sea control with assets assigned.

For further details on C2 of Navy forces, see JP 3-32, Command and Control for Joint Maritime Operations.

d. **Landing Forces.** The LF consists of ground combat units and any of its combat support and combat service support units. The LF may be composed of Marine Corps and/or Army forces, other US forces, and multinational forces. If LF capabilities are required by the CATF, the CLF will make decisions as to the appropriate LF capabilities to be made available TACON to the CATF. If US Army forces comprise part of the LF, the Army maneuver battalion, brigade, division, or corps will also be task-organized with appropriate combat and combat service support (CSS) capabilities. When Marine Corps forces are employed as the LF, they will be task organized into a Marine air-ground task force (MAGTF), the Marine Corps' principal organization for missions across the range of military operations. The MAGTF is functionally grouped into four core elements: a command element (CE), a ground combat element (GCE), an aviation combat element (ACE), and a logistics combat element (LCE). The basic structure of the MAGTF never varies, but the number, size, and type of Marine Corps units comprising each of the four elements are always mission dependent. Notional task organizations include the Marine expeditionary force (MEF), Marine expeditionary brigade (MEB), MEU, and in some cases, a special purpose Marine air-ground task force (SPMAGTF).

(1) **Marine Expeditionary Force.** A MEF is the largest MAGTF and is the Marine Corps' principal warfighting organization, and is normally commanded by a lieutenant general. The size and composition of a deployed MEF can vary greatly depending on the requirements of the mission. A MEF is normally built around a division, a Marine aircraft wing, and a Marine logistics group; the largest respective Marine Corps ground, air, or logistic units. **A MEF is capable of missions across the full range of military operations, including amphibious assault and sustained operations ashore in any environment.** It can operate from a sea base, land base, or both, and typically deploys with more than 45,000 personnel with up to 60 days of sustainment. It is normally built around a GCE of an infantry division. The ACE consists of a Marine aircraft wing with fixed- and rotary-wing groups. The LCE is a combat logistics force that is organized to provide the full range of combat service support to the MEF. The MEF headquarters can serve as a JTF headquarters. When operating as part of a JTF, the MEF commander can operate as a functional component commander. MEFs are capable of self-sustained forcible entry to overcome challenges to access. It can seize and hold beachheads, airfields, and

ports to enable the introduction of follow-on forces. The MEF can then remain in theater to conduct the full range of military operations in support of the joint campaign.

(2) **Marine Expeditionary Brigade.** The MEB is a mid-sized MAGTF that is usually commanded by a brigadier or major general, and is comprised of 8,000 to 18,000 Marines. The MEB varies in size and composition and is task-organized to meet the requirements of a specific situation. It is normally built around a GCE of a reinforced infantry regiment. The ACE consists of a Marine aircraft group with fixed- and rotary-wing squadrons. The LCE is a combat logistics regiment that is organized to provide the full range of CSS to the MEB. A MEB is capable of rapid deployment and employment via amphibious shipping and intratheater airlift and sealift. It can operate by itself with a self-sustainment capability of 30 days. The MEB can conduct forcible entry operations. The MEB is designed to aggregate with other MEBs, MEUs, and other pre-positioning force assets to fight as the MEF.

(3) **Marine Expeditionary Unit.** A MEU is organized as a MAGTF with approximately 2,200 Marines and Sailors. It is normally commanded by a Marine colonel, and consists of a CE, a reinforced infantry battalion, a reinforced composite aviation squadron, and a task-organized LCE. The forward-deployed MEU is uniquely organized, trained, and equipped to provide the JFC with an expeditionary force. It fulfills the Marine Corps' forward, sea-based deployment requirements and deploys with up to 15 days of supplies. Two to three MEUs are normally deployed forward supporting geographic combatant commander requirements, prepared to deploy in response to crisis situations as required. They can rapidly deploy and employ via amphibious shipping, by airlift, through marshalling with maritime pre-positioning force (MPF) assets, or any combination thereof. In terms of employment, **a MEU does not regularly conduct opposed amphibious operations and can only conduct amphibious operations of limited duration and scope**. Its expeditionary warfare capabilities make it extremely useful for crisis response, immediate reaction operations such as NEO, humanitarian and civic assistance, limited objective attacks, raids, and for acting as an advance force for a larger follow-on MAGTF. The special operations capable designation of a MEU (special operations capable) indicates the presence of a Marine special operations company (MSOC). This MSOC is typically chartered to perform three core missions: direct action, special reconnaissance, and foreign internal defense. The MSOC is OPCON to the geographic combatant commander, normally executed through the theater special operations command commander.

(4) **Special Purpose Marine Air-Ground Task Force.** The SPMAGTF is organized, trained, and equipped with narrowly focused capabilities. It is designed to accomplish a wide variety of expeditionary operations, but its missions are usually limited in scope and duration. It is configured to accomplish specific mission(s) for which a MEF/MEB/MEU would be inappropriate or too large. A SPMAGTF may be any size, but is usually a small force, MEU-sized, or smaller.

(5) **Landing Force Organizational Shifts.** The amphibious operation requires that the LF be organized at various times in one of three functional forms.

(a) **Organization for Embarkation.** The organization for embarkation is a temporary administrative task organization of forces established to simplify planning and facilitate execution of embarkation at all levels of command. This organization is used by the LF during the movement phase of the amphibious operation.

For more information see Chapter III, "Conduct of Amphibious Operations," *Section B* "Embarkation," *and JP 3-02.1,* Amphibious Embarkation and Debarkation.

(b) **Organization for Landing.** The organization for landing represents a specific tactical grouping of forces that facilitates landing and actions to accomplish the assigned mission.

For more information see Chapter III, "Conduct of Amphibious Operations," *Section E* "Action."

(c) **Organization for Combat.** The task organization of LF units for accomplishment of missions ashore is employed as soon as possible following the landing of various assault elements of the LF. It involves the combination of combat, combat support, CSS, and other units that the CLF determines will best accomplish the assigned mission.

<u>1</u>. External fire support means made available to the LF may be organized to support the specified task groups formed. Such forces normally include artillery units (not organic to the division), naval surface fire support (NSFS), and joint aviation.

<u>2</u>. **CSS installations and units are organized and located to support the LF and combat support forces.** Centralized control of CSS is efficient, but it is often necessary to decentralize control to those elements that support the tactical elements, particularly when these task organizations have been assigned independent missions.

4. **Operational Areas**

a. **General. Amphibious operations normally require a three-dimensional geographic area, within which is located the AF's objective(s).** The operational area must be of sufficient size to conduct sea, land, and air operations to execute the mission of the AF. In addition, JFCs employ various maneuver and movement control and fire support coordination measures (FSCMs) to facilitate effective joint operations. These measures include boundaries, phase lines, objectives, coordinating altitudes to deconflict air operations, air defense areas, amphibious objective areas (AOAs), submarine operating patrol areas and minefields. JFCs may use boundaries to define areas of operations (AOs) for land and maritime forces. Within the designated operational area, the designated commander will synchronize maneuver, fires, and interdiction. The operational areas that may be assigned to an AF in an initiating directive are an AOA or an AO normally in conjunction with a high-density airspace control zone (HIDACZ).

(1) **An AOA** is a geographical area (delineated for C2 purposes in the initiating directive) within which is located the objective(s) to be secured by the AF. This area must be of sufficient size to ensure accomplishment of the AF's mission and must provide sufficient area for conducting necessary sea, air, and land operations in direct support of the amphibious operation.

(2) **An AO** is an operational area defined by the JFC for land and maritime forces and should be large enough for component commanders to accomplish their missions and protect their forces.

For additional guidance on boundaries and synchronization of joint efforts within land and naval AOs, refer to JP 3-0, Joint Operations.

b. **Assigned Area.** The commander designated in the initiating directive is responsible for airspace control, defense of friendly forces, and direction and deconfliction of supporting arms. The initiating directive will also specify the degree of authority that the designated commander has over supporting forces entering the assigned geographic area. The designated commander will request the airspace coordinating measures (ACMs) required for inclusion in the establishing directive (for a support relationship) or in the CONOPS to further ensure success of the mission.

c. **Disestablishment of Assigned Area.** Once the type of operational area (AOA or AO) is defined, it is not necessarily dissolved upon termination of the amphibious operation. The operational area may be required for the coordination of follow-on logistic support of the operation or other missions as assigned. As with its establishment, **disestablishing the area is the decision of the establishing authority** (with CATF or CLF recommendations) and should be delineated in the initiating directive or in follow-on orders.

SECTION B. AMPHIBIOUS AIR OPERATIONS

"The doctrine and performance of Marines and airmen matured in Pacific campaigns as the hesitancy and missteps of Guadalcanal, New Guinea, and Tarawa were heeded. Coordinated amphibious assault and air warfare became irrepressible."

"Struggle for the Marianas," Captain Bernard D. Cole, US Navy
***Joint Force Quarterly*, Spring 95**

5. Joint Air Operations

Joint air operations in support of the AF, are performed with air capabilities and forces made available by components in support of the JFC's or AF's objectives. **To create synergy and avoid duplication of effort, the JFC synchronizes and integrates the actions of assigned, attached, and supporting capabilities and forces in time, space, and purpose.** The JFC normally accomplishes this through designation of a joint force air component commander (JFACC), area air defense commander (AADC), and airspace control authority (ACA) for the joint operations area (JOA). The JFACC uses joint air to support amphibious operations within the AOA. It is within this context that joint air tasking, air defense activities, and airspace control are conducted during amphibious operations.

For more information, see JP 3-30, Command and Control for Joint Air Operations.

6. **Defensive Counterair**

a. **The AADC bears overall responsibility for air defense activities of the joint force.** The AADC may, however, designate subordinate regional air defense commanders (RADCs) for specific geographic regions to accomplish the joint force mission. Additionally, sector air defense commanders (SADCs) may be designated within and subordinate to RADCs. **The RADC is normally established within the ATF organization and is responsible for the airspace allocated for amphibious operations, including but not limited to the AOA (if established).** The CATF will coordinate joint air requirements in support of active defense plans and procedures with the AADC and attack operations with the JFACC. The CATF usually assigns an air defense commander (ADC), normally located on the most capable air defense platform, to actually carry out air defense operations. The ADC coordinates with the Navy tactical air control center (Navy TACC) to maintain a current air picture.

b. **When an AOA is established, the airspace assigned to the AF usually includes a margin of airspace surrounding the AOA called the amphibious defense zone (ADZ).** An ADZ is the area encompassing the AOA and the adjoining airspace required by accompanying naval forces for the purpose of air defense. The actual size and shape of an ADZ is dependent upon the capabilities of air defense platforms assigned to the CATF; the size of the AOA; and agreement between the AF's RADC, the AADC, and adjacent ADCs. Within the ADZ, the AF air defense agency maintains positive identification of all aircraft and conducts air defense with the authority to engage in accordance with established rules of engagement (ROE) and AADC established procedures.

c. **Planning Considerations**

(1) A coherent air defense plan requires the designated commander to conduct coordinated planning with all supporting and adjacent commanders and the JFC to establish a robust C2 arrangement. Effective air defense operations require a control system that functions despite a high volume of all types of friendly aircraft operations within the operational area and the difficult overland target detection environment present in amphibious operations.

(2) The area air defense plan must be written with detailed engagement procedures that are consistent with the airspace control plan (ACP) and operations in the combat zone. The geographic arrangement of weapons and the location of specific types of air defense operations, as well as specific procedures for identification of aircraft, are important factors to include in planning.

Refer to JP 3-09.3, Close Air Support, *and JP 3-01,* Countering Air and Missile Threats, *for additional information.*

Other key factors to consider are described in JP 3-52, Joint Airspace Control.

7.   **Airspace Control in Amphibious Operations**

a. Assignment of airspace allows the JFC to exercise C2 of forces, deconflict high volumes of different types of aircraft and missiles, and defense forces. During amphibious operations, **the ACA will normally further delegate the control authority for a specific airspace control area to the CATF**. The further delegation of roles typically includes regional air defense responsibilities. The complexity and size of an amphibious operation directly affects the amount of airspace allocated.

See JP 3-52, Joint Airspace Control in the Combat Zone, *for further information on control authority designation.*

b. **A HIDACZ** is airspace in which there is a concentrated employment of numerous and varied weapons, such as artillery, missiles, and NSFS, and airspace users. A HIDACZ has defined dimensions that usually coincide with specific geographical features or navigational aids. Access to a HIDACZ is normally controlled by the Navy TACC.

c. The level of air control allocated to the AF depends on the degree of air control measures. The ACA approves these measures on behalf of the JFC. A HIDACZ is an effective means of airspace control that is typically initiated by the primary user (CATF). Considerations for establishing a HIDACZ include:

(1) Airspace control capabilities of the AF.

(2) Minimum risk routes into and out of the HIDACZ and to the target area.

(3) Air traffic advisory as required. Procedures and systems must also be considered for air traffic control service during instrument meteorological conditions.

(4) Procedures for expeditious movement of aircraft into and out of the HIDACZ.

(5) Coordination of fire support, as well as air defense weapons control orders or status within and in the vicinity of the HIDACZ.

(6) Range and type of NSFS available.

(7) Location of enemy forces inside and in close proximity to the HIDACZ.

(8) The HIDACZ should cover the ATF's sea echelon areas and extend inland to the LF's fire support coordination line (FSCL). Optimally, it should extend beyond the

FSCL so that the CLF can fight the deep battle. Additionally, the HIDACZ should be large enough to accommodate the flow of fixed- and rotary-wing aircraft, to include unmanned aircraft systems (UASs), into and out of the amphibious airspace.

d. Under the ATF, **the Navy TACC typically onboard the amphibious flagship, will normally be established as the agency responsible for controlling all air operations** within the allocated airspace regardless of mission or origin, to include supporting arms and assault breaching. An aircraft or surface combatant with the requisite air C2 capabilities may also serve this function. Regardless of where actual airspace control is exercised, close and continuous coordination between airspace control and air defense agencies is essential. Emphasis will be placed on simple, flexible air traffic control plans and a combination of positive and procedural airspace control. There are three levels of control: procedural, positive, and a combination of the two. AFs operating in a non-radar environment will rely exclusively on procedural control. **Amphibious air control plans employ a combination of positive and procedural control methods.**

(1) **Positive Airspace Control.** Positive airspace control uses radar; electronic warfare support; identification, friend or foe/selective identification feature; visual means; digital data links; and elements of the air defense network communications system to positively identify, track, and direct air assets.

(2) **Procedural Airspace Control.** Procedural control methods supplement those methods utilized in positive airspace control. Procedural control will be used when electronic or visual identification, tracking, or communication means are unavailable or inadequate to provide positive airspace control. These methods are often used when adequate coverage does exist to complement positive control methods. Procedural airspace control relies on a combination of previously agreed upon and promulgated orders and procedures.

See JP 3-52, Joint Airspace Control in the Combat Zone, *for more details.*

e. To ensure unity of effort and minimal interference along adjacent boundaries, the AF air control agency coordinates the items listed in Figure II-2 with the ACA. **Navy TACC prepares and submits ACMs for the AF to the ACA for inclusion in the JFC's ACP.** The ACP provides the basic information needed to operate within the amphibious airspace. Changes to established procedures will be coordinated with all airspace users. The airspace control order (ACO) and SPINS to the air tasking order (ATO) may contain changes to airspace control procedures and must be reviewed daily by all users of amphibious airspace.

8. **Navy Tactical Air Control Center**

The senior Navy amphibious air control agency is the Navy TACC. The functions of the Navy TACC may be spread across several ships. The Navy TACC possesses the functionality of future plans and current operations. **During amphibious operations, the Navy TACC coordinates the types of ACMs and controls all air operations within the**

operational area until a land-based air control agency is established ashore. Once a land-based air control agency receives control of all LF air operations, the Navy TACC may become a tactical air direction center (TADC) supporting the land-based air control agency. The supporting arms coordination center (SACC) is a single location on board an amphibious assault ship (general purpose) (LHA) or amphibious assault ship (multipurpose) (LHD) in which all communication facilities incident to the coordination of fire support from artillery, air, and NSFS are centralized. This is the naval counterpart to the fire support coordination center (FSCC) and direct air support center (DASC) used by the LF. The Navy TACC has five sections, four of which control and integrate aircraft.

a. **Air Traffic Control Section (ATCS).** The ATCS is located in the Navy TACC and provides initial safe passage, radar control, and surveillance for close air support (CAS) aircraft in the operational area. The ATCS also controls and routes rotary-wing CAS aircraft and assault support aircraft and coordinates with individual shipboard helicopter direction centers (HDCs) and the amphibious air traffic control center (AATCC) onboard the large deck amphibious ship(s) during amphibious operations. In amphibious operations, the HDC is the primary direct control agency for the helicopter group/unit commander operating under the overall control of the Navy TACC.

b. **Helicopter Coordination Section (HCS).** The HCS coordinates rotary-wing air operations with all HDCs and AATCC(s) in the amphibious task force. HCS tasks are to:

(1) Ensure all assault support requests are coordinated.

(2) Coordinate ship-to-shore movements.

(3) Resolve conflicts in rotary-wing tasking.

COORDINATION RESPONSIBILITIES

- Procedures for coordination of flight information

- Clearance of aircraft to enter and depart the airspace sector

- Procedures for assisting and coordinating with airspace control elements that respond to adjacent or supporting component commanders

- Procedures for deconfliction of operations during transitional operations and during operations in overlapping airspace areas

Figure II-2. Coordination Responsibilities

c. **Air Support Coordination Section (ASCS).** The ASCS is located in the SACC and is the section of the Navy TACC designated to coordinate, control, and integrate all direct support aircraft (i.e., CAS) and assault support operations.

d. **Air Defense Section (ADS).** The ADS, located in the Navy TACC, provides liaison with air defense commanders and provides early detection, identification, and warning of enemy aircraft.

e. **Plans, Execution, and Support Section.** The plans cell participates in the targeting effort as air operations subject matter experts through the targeting board. The section's planning will coincide with the ATO process. The section forwards excess air sorties and air support requests to the establishing authority for tasking and allocation. The input from the targeting board is processed by the ATO planning, production, and execution cell. This cell normally produces the following amphibious products: the ACO, the ATO, SPINS, and additional fire support asset requests. If the Navy TACC is acting as the joint air operations center for an enabling JFACC, the plans cell section may be required to produce the air apportionment recommendation for the JFC.

9. Marine Corps Tactical Air Command Center

The Marine Corps tactical air command center (Marine TACC), **when established ashore, provides the facilities for the ACE commander and staff to conduct air operations.** Other Services' comparable agencies include the US Air Force air and space operations center and the Navy TACC. If the ACE is afloat, the Marine TACC may be incrementally phased ashore. Initially, a Marine TADC is established ashore subordinate to

The air traffic control section provides initial safe passage, radar control, and surveillance for close air support aircraft in the operational area.

the Navy TACC and is responsible for air operations in the landward sector of the operational area. Upon completion of its build-up and when airspace management functions are passed from afloat to ashore, the Marine TADC assumes the title and responsibilities of the Marine TACC. The Navy TACC then may become a TADC, in support of the Marine TACC.

10. Direct Air Support Center

The DASC is an organization within the Marine air command and control system (MACCS) that serves as the central coordination point for all direct support air requests. Based upon the tactical situation, the DASC is normally located with either the senior GCE, FSCC, or the MAGTF force fires coordination center (FFCC). The DASC assigns direct air support aircraft to terminal control agencies, provides aircraft ingress and egress route instructions, and disseminates advisory information. When control is afloat, the Navy TACC supervises the DASC's operations. When control is ashore, the Marine TADC or Marine TACC supervises the DASC's operations. The DASC is normally the first major LF air control agency to come ashore, typically landing in the same wave as the FSCC.

11. Tactical Air Operations Center

The tactical air operations center (TAOC) provides safe passage, radar control, and surveillance for CAS aircraft en route to and from target areas. Until the Marine TADC or Marine TACC is established ashore, the TAOC normally reports to the Navy TACC. The TAOC, or elements thereof typically deploy with the land elements of a MEB or a MEF. The TAOC's capabilities incrementally increase as the size of the land force component increases (i.e., MEB or MEF size land force).

12. Air Command and Control Procedures and Coordination

The air C2 procedures described below are frequently associated with an established AOA; however, the underlying principles apply for most amphibious operations, whether an AOA is established or other airspace allocation methods are used.

a. **Pre-D-day Operations. Prior to the commencement of amphibious operations, airspace control and air defense operations throughout the operational area will be the direct responsibility of the ACA and AADC, respectively, as designated by the JFC.** Control is exercised through the designated air control agency which, as described earlier, could be an aircraft, surface ship, or Navy TACC. Subordinate TADCs, as designated, monitor air control circuits in readiness to assume all or part of the duties of the air control agency, if necessary.

b. **Advance Forces.** An advance force is a temporary organization within the AF which precedes the main body to the objective area. Its function is to participate in preparing the objective for the main assault by conducting such operations as reconnaissance, seizure of supporting positions, mine countermeasures (MCM), preliminary bombardment, underwater demolitions, and air support. **If advance force operations are** conducted in the operational area, the designated commander normally exercises air C2 through an advance force commander. The advance force commander controls operations in the designated area through an air control agency tailored and trained for the mission. CATF typically assumes responsibility for local airspace control and air defense operations upon arrival of the main body of the AF in the operational area.

c. **Control by Attack Groups.** When subordinate attack groups are formed for operations in widely separated landing areas, **the designated commander normally delegates to each attack group commander authority for control of airspace and air operations in the immediate area surrounding the respective landing areas**. An attack group is a subordinate task organization of the Navy forces of an ATF. It is composed of assault shipping and supporting naval units designated to transport, protect, land, and initially support a landing group. In amphibious operations, a landing group is a subordinate task organization of the LF capable of conducting landing operations, under a single tactical command, against an objective or group of objectives. The attack group commander exercises control through a local air control and defense agency consisting of airborne elements, an escorting surface combatant, or a TADC on the appropriate attack group ship. Overall direction of air operations as they apply to the amphibious mission is normally retained by the CATF and exercised through the designated air control agency.

d. **Air Tasking. The commander designated in the initiating directive is responsible for coordinating the air support requirements for the AF.** The commander coordinates the submission of air support requests through preparation of an air allocation request (ALLOREQ). An ALLOREQ message provides, among other things, the vehicle for requesting additional air support beyond the capability of the AF and its direct support components.

For more information see, JP 3-30, Command and Control for Joint Air Operations, *and Chapter V, Section B, "Fire Support," for more discussion of the joint air tasking cycle, and Chapter IV,* "Amphibious Operations Against Coastal Defenses," *for amplification on assault breaching.*

e. **Air Defense Transition Ashore.** As sufficient air defense assets are established ashore, the CLF will coordinate with the CATF to assume SADC responsibility in the landward sector of the operational area, the dimensions of which will have been predetermined during the planning phase of the operation.

f. **Termination of the Amphibious Operation.** Upon termination of the amphibious operation, the AF will be dissolved, and air control and defense responsibilities in the area passed to the appropriate commander in accordance with the establishing authority's guidance.

13. Transition from Tactical Air Control Center to Tactical Air Command Center

Both the Navy and the Marine Corps air control systems are capable of independent operations; however, in the conduct of an amphibious operation, elements of both systems are used to different degrees from the beginning of the operation until the control is phased ashore. Under the ATF commander, the TACC, typically on board the LHA or LHD, will normally be established as the agency responsible for controlling all air operations within the allocated airspace regardless of mission or origin, to include supporting arms. As the operation progresses, the LF commander, having the capability to control air operations, may establish C2 systems ashore and incrementally accept responsibility for various C2 functions from the ATF commander. When full capability is achieved, the CLF may assume full air control responsibility from the ATF commander (i.e., Navy TACC). In some cases it might be neither necessary nor desirable to transfer authority ashore. As the amphibious operation proceeds, C2 of aviation operations is transitioned ashore as MACCS agencies are established on the ground. Air C2 functions are traditionally sequenced ashore in five phases.

a. Phase one is characterized by the arrival of various "supporting arms controllers" ashore; namely the tactical air control party (TACP), forward observers, air support liaison teams, and NSFS spot teams.

b. In phase two, the DASC is normally the first principal air control agency established ashore. When control is afloat, the Navy TACC supervises the DASC's operations.

c. The movement of the TAOC ashore, although not directly related to CAS, is the principal event in phase three.

d. In phase four, the senior organization of the Marine air control group is established ashore and functions as the Marine TADC under control of the Navy TACC.

e. Phase five is characterized by the passage of command responsibility ashore. The Marine Corps TADC assumes the role of the Marine TACC. Once the Marine TACC receives control of all LF air operations, the Navy TACC may become the TADC (afloat) supporting the land-based air control agency. The CATF will normally be assigned RADC or SADC responsibility for the seaward sector of the operational area.

See Navy Tactics, Techniques, and Procedures (NTTP) 3-02.1.3, Amphibious/Expeditionary Operations Air Control, for more details.

CHAPTER III
CONDUCT OF AMPHIBIOUS OPERATIONS

> *"Amphibious flexibility is the greatest strategic asset that a sea-based power possesses."*
>
> **B.H. Liddell Hart, *Deterrence or Defense*, 1960**

1. Overview

An amphibious operation applies maneuver principles to expeditionary power projection by establishing a LF ashore. The AF executes rapid, focused operations to accomplish the JFC's objectives. Regardless of the type of amphibious operation, the CLF and CATF plan and execute operations based on maneuver warfare philosophy and the following general concepts.

a. All actions **focus on achieving the commander's objectives**. The CONOPS guides the decisive actions to exploit enemy vulnerabilities and attack enemy COGs and selected decisive points.

b. **The use of the sea offers maneuver space.** Operations should create freedom of action for the AF, while **creating a tempo greater than the enemy can withstand**. The AF commander should exploit evolutionary advances in electronic warfare (EW), precision targeting systems, waterborne/airborne transportation craft, and anything else that allows for the introduction of the AF at the time and place of his choosing. Maneuver can begin long before closing the shoreline as the sea offers many avenues of approach.

c. The key to successful LF operations is the rapid build up of combat power ashore. Therefore, it is imperative that commanders **seek to pit friendly strength against enemy weakness**.

d. The preferred tactic for AFs operating against coastal defenses is to avoid or bypass the strong points if unable to exploit gaps in these defenses. Operations that **emphasize intelligence, deception, and flexibility** will help identify and create gaps while also enhancing the force protection of the entire joint force. If unable to bypass the strong points, the AF will be required to neutralize an adversary's anti-access systems.

e. The complexity of amphibious operations and the vulnerability of the AF as it builds combat power ashore require the **full integration of organic assets as well as those of other joint and multinational forces**. The AF realizes maximum effectiveness by using all available capabilities.

f. This chapter has been structured to follow the phases of an amphibious operation as discussed in Chapter I, "Overview." The phases are: planning, embarkation, rehearsals, movement, and action (also known as PERMA). The action phase has been further divided into the five types of amphibious operations.

SECTION A. PLANNING

2. General

The planning process described herein is designed for use by any size AF while conducting any operation. This tool assists commanders, who make the decisions (see paragraph 6, "Primary Decisions"), required in most amphibious operations. **The focus of the planning process is the development of a plan that accomplishes the mission.** It links the employment of the AF to the attainment of operational and strategic objectives through the design, organization, integration, and conduct of the amphibious operation within the JFC's overall operation or campaign. The nature of amphibious warfare gives rise to planning procedures that are both intricate and unique. Planning intricacy stems from the complex detail required to fully coordinate the assault landing of troops, equipment, and supplies; maximize maneuver, speed, and available fire support; and minimize the vulnerability of the assault forces and naval shipping. The uniqueness of amphibious planning stems from the interrelationships between the components of the AF; between the AF and the joint force; and between the AF and supporting organizations and agencies.

3. Tenets of Amphibious Planning

Planning for an amphibious operation is continuous, from the receipt of the initiating directive through the termination of the operation. Amphibious planning requires concurrent, parallel, and detailed planning by all participating forces. The planning pattern is cyclical in nature, composed of a series of analyses and judgments of operational situations, each stemming from those that have preceded. The tenets of successful amphibious planning are commanders' involvement and guidance, unity of effort, and an integrated planning effort.

a. **Commanders' Involvement and Guidance. The complexity of amphibious operations requires AF commanders to drive the planning process.** Their guidance and intent are central to planning and must be translated into a design for action by subordinates. Their decisions (e.g., AF area of operations, AF objectives, AF CONOPS, landing beaches, commanders' critical information requirements, and promulgated essential elements of friendly information) are required before additional steps in the process can proceed.

b. **Unity of Effort.** Unity of effort allows the AF commanders to effectively focus their forces on mission accomplishment. **They must view their operational environment as an indivisible entity**, for operations or events in one area may have profound and often unintended effects on other areas and events.

c. **Integrated Planning.** Integrated planning in amphibious operations has two parts. **The first part is the assembly of the AF commanders and their staffs in the same locality.** When such arrangements are not practicable, the exchange of liaison officers qualified to perform planning functions and the use of advanced technology, collaborative planning aids, and video teleconferencing are necessary. During planning, and particularly in CAP, AF commanders ensure that their planning efforts are parallel and concurrent with each other and those of their higher headquarters. The same degree of integration by AF commanders and their staffs must also be achieved with subordinate units to ensure a coordinated and thorough plan. **The second part of integrated planning occurs across functional areas.** An integrated operational planning team, consisting of cross functional representatives, is necessary. The use of functional areas, C2, intelligence, fires, movement and maneuver, protection and sustainment, enable commanders to integrate the planning effort and supervise the plan. The use of functional areas facilitates the consideration of all relevant factors and minimizes omissions. The key to this part of integrated planning is the assignment of appropriate personnel to represent each functional area. Integrated planning is facilitated by the use of operational planning teams which are dynamic, ad hoc organizations formed around planners from functional areas, appropriate staff representatives, subordinate and supporting command liaison officers, and other subject matter experts.

See JP 5-0, Joint Operation Planning, *and JP 3-33,* Joint Task Force Headquarters.

4. **Planning Directive**

Following receipt of the initiating directive, the AF commanders issue a coordinated planning directive to harmonize staff actions, and complete required planning in the time allowed. **The planning directive specifies the plan of action and milestones to complete each major step in the planning process,** and the timeline for the development of OPLANs, OPORDs, operational general matters (OPGENs), operation tasks (OPTASKs) and other products.

5. **Planning Methods**

Amphibious planning is conducted as part of the Joint Operation Planning and Execution System (JOPES) planning activities that occur either as contingency planning or CAP.

a. **Contingency Planning.** Contingency planning occurs in response to a hypothetical situation and is based on requirements identified in the *Guidance for Employment of the Force, Joint Strategic Capabilities Plan*, or other planning directives. It is performed well in advance of expected execution, often during peacetime or before initiating an operation.

b. **Crisis Action Planning.** CAP is the JOPES process involving the time-sensitive development of joint OPLANs and OPORDs for the deployment, employment, and sustainment of assigned and allocated forces in response to an imminent situation. CAP is based on up-to-date actual circumstances that exist at the time planning occurs.

For more detailed information on contingency planning and CAP refer to CJCSM 3122.01 Series Joint Operation Planning and Execution System.

c. **Amphibious Planning Process.** The cornerstone of amphibious operations execution is the six-step planning process. It is modeled upon the joint operation planning process found in JP 5-0, *Joint Operation Planning.* The six steps of the process are mission analysis, COA development, COA wargame, COA comparison and decision, orders development, and transition (see Figure III-1). This planning process provides logical procedures to follow from receipt of the initiating directive through the development of OPLANs, OPORDs, OPTASKs, and other products. The process also provides the AF

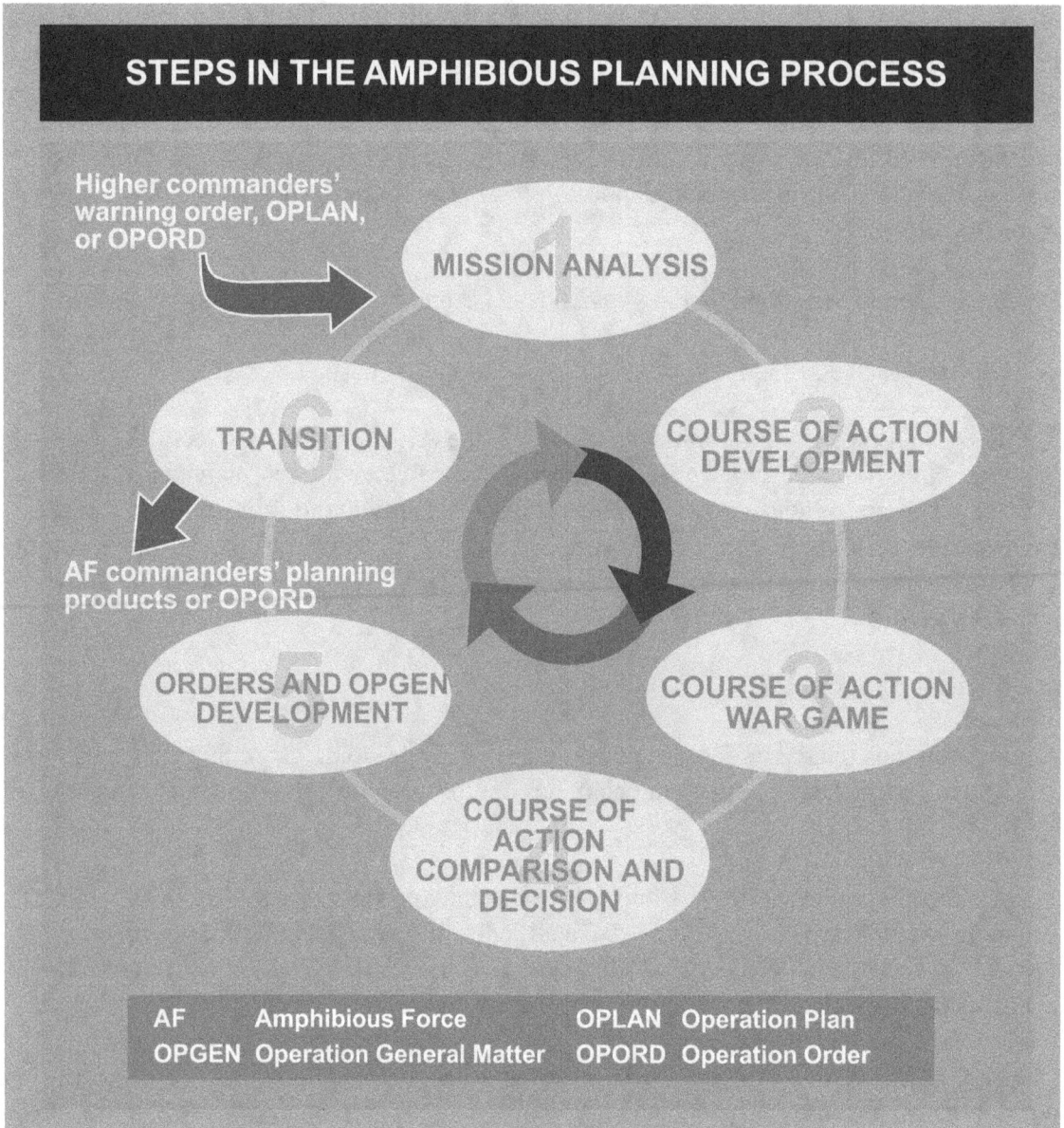

Figure III-1. Steps in the Amphibious Planning Process

commanders and their staffs with a means to organize planning activities, transmit plans to subordinate commands, and share a common understanding of the mission and the commanders' intents. Staff interactions, processes, and compatible system interfaces, and the overlap between various planning steps allow a concurrent, coordinated effort that maintains flexibility, makes efficient use of available time, and facilitates continuous information sharing. It enhances the commanders' ability to make timely decisions.

6. Primary Decisions

AF commanders make certain primary decisions during the planning process before further planning for an amphibious operation can proceed. In some cases, these decisions may have been made by the establishing authority and promulgated in the initiating directive. The decisions and who makes them are described below. **In the case of mutual decisions, both commanders must concur or the decision is referred to the establishing authority for resolution** (see Figure III-2).

a. During **"mission analysis,"** the following decisions are made:

(1) **Determine AF Mission(s).** AF commanders may decide on a coordinated mission statement or develop separate but supporting mission statements. The determination of a coordinated AF mission statement is a mutual decision. If separate but supporting mission statements are chosen, then each commander must develop his or her respective mission statement.

(2) **Select AF Objective(s). AF objectives are physical in nature such as: terrain, infrastructure (e.g., ports or airfields), or forces that must be seized, secured, or destroyed in order to accomplish the mission.** AF objectives are designated in alphabetic order (e.g., AF Objective A and AF Objective B). The selection of AF objectives is a mutual decision.

b. During **"COA Development,"** AF staffs **further develop COAs** based on the guidance from the AF commanders. Normally, the LF planners will provide an LF COA for the ATF planners to build a supporting COA. At a minimum, COAs include the general area for a landing (which may already be specified by higher headquarters), designation of the main effort, the scheme of maneuver, and the task organization. The selected COAs will be wargamed and compared based on criteria established by the commanders. The selection of AF COAs is a mutual decision.

c. **COA analysis and wargaming** follows JP 5-0, *Joint Operation Planning.*

d. No later than during **"COA comparison and decision"** the following decisions must be made:

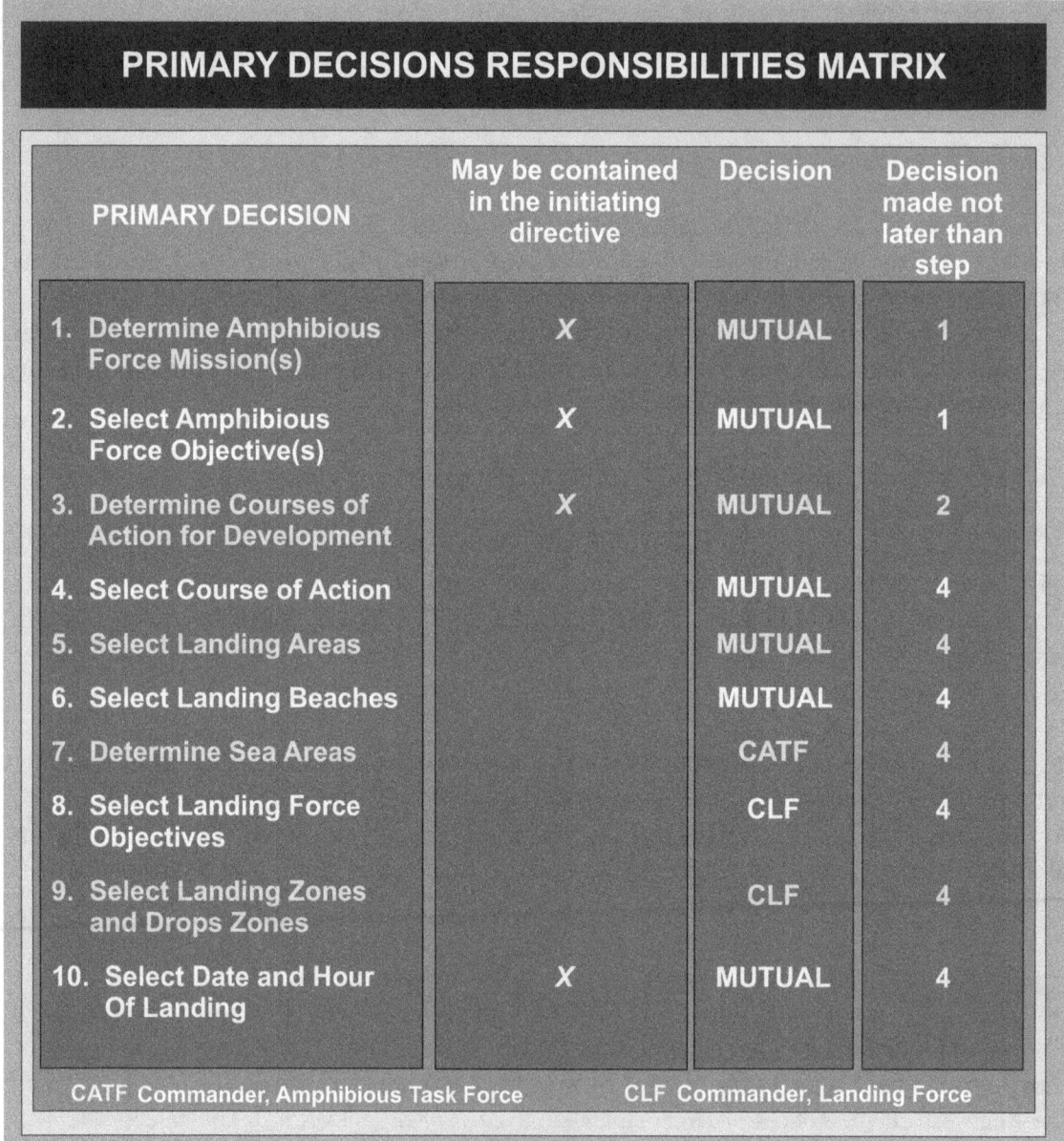

PRIMARY DECISIONS RESPONSIBILITIES MATRIX

PRIMARY DECISION	May be contained in the initiating directive	Decision	Decision made not later than step
1. Determine Amphibious Force Mission(s)	X	MUTUAL	1
2. Select Amphibious Force Objective(s)	X	MUTUAL	1
3. Determine Courses of Action for Development	X	MUTUAL	2
4. Select Course of Action		MUTUAL	4
5. Select Landing Areas		MUTUAL	4
6. Select Landing Beaches		MUTUAL	4
7. Determine Sea Areas		CATF	4
8. Select Landing Force Objectives		CLF	4
9. Select Landing Zones and Drops Zones		CLF	4
10. Select Date and Hour Of Landing	X	MUTUAL	4

CATF Commander, Amphibious Task Force   CLF Commander, Landing Force

Figure III-2. Primary Decisions Responsibilities Matrix

(1) **Select Course of Action.** At this point a COA is selected and the CONOPS (including fire support planning guidance) is prepared. The CONOPS is usually a written and graphic representation, in broad outline, of the intent of both of the commanders with respect to their portion of the operation. It gives an overall picture of the operation, including the transit, formation for landing, and the scheme of maneuver for accomplishing the AF objectives. Both commanders prepare mutually supporting CONOPS.

(2) **Select Landing Areas. The landing area** includes the beach, the approaches to the beach, the transport areas, the fire support areas, the airspace above it, and the land included in the advance inland to accomplish the initial objectives. The selection of the landing area is a mutual decision (see Figure III-3). The beach is the area extending from

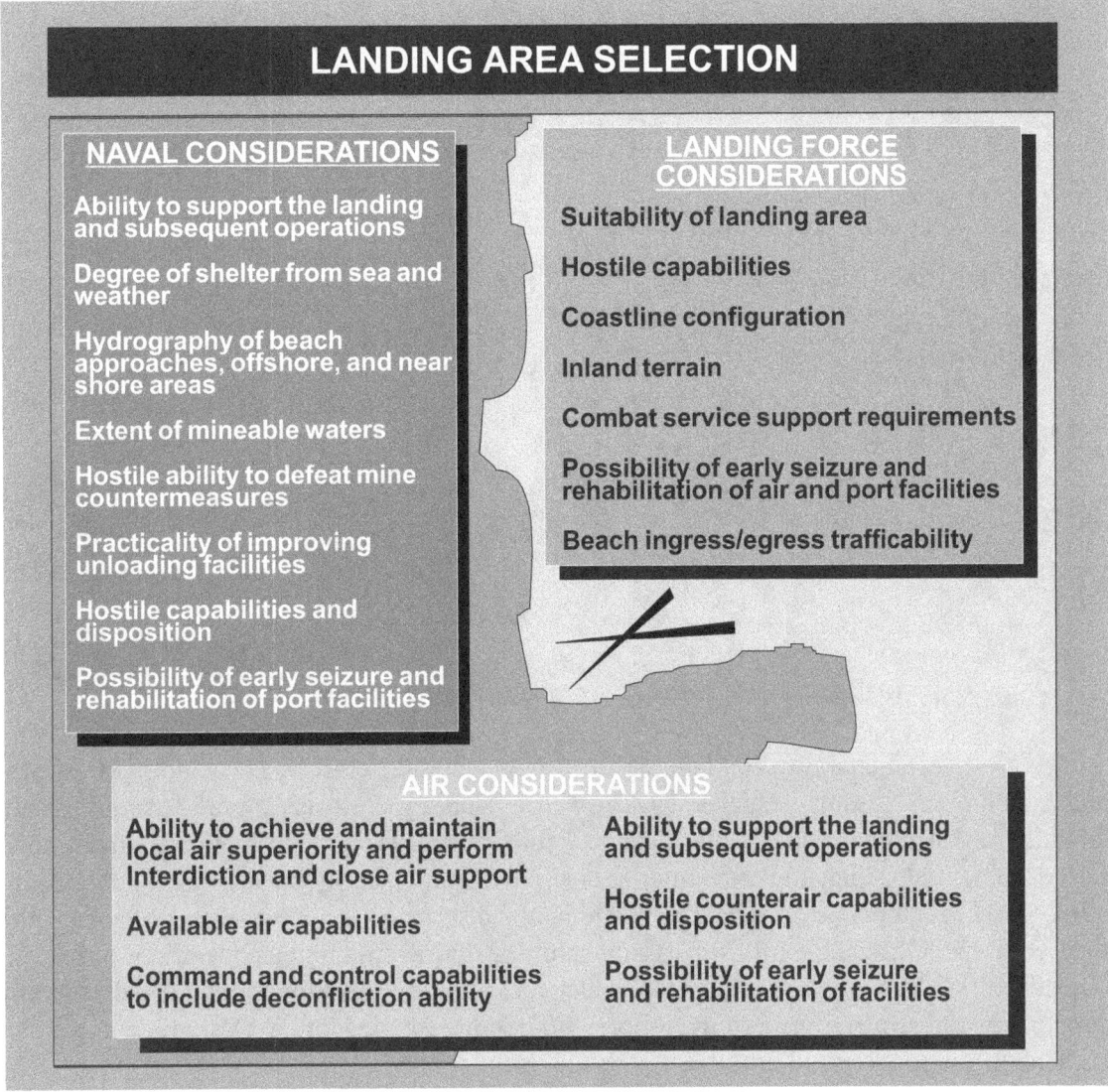

LANDING AREA SELECTION

NAVAL CONSIDERATIONS

Ability to support the landing and subsequent operations

Degree of shelter from sea and weather

Hydrography of beach approaches, offshore, and near shore areas

Extent of mineable waters

Hostile ability to defeat mine countermeasures

Practicality of improving unloading facilities

Hostile capabilities and disposition

Possibility of early seizure and rehabilitation of port facilities

LANDING FORCE CONSIDERATIONS

Suitability of landing area

Hostile capabilities

Coastline configuration

Inland terrain

Combat service support requirements

Possibility of early seizure and rehabilitation of air and port facilities

Beach ingress/egress trafficability

AIR CONSIDERATIONS

Ability to achieve and maintain local air superiority and perform Interdiction and close air support

Available air capabilities

Command and control capabilities to include deconfliction ability

Ability to support the landing and subsequent operations

Hostile counterair capabilities and disposition

Possibility of early seizure and rehabilitation of facilities

Figure III-3. Landing Area Selection

the shoreline inland to a marked change in physiographic form or material, or to the line of permanent vegetation (coastline).

(3) **Select Landing Beaches.** A landing beach is usually the portion of a shoreline required for the landing of a battalion landing team (BLT). In an amphibious operation, a BLT is an infantry battalion normally reinforced by necessary combat and combat support elements; the basic unit for planning an assault landing. Landing beaches are selected from within the selected landing areas. Landing beaches are named by color and are typically 1000 meters wide. Principal factors in the selection of landing beaches (in addition to those previously described for selection of landing areas) include:

The commander, landing force selects landing and drop zones.

(a) Suitability for landing craft (e.g., landing crafts, air cushion [LCACs]) and amphibious assault vehicles (AAVs). A landing craft is a craft employed in amphibious operations, specifically designed for carrying troops and their equipment and for beaching, unloading, and retracting. It is also used for resupply operations. The AAV is a fully tracked, amphibious vehicle tasked to land the surface assault elements of the LF and their equipment in a single lift from assault shipping during amphibious operations to inland objectives. AAVs are also used to conduct mechanized operations and related combat support in subsequent operations ashore. The three types of AAVs are command, personnel, and recovery.

(b) Offshore approaches and tidal conditions.

(c) Number, location, and suitability of beach support areas, beach exits, and nearby infrastructure. In amphibious operations, the beach support area is to the rear of a LF or elements thereof, established and operated by shore party units, which contains the facilities for the unloading of troops and materiel and the support of the forces ashore; it includes facilities for the evacuation of wounded, enemy prisoners of war (EPWs), and captured materiel. Landing beaches are designated by color, and subdivisions are further designated with the addition of a number (Green Beach, Red Beach 1, and Red Beach 2). The selection of landing beaches is a mutual decision.

(d) **Determine requirement and feasibility of OTH operations.** Consider threat, environmental conditions, likelihood of achieving surprise, and friendly force capabilities (e.g., power projection and sustainment). See paragraph 21, "Over-the-Horizon Amphibious Operations."

(4) **Determine Sea Areas and the Sea Echelon Plan.** A sea echelon is a portion of the amphibious shipping that withdraws from, or remains out of, the transport area during a landing or an operation. It operates in designated areas to seaward in an on-call or unscheduled status. The sea echelon plan provides for the dispersion of amphibious shipping to minimize losses due to enemy attacks and to reduce the area that must be cleared for mines. Amphibious shipping consists of organic navy ships specifically designed to transport, land, and support landing forces in amphibious assault operations and capable of being loaded or unloaded by naval personnel without external assistance in the AOA. In amphibious operations, the transport area is an area assigned to a transport organization for the purpose of debarking troops and equipment. The CATF determines the sea echelon plan. The design of the amphibious airspace must take into account, as a general rule, the lateral limits of the amphibious area above the sea echelon areas.

(5) **Select LF Objectives. LF objectives facilitate the attainment of AF objectives and/or uninterrupted landing of forces and materiel.** LF objectives are normally designated by LF and a number (e.g., LF Objective 1). LF objectives are selected by the CLF.

(6) **Select Landing Zones (LZs) and Drop Zones (DZs).** An LZ is a specified zone used for the landing of aircraft. An LZ may contain one or more landing sites. A DZ is a specific area upon which airborne troops, equipment, or supplies are air dropped. LZs and DZs are designated when airborne or air-transported forces are employed. The CLF selects LZs and DZs.

(7) **Select Date and Hour of Landing.** The date and hour of the landing are selected unless they are specified in the initiating directive. **H-hour**, in amphibious operations, is the time the first assault elements are scheduled to touchdown on the beach or an LZ. **L-hour** is defined in amphibious operations as the time at which the first helicopter of the helicopterborne assault wave touches down in the LZ. H- and L-hour are confirmed prior to commencement of the landing based on the weather, enemy situation, and other pertinent factors. If not specified in the initiating directive, this is a mutual decision. Landing considerations include:

(a) Is it preferable to land at high tide or low tide?

(b) Is it preferable to land during the day or night, and if at night, which nights or when during the night based on luminescence?

(c) Is it preferable to land on a certain day due to religious and cultural events?

(d) Is it preferable to land in a certain month due to better weather?

(e) Is it preferable to land immediately after certain countermine operations, which are more effective at low tide, have been conducted or is it better to wait for high tide?

(f) Is it preferable to have the helicopters land at the same time as the surface assault?

e. **Orders and OPGEN Development. OPGENs and OPTASKs are messages, used by commanders of Navy forces to transmit orders, fragmentary orders, and tactical and operational tasks to elements of the ATF. Orders and OPGENs/OPTASKs serve as the principal means by which the commanders express their decisions, intents, and guidance.**

(1) **Order and OPGEN/OPTASK Crosstalk.** After the primary decisions have been made and step four of the planning process is completed, the AF commanders develop their OPLANs, OPORDs, OPGENs, or OPTASKs. The staffs must maintain constant communication to ensure continued harmonization of their concurrent planning efforts. **Depending upon time available, once final drafts of the OPORD and OPGEN/OPTASK have been completed a crosstalk and confirmation brief should be conducted between the commanders and staffs.** The purpose of the crosstalk is to compare these documents with higher and adjacent orders to ensure unity of effort and to identify any discrepancies or gaps. Following the staff's correction of any discrepancies identified during the crosstalk, the OPORD and OPGEN will be submitted for approval, and a confirmation brief is scheduled.

(2) **Confirmation Brief.** A confirmation brief is given by a subordinate commander and his staff once planning is complete. The participants brief their scheme of maneuver and fire support plan and the relationship between their unit's mission and the other units in the operation. The confirmation brief allows the higher commander to identify discrepancies between his order and the subordinates' plan(s) and allows for corrective actions, if required, prior to execution.

f. **Transition.** Transition is an orderly handover of an OPLAN, OPORD, OPGEN, or OPTASK as it is passed to those tasked with execution of the operation. It provides those who will execute the plan or order with the situational awareness and rationale for key decisions necessary to ensure that there is a coherent shift from planning to execution.

7. Assessment

Assessment is a process that measures progress of the AF toward mission accomplishment and occurs at all levels. The assessment process begins during mission analysis when the commander and staff consider what to measure and how to measure it to determine progress toward accomplishing a task, creating an effect, or achieving an objective. Assessment actions and measures help commanders adjust operations and resources as required, determine when to execute branches and sequels, and make other critical decisions to ensure current and future operations remain aligned with the mission and end state. As a general rule, the level at which a specific operation, task, or action is directed should be the level at which such activity is assessed. Assessment at the operational level typically is broader than at the tactical level (e.g., combat assessment) and uses measures of effectiveness (MOEs) that support operational mission accomplishment. Commanders use MOEs to determine progress toward success in those operations for which tactical-level combat assessment ways, means, and measures do not apply. Tactical-level assessment typically uses measures of performance to evaluate task accomplishment. The results of tactical tasks are often physical in nature, but also can reflect the impact on specific functions and systems. Tactical-level assessment may include assessing progress by phase lines; neutralization of enemy forces; control of key terrain or resources; and security, relief, or reconstruction tasks. Assessment of results at the tactical level helps commanders determine operational and strategic progress, so JFCs must have a comprehensive, integrated assessment plan that links assessment activities and measures at all levels.

For more information refer to JP 5-0, Joint Operation Planning.

8. **Movement Planning Responsibilities**

a. **Movement Plan.** The CATF is responsible for preparing a movement plan. In operations involving several attack groups, the CATF usually prepares a general movement plan in which coordination measures are included as necessary. Subordinate force and group commanders will prepare their own detailed movement plans. **Because details of**

USS San Antonio (LPD-17) transits the Suez Canal en route to the operational area.

the movement depend on overall requirements of the operation, the movement plans are generally among the last to be completed. Each movement plan is normally included as an annex to the appropriate OPLAN or OPORD.

b. **Coordination with Other Forces.** Coordination measures between forces supporting the amphibious operation and the AF will normally be provided in planning guidance issued by the JFC or designated commander.

c. **Postponement Plan.** Postponement may be necessary because of weather conditions, unexpected movement of major enemy forces, or failure to meet go/no-go criteria after the AF has started its movement from final staging areas toward the operational area. This contingency is provided for in the postponement plan. **Usually, postponement is on a 24-hour basis, which involves backtracking or diversion of ships into a designated sea area.** A longer postponement may involve redeployment of the force to a staging area. The postponement plan will be prepared by the CATF and is usually promulgated as part of the OPLAN. Execution of the postponement plan will normally be controlled by the JFC or designated commander, based on the recommendations of the CATF and CLF.

d. **Alternate Plans.** The alternate plan for an amphibious operation may differ from the preferred plan and necessitate separate movement or approach plans. It is seldom possible to determine far in advance the time at which an alternate plan will be placed in effect. Movement plans must therefore be flexible enough for execution of alternate plans at any point between the final staging area and the operational area.

9. **Sea Routes**

a. **En route to the Operational Area. Sea routes and route points to the operational area will normally be planned by the CATF.** Routes selected should lead from all possible ports of departure to the operational area. Alternate routes should also be provided to avoid interference between forces and to permit diversion should the threat of enemy attack or weather prevent use of primary routes. Routes and route points should be named to facilitate reference. Small-scale charts, which show sea routes and route points, are prepared and included in the operation plans and orders of appropriate ATF echelons. All sea routes should be wide enough for a movement group commander to maneuver his group without interfering with the movement of other groups.

b. **Within the Operational Area. CATF determines sea routes in the operational area.** During planning, sea route selection must take into consideration the missions of various task forces, groups, units, and elements in the AF, so they may proceed expeditiously to their assigned stations without interference. Sea routes to the operational area will connect with sea routes within the operational area at designated points just outside the area screen to minimize interference during the deployment and movement of forces from their cruising or approach formations to assigned stations or areas. Sea routes in the operational area should be selected that:

(1) Ensure a minimum of interference among ships and formations.

(2) Are clear of mines and navigational hazards to the maximum extent possible.

(3) Provide sufficient dispersion to prevent concentrations that would make the AF a desirable target for chemical, biological, radiological, and nuclear (CBRN) attack.

(4) Provide for economy of screening forces.

10. Staging Areas

Plans will be made by the CATF, in consultation with the CLF, to use staging areas while en route to the operational area. The AF may stage at one or more intervening ports for logistic support, emergency repairs, or final rehearsals. **The CATF will select the staging area required** and will ensure that:

a. Necessary service craft are available.

b. A general logistics schedule is promulgated.

c. Anchorages are assigned based on consideration for expediting logistics while facilitating entry and sortie of movement groups staging through the area and avoiding vulnerable concentrations.

d. Provision is made for replacement or repair of critical supplies or equipment expended or damaged during rehearsal.

11. Sea Areas

a. To minimize the possibility of interference between various elements of the AF and other supporting forces, sea areas in the vicinity of the landing area will be selected by the CATF and designated by the higher commander. The sea areas will be divided into a number of operating areas as depicted in Figure III-4 and described below.

b. **Ocean Operating Areas.** Two kinds of ocean operating areas may be selected.

(1) **Close support area.** Defines the portion(s) of the ocean operating area nearest to, but not necessarily in, the objective area. They are assigned to carrier strike groups, surface action groups, surface action units, and certain logistic CSS elements.

(2) **Distant retirement area.** Located to seaward of the landing area and divided into a number of operating areas in which assault ships may retire and operate in the event of heavy weather or to prevent concentration of ships in the landing area.

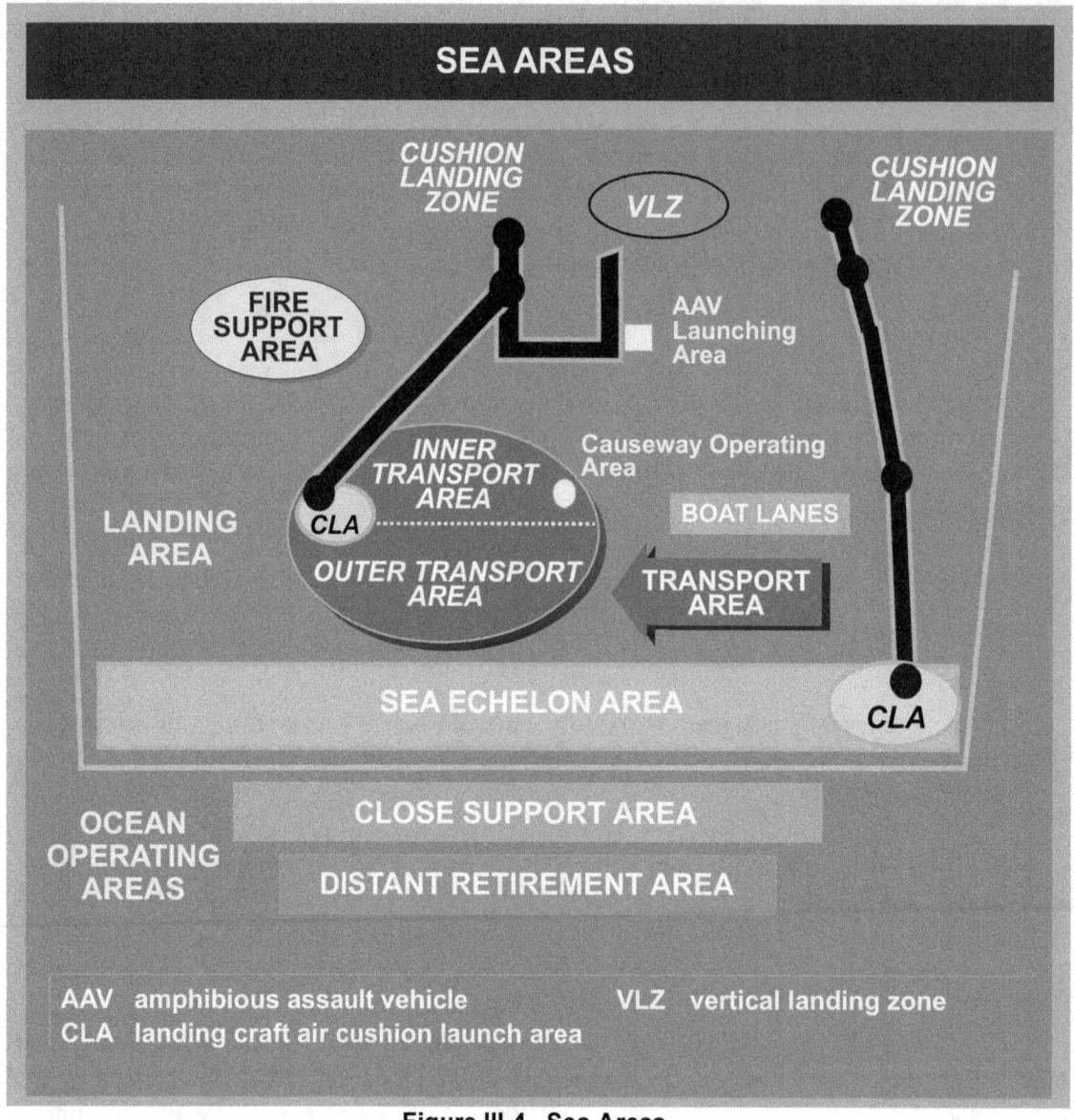

SEA AREAS

CUSHION LANDING ZONE

VLZ

CUSHION LANDING ZONE

FIRE SUPPORT AREA

AAV Launching Area

INNER TRANSPORT AREA

Causeway Operating Area

LANDING AREA

CLA

BOAT LANES

OUTER TRANSPORT AREA

TRANSPORT AREA

SEA ECHELON AREA

CLA

OCEAN OPERATING AREAS

CLOSE SUPPORT AREA

DISTANT RETIREMENT AREA

AAV amphibious assault vehicle
CLA landing craft air cushion launch area
VLZ vertical landing zone

Figure III-4. Sea Areas

c. **Sea Areas Within the Landing Area**. Areas in the landing area extending outward to the inner limits of the close support areas.

(1) **Sea Echelon Area.** An area to seaward of a transport area from which assault ships are phased into the transport area and to which assault ships withdraw from the transport area. The use of a sea echelon area allows for dispersion as a defense against attack.

(2) **Transport Area.** In amphibious operations, an area assigned to a transport organization for the purpose of debarking troops and equipment. It consists of mine cleared lanes, areas, and channels leading from a sea echelon area to the beaches. The maximum number of ships in the transport area is determined by dispersion requirements, availability

of forces for MCM operations, and local hydrography and topography. Transport landing areas include:

(a) **Outer Transport Area. An area inside the antisubmarine screen to which assault transports proceed initially after arrival in the objective area.**

(b) **Inner Transport Area.** Area located close to the landing beach which transports may utilize to expedite unloading. Considerations are: depth of water, navigational hazards, boat traffic, and enemy action.

(3) **Landing Craft Air Cushion Launch Area (CLA).** CLAs are located in the transport area and sea echelon area. The CLA (the sea component) and landing craft air cushion landing zone (CLZ) (the beach component) are connected by transit lanes.

(4) **AAV Launch Area.** Areas located near and to seaward of the line of departure (LOD) to which landing ships proceed to launch AAVs.

(5) **Causeway Operation Area.** The causeway launching area is an area located near the LOD but clear of the approach lanes to an area located in the inner transport area.

(6) A boat lane is a lane for amphibious assault landing craft, which goes from the LOD at sea to the landing beaches. The width of the boat lane is determined by the number of craft that need to safely transit the boat lane. The beach can be wider than the boat lane and several boat lanes can serve one beach.

(7) **Fire Support Areas (FSAs)/Fire Support Station.** A maneuver area or exact location assigned to fire support ships from which surface fire support is delivered.

12. Geographic Reference Points

A complete system of geographic reference points for the operational area and surrounding ocean area should be formulated during planning. The points may be used to indicate routes (particularly where the direction of the routes changes), to depict the shape and location of the areas discussed above, and for certain locations not related to areas or routes. Reference points will be encoded and defined by exact latitude and longitude.

13. Intelligence En Route

a. The AF, or elements thereof, may receive significant intelligence information while en route to the operational area. This is particularly true in situations where advance forces or forces external to the AF, conduct pre-D-day operations in the operational area or where remote sensor data is provided.

b. The AF's intelligence center is responsible for timely dissemination of pertinent intelligence information to the CATF and CLF. ATF ships receiving such information are responsible for passing it to the embarked landing forces.

14. Coordination During Passage

a. Forces not a part of the AF that are supporting the AF must coordinate their movement within the AOA with the ATF. This coordination must be delineated in the plans of the JFC or designated commander.

b. Individual commanders must remain aware of the need for maintaining the schedule and proceeding along prescribed routes. If deviation is required, the commander of the group will determine whether to break EMCON to advise other commands of the situation. In certain situations, there may be serious consequences if friendly land or carrier-based search aircraft observe a force in a position not indicated in the aircrew briefing. All commanders must be fully cognizant of the general scheme and operational areas of other forces.

15. Approach to the Operational Area

a. Approach to the operational area includes the arrival of various task groups in the vicinity of the operational area and deployment of task groups from cruising formations, aggregating as necessary according to assigned tasks and proceeding to designated positions in the operational area. During this critical period, additional protective measures may be necessary. These provisions should encompass:

(1) Counterair measures, including timely air strikes against enemy airfields within range of the landing area.

(2) Location and neutralization of enemy submarines, surface craft, minefields, and shore batteries that can interfere with the approach.

(3) Selection of approach routes that avoid lengthy exposure to fire from enemy shore batteries.

b. Approach of the main body is usually more complicated than the advance force because it involves a greater number of ships and because the arrival of the main body must be carefully timed relative to H-hour. However, if an advance force has been employed, protective measures for the main body during the approach may be easier because the advance force may have been in the area for some time and implemented many of the necessary protective measures. In particular, minesweep assets of the advance force will normally have swept enough of the landing area to permit the main body to approach with less risk. The same considerations apply to the approach of the demonstration force as to the approach of the main body.

c. Proper coordination and timing is of utmost importance in the final stages of the approach of all elements of each movement group to prevent interference between elements and permit each to arrive at its assigned position at the proper time to commence its task. Careful, precise, and accurate navigation is essential. The presence of advanced force elements already in the landing area may increase the complexity of the amphibious landing. The advance force commander is responsible to ensure that elements of the advance force do not interfere with the approach of the main body. When the AF is composed of two or more task groups, the CATF normally coordinates the approach of the various task groups, but the task group commander is responsible for the movements of each individual task group.

16. Ship-to-Shore Movement Considerations

a. The plan for ship-to-shore movement is developed by the CATF and CLF to ensure that troops, equipment, and supplies are landed at the prescribed times, places, and in the formation required to support the LF scheme of maneuver. Ship-to-shore movement is that portion of the assault which includes the deployment of the LF from the assault shipping to designated landing areas. The element of a force comprised of tailored units and craft assigned to conduct the initial assault on the operational area is known as the **assault echelon (AE)**. Assault troops, vehicles, aircraft, equipment, and supplies that are not needed to initiate the assault, but are required to support and sustain the assault are known as **the assault follow-on echelon (AFOE)**. The AFOE will, therefore, usually come in after the AE has conducted the initial assault. **Ship-to-shore movement is perhaps the most critical part of the action phase of amphibious operations.** During this period, the LF and assault shipping are most concentrated. Landing craft, AAVs, and helicopters are vulnerable to adversary fire, not to mention the natural hazards of weather, sea state, and surf conditions. Movement control requirements are complex and must be coordinated precisely with supporting arms.

> "It was to be a brutal day. At first light on 15 June 1944, the Navy fire support ships of the task force lying off Saipan Island increased their previous days' preparatory fires involving all caliber of weapons. At 0542, Vice Admiral Richmond K. Turner ordered, "Land the landing force." Around 0700, the landing ships, tank (LSTs) moved to within approximately 1,250 yards behind the line of departure. Troops in the LSTs began debarking from them in landing vehicles, tracked (LVTs). Control vessels containing Navy and Marine personnel with their radio gear took their positions displaying flags indicating which beach approaches they controlled."
>
> **John C. Chapin:**
> **Breaching the Marianas: The Battle for Saipan**

b. Organizations and agencies may be established to support the ship-to-shore movement plan. These organizations and agencies (i.e., terminal service battalion, amphibious construction battalion, or cargo handling and port group units) may be required to support the offload of merchant ships. An amphibious construction battalion is a permanently commissioned naval unit, subordinate to the commander, naval beach group, designed to provide an administrative unit from which personnel and equipment are formed in tactical elements and made available to appropriate commanders to operate pontoon causeways, transfer barges, warping tugs, and assault bulk fuel systems, and to meet salvage requirements of the naval beach party. The beach party is the Navy component of the landing force support party (LFSP) under the tactical control of the LFSP commander. As developed seaports and airports become available, they are used to supplement traditional beach operations. Unloading operations are divided into two periods.

(1) **The initial landing and unloading period** is a tactical evolution and must provide rapid build-up of combat forces ashore and quick response to LF requirements.

(2) **The selective and general unloading period. Selective unloading is tactical in nature and used to satisfy immediate support requirements when a full general unloading period is unnecessary or not feasible.** General unloading is primarily logistic-oriented and emphasizes speed, volume, and rapid completion of the unloading of required personnel and materiel. It encompasses the unloading of units and cargo from the ships as rapidly as cargo handling facilities on the beach or ashore permit. It proceeds without regard to class, type, or priority of cargo.

c. **Conduct of Ship-to-Shore Movement**. All ship-to-shore movement is controlled by CATF. For large operations, there will be a central control officer (CCO) who will control all ship-to-shore movement by surface. The primary control officer (PCO) will control all ship-to-shore movement to a colored beach and works for the CCO. If the operation does not require a CCO, then the PCO will work directly for CATF. A parallel organization exists with air with all air ship-to-shore movement controlled by the tactical air officer (TAO) and the HCS will control all flights into a helicopter landing zone (HLZ). If the operation does not require a TAO, then the HCS will work directly for CATF. The commencement of landing craft and aircraft loading operations and the timing of other ship-to-shore movement preparations are dependent on the designated H-hour and L-hour. All elements must be prepared to modify plans on short notice to conform to changes in H-hour. Prior to H- or L-hour, surface movement control group personnel are cross-decked, as required, to ships of the control group. Helicopter movement control groups take assigned stations and initiate actions as required to meet the time schedule for initial landings. The loading of personnel, equipment, and supplies of the scheduled waves is tedious work and time consuming. Whether using landing craft, amphibious vehicles, or helicopters, the LF must develop and adhere to a strict time schedule based on the established H-hour. Preparations are made for debarkation of on-call and nonscheduled units and for dispatching these units when required.

(1) **Scheduled Waves (Waterborne).** Once H/L-hour are confirmed by CATF and CLF, scheduled waves are landed according to plan. When practicable, the first scheduled wave is dispatched by the CCO with other waves being regulated by the various PCOs.

(2) **On-call Waves (Waterborne).** The landing of on-call waves and pre-positioned emergency supplies is initiated when called by the LF and continues until these categories are ashore. When the commander ashore desires the landing of an on-call unit, he notifies his tactical-logistical (TACLOG) group of the desired place and time (if appropriate) of landing. The Navy control officer then directs the landing of the unit. Pre-positioned emergency supplies are located in proximity to the appropriate control officer who directs their landing as requested by the troop commander concerned.

(3) **Nonscheduled units and remaining LF supplies**. Nonscheduled units and remaining LF supplies are landed in accordance with the requirements of the LF. On rare occasions, these categories may be landed before completion of on-call waves and pre-positioned emergency supplies. Nonscheduled units and previously designated supplies are normally requested by serial until the commencement of general unloading. The responsibility for their landing is assigned by the CATF to the commanders of the cognizant control organizations. In the landing of nonscheduled units, the maximum coordination between LF and ATF control organizations is essential to ensure responsiveness and efficient use of landing ships and craft. The control officers concerned regulate the movement of the ships and craft in accordance with instructions from appropriate commanders and requests from the TACLOG group. Any changes in the landing sequence, no matter how slight they may seem, will invariably disrupt the flow of the offload and may result in unintended delays. The CLF requests the landing of the nonscheduled units and notifies the CATF of any requested modifications to the landing sequence as soon as possible. The CLF continually reviews the progress of the landing and submits periodic and timely requests to the CATF for landing needed units and items of supply.

(4) **Scheduled waves (helicopterborne).** Helicopterborne ship-to-shore movement is normally completed during the initial unloading period. In fact, helicopters usually must make several trips to land and supply the LF units going ashore. Scheduled waves are launched on a prescribed time schedule to ensure the timely arrival in the LZs in accordance with the LF OPLAN. The prescribed launch times will be based on many factors such as distance to the LZ, speed of the aircraft, prevailing weather (wind) conditions, etc.

(5) **On-call waves (helicopterborne).** Because of the urgency that may be attendant to landing on-call waves, elements or items in other landing categories may be preempted to permit their landing. The number of on-call units or items must be kept to a minimum if their high-priority status is to be preserved.

(6) **Nonscheduled waves (helicopterborne).** The landing of nonscheduled, helicopterborne waves commences upon completion of scheduled landings into the LZs. Once started, this process may be interrupted to permit the landing of on-call or other selected units or supplies based on the request of the appropriate LF commander. Furthermore, unforeseen circumstances such as the requirement for LF helicopters to support other tactical missions, may also interrupt the landing of nonscheduled waves. Once the helicopterborne ship-to-shore movement is completed, transport helicopters are employed to meet tactical and logistical requirements of LF operations ashore as directed by the CLF. Helicopter movement in these operations will be controlled by appropriate tactical air control agencies.

d. Amphibious operations involve complex interrelationships between the LFs, ATF, and other assigned and supporting forces, especially during the action phase. Planning is a synergistic effort which must ensure that ATF's, LF's, and other forces' considerations are adequately addressed. **The CATF is responsible for preparation and coordination of**

the ship-to-shore movement plan. The CATF is responsible for the ship-to-shore movement, but will coordinate with the CLF for changing situations that affect the amphibious operation as revealed by intelligence sources or landing forces ashore.

17. Relationship to Other Planning

Detailed planning for the ship-to-shore movement can begin only after the LF scheme of maneuver ashore is determined. The landing and fire support plans must be carefully integrated. The landing plan should provide for requisite logistic support of all forces. Maximum attention will be given to preserving operations security (OPSEC) during planning.

18. Responsibilities

a. The CATF, in close coordination with the CLF, is responsible for the preparation of the overall ship-to-shore movement and landing plan. Included in the planning is the selection of necessary approach and retirement lanes, check points, rendezvous areas, and aids to navigation to facilitate movement of airland troops. In an amphibious operation, a rendezvous area is the area in which the landing craft and amphibious vehicles rendezvous to form waves after being loaded, and prior to movement to the LOD. Where appropriate, other force commanders participate in this process. **The CATF is responsible for debarkation until termination of the amphibious operation**, at which time the responsibilities for offload of follow-up ships and logistics over-the-shore (LOTS) operations may be passed to another organization designated by higher authority. In the case of an amphibious assault, the operation will normally be terminated only after the entire AFOE is ashore. **The CLF is responsible for determining LF requirements for the ship-to-shore movement and presenting them to the CATF.** The CLF provides information on the availability of organic assets (helicopters and amphibious vehicles) to the CATF and prepares the documents contained in the LF landing plan.

b. Commanders of other forces assigned to the AF (including those assigned for movement to the operational area for tasks not part of the amphibious operation) are responsible for determining and presenting their requirements to the CATF.

c. Hydrographic conditions. The Navy's fleet survey team conducts quick response hydrographic surveys and produces charting products in the field for maritime requirements. It provides high resolution hydrographic surveys for use in nautical or tactical charting and support amphibious landings, mine warfare, or naval special warfare with bathymetry and other collected hydrographic information. C-130 deployable detachments from this team can conduct navigation quality surveys or clearance surveys to provide access to ports and waterways in support of amphibious operations.

For more information, see JP 3-34, Joint Engineer Operations.

THE INVASION OF NORMANDY

The invasion of Normandy was without question the most important battle fought in western Europe in the Second World War. The Allies' success in landing their troops and securing a beachhead on June 6, 1944, doomed Hitler. The landings at Anzio only a few months earlier had shown that success was by no means certain. Amphibious landings were inevitably extremely risky operations. Years of careful planning — and a certain amount of luck at the last moment — led to the Allied victory in Normandy.

Allied strategists meeting in Washington in May 1943 set the date for the cross channel invasion of France as May 1, 1944. Due to a shortage of landing craft, however, the invasion date would be postponed from May to June 1944. Planning for the invasion had been going on since 1942. The raid at Dieppe had provided an early and disastrous dress rehearsal. The fighting in North Africa, Sicily, and Italy had taught the Allies valuable lessons. If there was one lesson above all that the Allies had been forced to learn, it was not to underestimate the abilities of their enemy.

The Allies had decided in July 1943 that the Cotentin peninsula of Normandy offered the best location for the invasion. The Germans, who had 3000 miles of coastline to defend, did not know where the invasion would come. They put up their heaviest defenses in the Calais region of the French coast. Nazi leaders disagreed on the most likely site for the invasion and on the strategy for employment of their forces. This lack of unity in the German command would prove a great weakness to them.

In England the troops who would land on D-day went through endless rehearsals for the invasion. For veterans of combat in North Africa, Sicily, and Italy, the training seemed like a waste of time. Those who had never seen combat tried to imagine what the real thing would be like. In late May 1944, the rehearsals came to an end. Soldiers were confined to their quarters, then shipped to "concentration areas" near ports and airfields from which they would depart. For security reasons they were not told their ultimate destination. When they were safely at sea they would finally be told they were headed to Normandy.

By the end of the day of June 5, 1944, over 2500 ships carrying the Allied invasion force were heading toward the Normandy coast. More than 1000 planes and gliders were being readied to carry the airborne troops into battle. Every man who boarded a ship or plane for Europe was given a letter from Eisenhower with his order of the day.

"You are about to embark on a great crusade, toward which we have striven these many months. . . . The tide has turned. The free men of the
world are marching together to victory. . . ."

SOURCE: *World War II — America at War,* Maurice Isserman, 1991

19. Landing Plan

a. **Ship-to-shore movement planning for the LF is given final form and expression in the landing plan.** The landing plan is designed to support the LF's CONOPS, keeping in mind the inherent capabilities and operational characteristics of available amphibious ships and landing craft. It is prepared after the final allocation of means has been made. It represents the integrated sum of detailed plans for waterborne and airborne ship-to-shore movement prepared by corresponding ATF and LF commands at all levels. This plan should maximize range and speed capabilities of surface assault craft and aircraft (rotary, tilt-rotor, and vertical takeoff and landing [VTOL]) that allow a coordinated assault over a wide range. A flexible landing plan enables the AF to gain and retain tactical initiative, enhances operational flexibility, takes advantage of enemy force dispositions and weaknesses, and employs the element of surprise to the maximum extent. The landing plan is composed of certain specific documents that present, in detail, the numbers of land craft, helicopters, and surface craft available for use and the exact personnel and equipment that will be loaded on each, along with embarkation and landing times. These documents should be incorporated in annexes to operation and administrative plans and orders (Figure III-5). **The body of the landing plan is usually short, with only information of interest to all subordinate units.** The bulk of the plan is a compilation of documents included as tabs and enclosures that contain the facts and figures essential for the orderly and timely execution of the landing.

b. The landing plan is concerned primarily with establishing relative landing priorities among the various elements of the LF and with overall coordination of ship-to-shore movement planning. Specifically, it provides:

US Soldiers of the 8th Infantry Regiment, 4th Infantry Division, move out over the seawall on "Utah" Beach. (June 6, 1944).

LANDING PLAN DOCUMENTS

COMMANDER, AMPHIBIOUS TASK FORCE RESPONSIBILITY

- √ Naval Landing Plan
- √ Landing Craft Availability Table
- √ Landing Craft Employment Plan
- √ Debarkation Schedule
- √ Ship's Diagram
- √ Pontoon Causeway Plan
- √ Unloading Plan
- √ Approach Schedule
- √ Assault Wave Diagram
- √ Landing Area Diagram
- √ Transport Area Diagram
- √ Beach Approach Diagram
- √ Sea Echelon Area
- √ Landing Control Plan
- √ Medical Regulating Plan
- √ Amphibious Bulk Liquid Transfer System and Offshore Petroleum Discharge System Plan

COMMANDER, LANDING FORCE RESPONSIBILITY

- √ Landing Force Landing Plan
- √ Amphibious Vehicle Availability Table
- √ Landing Craft and Amphibious Vehicle Assignment Table
- √ Landing Diagram
- √ Landing Force Serial Assignment Table
- √ Landing Priority Table
- √ Landing Force Sequence Table
- √ Assault Schedule
- √ Amphibious Vehicle Employment Plan
- √ Helicopter Availability Table
- √ Heliteam Wave and Serial Assignment Table
- √ Helicopter Enplaning Schedule
- √ Helicopter Landing Diagram
- √ Helicopter Employment and Assault Landing Table
- √ Ground Combat Element Landing Plan
- √ Consolidated Landing and Approach Plan
- √ Aviation Combat Element and Landing Force Aviation Landing Plan

Figure III-5. Landing Plan Documents

(1) Priority for landing of elements of the LF.

(2) Allocation of resources.

(3) Allocation of serial numbers.

(4) Correlation of the sequence for landing of all units not being landed with assault elements, but landing before general unloading.

(5) Coordination of the landing plans of separate landing groups, if required.

c. **Landing plan documentation is a responsibility of both CATF and CLF.** Although some documents require joint preparation by ships' commanding officers (COs) and COs of troops (e.g., debarkation schedule and helicopter enplaning schedule), all landing plan documents are the responsibility of either the CATF or CLF.

d. After the available means for ship-to-shore movement have been assigned, LF plans are prepared in the following sequence:

(1) CLF allocates or specifies landing assets to subordinate elements on the basis of availability and in accordance with the CONOPS and scheme of maneuver ashore.

(2) CLF allocates blocks of serial numbers to elements of the force.

(3) CLF determines the relative landing priorities for the various elements of the force.

(4) Subordinate LF elements prepare a plan for landing based on assigned tasks and priorities. Landing plans for other forces not landing with ground combat forces are submitted to the LF commander.

(5) CLF correlates these recommendations and publishes them in the LF landing plan.

(6) Subordinate commands make pertinent extracts from the LF landing plan, as necessary, for control and coordination.

(7) Planning for the movement of supplies ashore, for the composition of floating dumps, and for the levels of supply ashore is conducted concurrently with other ship-to-shore movement planning.

e. **CATF develops the naval landing plan documents required to conduct ship-to-shore movement.** The information contained in several of these documents is vital to the CLF in the development of his own landing plan.

(1) The **landing craft availability table** lists the type and number of landing craft that will be available from each ship of the transport group, specifies the total required for Navy use, and indicates those available for troop use. The table is the basis for assignment

of landing craft for the ship-to-shore movement. It is prepared by the transport group commander, or in his absence, by the CATF.

(2) The **landing craft employment plan** provides for the assigned movement of landing craft from the various ships to satisfy Navy and LF requirements. It indicates the number of landing craft, their types, their parent ships, the ships to which they will report, the time at which they will report, and the period during which they will be attached. The plan is prepared by the transport group CO, or in his absence, by the CATF.

(3) The **debarkation schedule** is a plan that provides for the orderly debarkation of troops and equipment, and emergency supplies for the waterborne ship-to-shore movement. Prepared jointly by the CO of each ship and the CO of troops embarked, it is usually prepared after the troops are aboard and is distributed to all personnel responsible for control of debarkation. Debarkation schedules are not normally prepared for units landing in amphibious vehicles or aircraft (rotary, tilt-rotor, and VTOL). The debarkation schedule contains the following information:

(a) The sequence in which landing craft, by type, come alongside the debarkation stations, or depart the well deck.

(b) The individual boats and boat teams or supply loads that load from each troop debarkation station and the boats into which they are loaded.

(4) The **ship's diagram** supplements the debarkation schedule and graphically shows the location where each boat team will load.

(5) The **approach schedule** indicates the following for each scheduled wave: time of departure from the rendezvous area, LOD, and other control points; and time of arrival at the beach.

(6) The **assault wave diagram** displays the assault waves as they will appear at a specified time prior to H-hour. The diagram is consolidated jointly at the ATF/LF level and given wide distribution.

(7) The **landing area diagram** is prepared by the transport group commander or CATF as an overlay for an appropriately scaled chart. It shows graphically the most important details of the landing area: beach designations, boat lanes, LODs, landing ship areas, transport areas, and FSAs in the immediate vicinity of the boat lanes. The diagram contains extracts from other documents and may have numerous enclosures containing specific information required for orderly ship-to-shore movement.

(8) The **transport area diagram** is prepared as an overlay for a chart of the objective area. It shows the area extending from at least 1,000 yards off the beach to seaward and at least 1,000 yards to seaward beyond the outermost berth in the designated transport area. If both an outer and inner transport area are to be used, two diagrams will be required. Overlays will include the following information as appropriate:

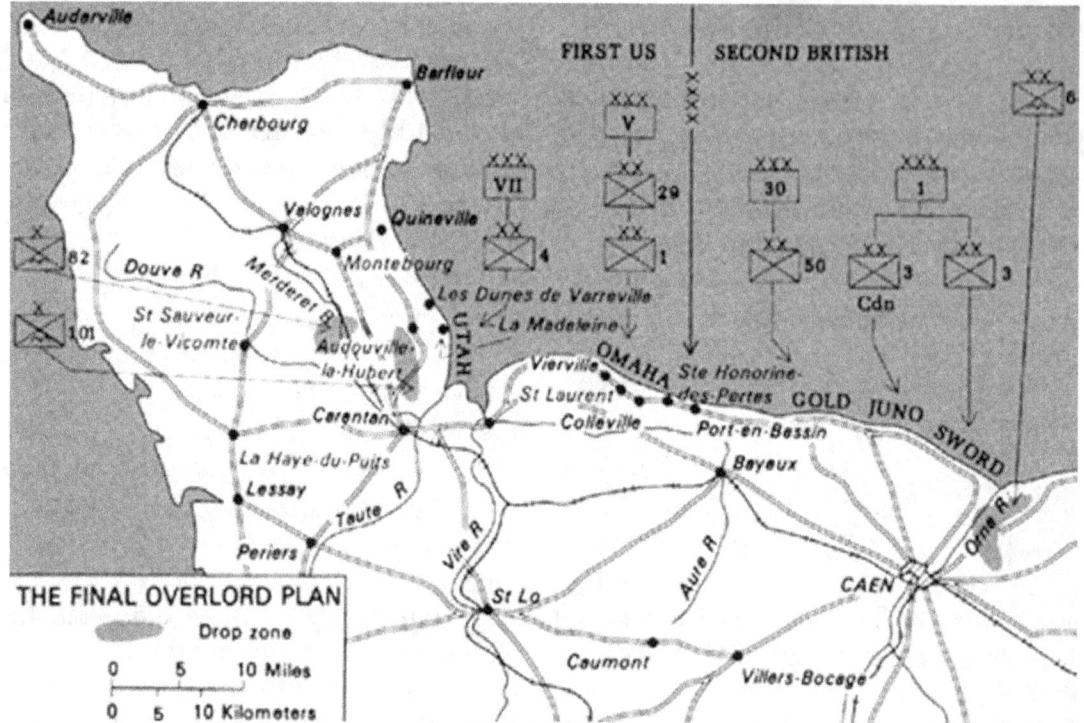

The general landing plan for Operation OVERLORD assigns beaches to US and Allied forces.

(a) Transport area(s) and assignment of all deep-draft ships to berths.

(b) Landing ship areas and assignment of all landing ships to berths.

(c) Inner transport area.

(d) Boat and approach lanes.

(e) LODs.

(f) AAV launching area.

(g) Causeway launching area.

(h) Beaches.

(i) Distances from the beach to the center of transport area, from the beach to the LOD, from the approach lane to the LOD, and the lengths of beaches.

(j) LCAC routes and areas such as LCAC collection area, LCAC departure point, LCAC control point, LCAC penetration point, and LCAC landing zone.

(9) A **beach approach diagram** is prepared by the transport group commander or CATF as an overlay for a large-scale chart of the landing beaches. The overlay depicts an area extending from each beach seaward to 300 to 500 yards beyond the LOD, showing the following:

(a) Designation and dimensions of landing beaches.

(b) LOD.

(c) Distance from beach to LOD.

(d) Position of control and medical ships and boats.

(e) Cargo transfer line information, if one is established.

(f) Return boat lanes.

(10) If a sea echelon is used, specific information relating to the **sea echelon area** is prepared as a diagram by the CATF in agreement with the CLF. The diagram contains the locations and limits of the sea echelon, swept transport lanes, LOD, primary control ships, and beaches.

(11) **The CLF is responsible for the LF landing plan.** It is the compilation of detailed plans prepared by the LF. The following documents designate the forces going ashore, and promulgate the means, organization, sequence, and landing priorities:

(a) The **amphibious vehicle availability table** is a list of the type and number of vehicles available for assault landings and for support of other elements of the operation. It also indicates the ships in which the AAVs are carried to the objective area.

(b) The **landing craft and amphibious vehicle assignment table** indicates the organization of LF units into boat teams and the assignment of boat teams to scheduled waves, on-call waves, or nonscheduled units. It may also include instructions for assigning floating dump supplies to landing craft or amphibious vehicles AAVs. The table, together with the debarkation schedule, furnishes the ship's CO with information for debarking troops and floating dump supplies. The landing craft and amphibious vehicle AAV assignment table is prepared and promulgated at the same time as the landing diagram. Both tables are prepared by the CLF. Following are some key considerations for the assignment of units and personnel to landing craft and amphibious vehicles:

1. A deck space or deck loading is the space and weight factor used to determine the capacity of boats, landing craft, and amphibious vehicles, based on the requirements of one person with individual equipment.

2. Allowance of deck spaces must be made for troop equipment, such as mortars, machine guns, vehicles, and heavy equipment. A smaller number of personnel

embark in craft carrying such equipment. The number of deck spaces the equipment occupies is included in a separate column of the table.

3. Tactical integrity required by the tactical plan must be maintained. Units must land in proper tactical formations.

4. The assignment of command elements and any attached or supporting troops (such as forward observers, naval gunfire spotters, or communications personnel) is made to the craft carrying the infantry units to which they are attached or directly support. If such units are assigned to separate craft, the craft are given positions in the waves that will facilitate small unit employment on beaching. A separate wave may be organized for command elements, supporting arms, and/or antitank units.

5. Distributing elements of command and liaison personnel among two or more landing craft reduces the risk of heavy losses in command elements. Personnel and equipment from key elements such as communications units are similarly distributed.

6. The priority of craft assignment is in the following order: assault units, supporting units, and reserve units.

(c) The **landing diagram** provides information on the tactical deployment of units for the landing. Based on the recommendations of subordinate commanders, the landing diagram is prepared and promulgated at the same time as the landing craft and amphibious vehicle assignment table. It is distributed to all personnel responsible for controlling the formation of the boat group and its waves during ship-to-shore movement, and the information it contains is used in the preparation of assault schedules.

(d) The **LF serial assignment table** reflects the organization of the LF for ship-to-shore movement.

1. A serial is a group of LF units and their equipment that originate from the same ship and that, for tactical or logistic reasons, will land on a specified beach or a specified HLZ at the same time. A serial number is assigned to each serial (group).

2. Serial numbers are administratively assigned numbers and do not in themselves prescribe a priority in landing. They are assigned only for reference purposes and the assignment in no way precludes the use of code names, designations, or unit titles when expedient.

3. Early in the planning stage the CLF allocates a block of consecutive serial numbers on the basis of administrative organization to each LF unit and Navy element to be landed; regardless of their location in the AE or AFOE. Allocation begins at the highest echelon as each unit allocates a consecutive portion of its block to subordinate units. Allocation continues until each element within the LF has a block of consecutive numbers for assignment to its subordinate and attached elements.

<u>4.</u> After the landing and embarkation plans have been determined, each planning echelon assigns serial numbers from its allocated block to its units, parts of units, or groupings. It is important to note that, while allocation of blocks of serial numbers to units is based on the administrative organization, the actual assignment of individual serial numbers is based on the organization for landing. The method of assignment does not depend either on the priority or on the estimated sequence of landing of nonscheduled units.

<u>5.</u> The LF serial assignment table indicates the tactical units, equipment, and supplies that are to be loaded into each landing craft, amphibious vehicle, or aircraft, and may be further broken down into a serial assignment table (Surface) and a heliteam wave and serial assignment table.

(e) The **landing priority table** is a worksheet used at the LF level to prescribe the planned buildup of the LF ashore. It is based on the commander's tactical plan and provides a foundation for the orderly deployment of the LF in support of the plan. The table lists all major units to be landed, the order or priority, the planned time of landing, and the designated beaches and/or LZs. It is used principally when the LF is complex or when a phasing of LF units is required.

(f) The **LF sequence table** is a complete list of the estimated landing sequence of the nonscheduled units of the LF. It is the principal document for executing and controlling the ship-to-shore movement of these units and is the basis for their embarkation and loading plans. Unless specific requests for changes are made during the execution of ship-to-shore movement, the landing proceeds in accordance with the estimated sequence shown in the LF sequence table. The table provides the following:

<u>1.</u> A guide to the embarkation officer in preparing loading plans.

<u>2.</u> The commander's priorities in offloading nonscheduled serials.

<u>3.</u> The order vehicles and equipment of nonscheduled units should be loaded so as to be available when requested.

<u>4.</u> The preferred sequence for landing nonscheduled serials.

(g) The **assault schedule** prescribes the formation, composition, and timing of waves landing over each beach. The CLF prepares the assault schedule based on the recommendations of subordinate unit commanders.

(h) The **amphibious vehicle employment plan** shows the origin, number and type, wave, destination, and contents of amphibious vehicles in initial movement and subsequent trips from ship to the beach.

(i) The **helicopter availability table** shows the number and models of helicopters available for a proposed helicopterborne landing. Prepared by the helicopter unit commander, it lists the helicopter units, the number of helicopters available for first and subsequent lifts, their tentative load capacity, and the ships on which they are transported.

(j) The **heliteam wave and serial assignment table** is prepared by the helicopterborne unit commander in coordination with the ship's CO. It indicates the tactical units, equipment, and supplies that are to be loaded into each heliteam by its assigned serial number and the serial number of the flight and wave. It lists the weight of personnel and equipment and includes all landing categories — scheduled, on-call, and nonscheduled waves.

(k) The **helicopter enplaning schedule** plans for the orderly enplaning of troops, supplies, and equipment for the helicopterborne ship-to-shore movement. It shows the following:

1. The enplaning stations on the flight deck of the ship.

2. The sequence in which helicopters are spotted at the enplaning stations.

3. The serialized heliteam with equipment and supplies assigned to each helicopter in each designated flight.

(l) The **helicopter landing diagram** illustrates the routes to and from LZs. It includes the helicopter transport area, rendezvous points, approach and retirement routes, departure and initial points, other control points, LZs and sites, and other details as are necessary for clarity. The diagrams are prepared by the senior helicopter unit commander in coordination with the cognizant helicopter transport unit commanders, and are submitted via the chain of command to the CATF for approval and coordination.

(m) The **helicopter employment and assault landing table** is a detailed plan for the movement of helicopterborne troops, equipment, and supplies. It provides the landing timetable for the helicopter movement and indicates the assignment of specific troop units to specific numbered flights. Analogous to the assault schedule and landing sequence table prepared by surface-landed units, it is the basis for the helicopter unit's flight schedules and the control of helicopter movement by the appropriate air control agency. The helicopter employment and assault landing table is prepared in close coordination between the commanders of the helicopterborne and helicopter units.

(n) The **ground combat element landing plan** is developed by the senior GCE representative, who does the major portion of the detailed planning and immediate supervision of the waterborne and helicopterborne ship-to-shore movement on the part of the LF. It is developed in coordination with the related Navy organization and based on information provided by both CLF and CATF concerning forces to be landed and landing assets available. Subordinate units down to the battalion level prepare their own landing plans, including all relevant documents. These plans may be incorporated into the landing plan of the next higher unit as an appendix, or the information contained in the documents incorporated in the documents of the GCE landing plan.

(o) The **aviation combat element and LF aviation landing plan** does not provide information concerning aviation support to ship-to-shore movement, but rather outlines the commander's plans for establishing aviation units ashore in the landing area by both air and surface means. It provides detailed plans for the landing of aviation elements that are embarked in assault shipping and landed with assault units or as nonscheduled units.

1. The aviation landing plan contains the following:

a. Plans for the echelonment and landing sequence of all aviation units to be established ashore within the landing area.

b. Detailed landing documents for aviation elements that move ashore before general unloading.

c. Applicable ship-to-shore control provisions.

d. Information on pontoon causeways, fuel handling systems, and the landing of engineering elements and equipment necessary for aviation support ashore.

2. **Composition of Echelons.** Elements of air control squadrons and helicopter groups comprising the first echelon are landed by helicopter to initiate operations ashore. The second echelon of these units is landed over the beaches with the heavy equipment and personnel required for sustained operations.

a. Fixed-wing fighter and attack groups land in an initial echelon composed of personnel and heavy equipment for base operations and maintenance. This echelon is surface-lifted into the landing area and landed over the beaches. A second echelon composed of pilots, aircraft, and crew is flown into the area from land bases.

b. The LF aviation organization for landing will differ greatly from the task organization because of the division of air groups and squadrons into elements for landing and wide variation in the time and method of landing these elements. The landing plan must provide for a grouping of the aviation elements into a series of echelons based on time and method of landing. These echelons, and the time and manner of their movement to the landing area, are shown in the general paragraph in the body of the aviation landing plan. Detailed composition of echelons is in a separate appendix.

3. **Scheduled On-Call, and Nonscheduled Elements.** Air control units, elements of the LF aviation headquarters squadrons, aviation groups, headquarters support squadrons, air base, and aviation logistics squadrons may be landed before commencement of general unloading to initiate establishment of air facilities ashore. These

units are either embarked with and landed as part of the assault division(s) or are landed as nonscheduled units.

a. Detachments of the aviation units and the CSS elements that form part of the helicopter support teams (HSTs) are often landed in scheduled waves. Air support radar teams usually will be landed in on-call waves. Such elements are shown in the assault schedules (or helicopter employment and assault landing table, and helicopter wave and serial assignment table) of the division(s). Other aviation elements that are landed early in the ship-to-shore movement are serialized and shown in the division or LF landing sequence table.

b. The LF aviation landing plan lists separately those aviation elements that are landed in scheduled, on-call, or nonscheduled units. The landing plan also contains additional landing documents, as extracted from division and force landing plans, necessary to describe the method and sequence for landing these elements. This information is shown in the following enclosures:

(1) Extracts from appropriate assault schedules.

(2) Extracts from helicopter employment and assault landing tables.

(3) Extracts from helicopter wave and serial assignment tables.

(4) Serial assignment table.

(5) Landing sequence table.

(p) Serial numbers for nonscheduled aviation elements are allocated by the LF. The assigned serials and an itemized list of personnel and equipment of aviation elements that are to land in scheduled or on-call waves are submitted to the CLF for coordination and approval. The division is then furnished the necessary information to provide for landing non-scheduled aviation elements. These elements are incorporated into the force landing sequence tables.

(12) **Ship-to-Shore Control.** To monitor the landing of aviation elements early in the ship-to-shore movement, the LF aviation commander provides representatives to the senior TACLOG group. As changes or delays in the landing of aviation elements occur, the commander may then be apprised of the situation. Schedules and tables required by aviation representatives in the HDC and the Navy TACC, in addition to those in the LF aviation landing plan, may be in the air annex to the OPLAN or OPORD.

(13) **Airfields, Pontoon Causeways, Fuel Handling Systems, and Engineering Operations.** The availability of operational facilities required to establish aviation ashore determines the time of landing aviation elements. Information on the projected dates when

these facilities will be complete, or engineering work will begin, is provided in the landing plan when available. This information includes estimated dates for:

(a) Airfields achieving operational status.

(b) Installation of pontoon causeways for landing heavy aviation assets.

(c) Completion of fuel handling systems from the beach to the airfields or helicopter operating sites.

(d) Landing of engineers and commencement of work on airfields.

20. Considerations

Planning for the ship-to-shore movement follows a general sequence of development (see Figure III-6). Detailed planning for the ship-to-shore movement cannot begin until the LF CONOPS ashore is approved. Likewise, the completed landing plan will drive embarkation planning. Principal factors that influence ship-to-shore movement planning include the following:

a. Tactical integrity of the LF allows for unity of command and execution of proven tactics, techniques, and procedures during assaults on initial objectives. The organization

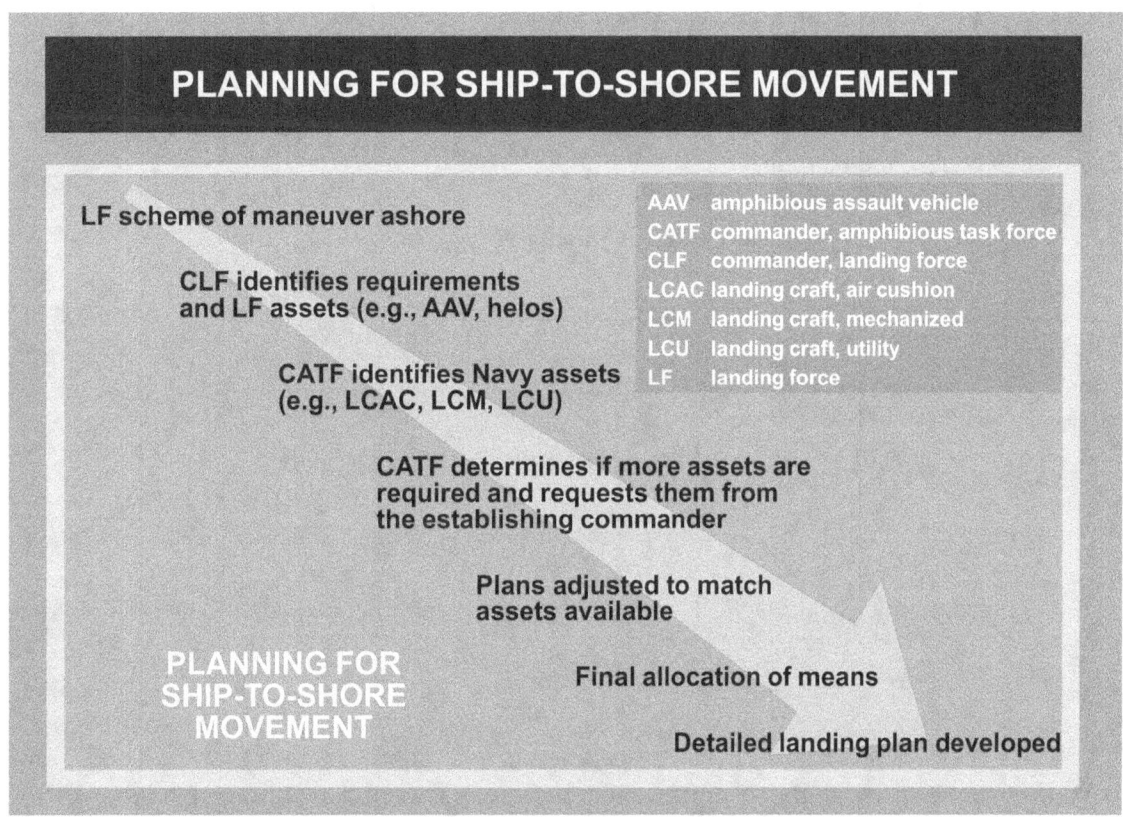

Figure III-6. Planning for Ship-to-Shore Movement

for landing must closely mirror the tactical formations of the LF and ensure adequate C2 for the respective commanders. As much as feasible, the LF should embark on assigned shipping, landing craft, AAVs, and helicopters along normal organizational lines.

b. Required degree of dispersion of assault shipping, to include contemplated employment of a sea echelon plan. Assault shipping is shipping assigned to the ATF and utilized for transporting assault troops, vehicles, equipment, and supplies to the objective area.

c. Available assault shipping and ship-to-shore movement assets. The type and quantity of assault shipping and ship-to-shore movement craft will influence every aspect of the planning and execution of the operation. The inherent capabilities and characteristics of available ATF assets play a key role in the development of the LF CONOPS.

d. Protection of the AF. This is a matter of mutual concern to the CATF and CLF. At times, commanders and their staffs must consider the use of LF assets (such as aircraft, antiair missiles, crew-served weapons, etc.) in the defense of the ATF. Protection comprising both active and passive measures must be provided during all phases of the amphibious operation, but particularly during the vulnerable period of ship-to-shore movement. **Active protection** includes defense counterair operations, antisubmarine and anti-small-boat screens, covering forces, electronic countermeasures, smoke, and NSFS. **Passive protection** places major emphasis on dispersion and mobility.

See Chapter V, "Support to Amphibious Operations," *Section E* "Protection."

e. Flexibility. The ship-to-shore movement plan must have sufficient flexibility to exploit adversary critical vulnerabilities that may become apparent only after the commencement of the landing.

f. Availability and planned utilization of supporting arms.

g. Need for speed and positive centralized control.

h. MCM and obstacle reduction requirements.

i. Assault breaching operations in the surf zone (SZ) and on the beach.

j. Go/no-go criteria.

k. Hydrographic conditions.

21. Over-the-Horizon Amphibious Operations

a. **General.** An OTH amphibious operation is an amphibious operation initiated from beyond visual and radar range of the enemy shore. The goal of OTH operations is to achieve operational surprise through creation of multiple threats, and ultimately to shatter an enemy's cohesion through a series of rapid, violent, and unexpected actions that create a turbulent and rapidly deteriorating situation with which an adversary cannot cope. The decision to conduct OTH operations may also principally be a force protection decision to mitigate threats such as antiship missiles. See Figure III-7 for advantages and disadvantages inherent to an OTH operation.

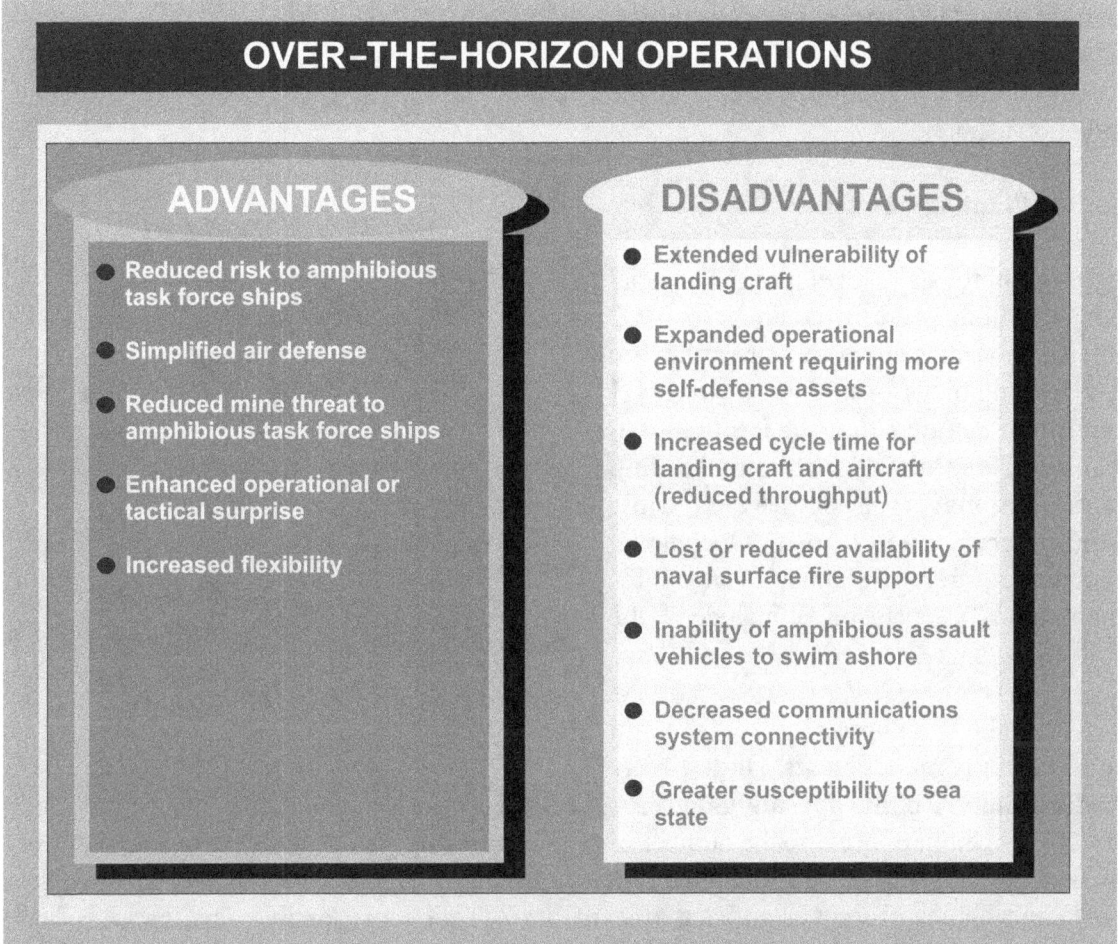

Figure III-7. Over-the-Horizon Operations

b. **Scope.** An OTH operation is a tactical option to hide intentions and capabilities and to exploit the element of tactical surprise to achieve AF objectives. It provides greater protection to the AF from near-shore threats, and provides escort ships a greater opportunity to detect, classify, track, and engage incoming hostile aircraft and coastal defense missiles while expanding the shoreline the enemy must be prepared to defend. Conversely, the expanded OTH operational environment increases ship-to-shore transit distance and time, complicates C2, and may strain logistic sustainment of the LF. **Conceptually, the operation will still be viewed as a single integrated evolution rather than as two or three parallel operations** (e.g., airborne assault, conventional surface assault, LCAC assault). As the situation ashore develops, the CATF and CLF adjust the ship-to-shore maneuver to reinforce successes, and may change penetration points, vertical landing zones (VLZs), and CLZs to keep enemy forces off balance. To increase combat power, ease the logistic strain for forces ashore, and support follow-on forces, the designated commander may shift all or part of the AF to near-shore operations. This decision is based on the threat to forces afloat, CLF requirements, and the situation ashore.

c. **Planning Considerations.** While OTH techniques are applicable to any type of amphibious operation, special considerations are required. C2 interrelationships are even more critical in OTH amphibious operations. **An OTH operation requires that the landing plan be fluid, containing alternate landing sites that may even be selected while landing craft are in transit.** Operational requirements for planning an OTH amphibious operation include the following:

Landing craft, air cushion vehicles provide the over-the-horizon heavy lift capability for the landing force.

(1) **Developing and maintaining an accurate and timely tactical picture of the operational area.** The need for timely intelligence data is increased for OTH operations because the number of possible landing sites is increased. The seaward tactical picture, as it pertains to the presence or absence of enemy naval forces between the ATF and shore, plays a significant role in the selection of possible landing sites and therefore affects the scheme of maneuver. Using OTH tactics requires consolidation of the tactical picture of land and water to provide the CATF and CLF with a consolidated base from which to plan and make tactical decisions. Interoperable C2 systems for maintaining situational awareness and a common tactical picture for the CATF and CLF are absolutely essential in OTH operations.

(2) **Surveillance and reconnaissance of the operational area with emphasis on possible landing sites.** Positioning the AF OTH allows the landing site location to remain flexible. Landing sites may be chosen just before launching the first wave, which requires timely intelligence, surveillance and hydrographic reconnaissance of potential beach landing sites and HLZs.

(3) **Reliable communications and accurate navigation.** OTH operations planning is more complex than traditional amphibious planning because of the increased

distances between launch platforms, landing beaches, supporting fires, and control platforms. This in turn requires greater coordination and communications capability. Flexibility must be maintained throughout the operation since VLZs and CLZs may be widely separated. The vertical assault may land forces inland where they will be able to threaten key enemy positions, facilities, and lines of communications (LOCs). The surface assault points of entry are sites along the coastline where the hydrography, terrain, and enemy situation allow the LF to rapidly move ashore and thrust inland.

(4) **Naval surface fire support may be a requirement for successful prosecution of an amphibious assault.** However, since one underlying reason for an OTH assault is the strength of coastal defenses, the primary mission of NSFS may shift from destroying enemy forces at a defended landing beach to isolating the landing area(s). Preassault fire support in the vicinity of landing sites may also be restricted, especially prior to D-day and H-hour, to preserve tactical surprise. D-day is the unnamed day on which a particular operation commences or is to commence. NSFS ships may initially be OTH with the ATF, closing the beach along with the initial waves of landing craft. Although ships can use land attack missiles for OTH fire support, their quantities are limited. With no current capability to conduct OTH surface gun fire support, missions normally conducted by NSFS will initially rest with aviation assets.

22. Other Planning Considerations

Planning for supporting functions (e.g., fires, communications, logistics, health service support [HSS]) is discussed in Chapter V, "Support to Amphibious Operations."

SECTION B. EMBARKATION

23. Overview

a. **General. The embarkation phase is the period during which the forces, with their equipment and supplies, are embarked in assigned shipping.** The primary goal of this phase is the orderly assembly of personnel and materiel and their embarkation in assigned shipping in a sequence designed to meet the requirements of the LF CONOPS ashore. Detailed considerations and guidance on the organization for embarkation, planning, and execution of this phase of the operation can be found in JP 3-02.1, *Amphibious Embarkation and Debarkation.* Military Sealift Command (MSC) support to amphibious operations and associated special considerations, is provided in Navy Warfare Publication (NWP) 3-02.21, *MSC Support of Amphibious Operations.*

b. **Considerations.** Plans for assembly of assault shipping and movement of troops to embarkation points are prepared by the CATF and CLF, respectively, as separate documents in the form of movement orders and embarkation and loading plans. These plans must be coordinated and distributed as soon as possible to permit initiation of preliminary movements and preparations to ensure that the embarkation is begun without delay. Critical to embarkation planning is an understanding of the required amphibious lift, which is the total capacity of assault shipping utilized in an amphibious operation, expressed in terms of personnel, vehicles, and measurement or weight tons of supplies. The organization for embarkation is a temporary task organization within each element of the AF. The organization for embarkation conforms to the circumstances of the deployment and the requirements of the expected tactical situation. Upon completion of the embarkation phase, these task organizations dissolve. Assault shipping assigned to transport the LF to the AOA is formed into tactical groupings by the CATF. The number and types of ships assigned to each of these groupings is determined by the size and composition of the LF organization for embarkation. **The LF organization for embarkation consists of embarkation groups, units, elements, and teams.** Corresponding embarkation echelons are formed within the ATF.

c. **Responsibilities.** ATF and LF commanders' planning responsibilities are as follows:

(1) The CATF is responsible for:

(a) Allocating assault shipping and sealift.

(b) Providing ship's loading characteristics pamphlets to the CLF.

(c) Organizing Navy forces for embarkation.

(d) Preparing movement orders for ships.

(e) Approving LF embarkation and loading plans. Ships' commanding officers have the final determination of what and how the ship is loaded. They are personally responsible for the safety of their ships and must approve the load plan.

(f) Planning for external support.

(g) Advising CLF on US Navy support forces' embarkation requirements, for example explosive ordinance disposal teams, sea air-land team, assault craft unit, and beachmaster unit requirements.

(2) The CLF is responsible for:

(a) Determining LF requirements for assault shipping.

(b) Developing LF organization for embarkation.

(c) Determining embarkation support requirements.

(d) Preparing detailed embarkation and loading plans.

(3) Other commanders must:

(a) Provide their lift requirements.

(b) Organize their units for embarkation.

(c) Participate in embarkation planning meetings.

See JP 3-02.1, Amphibious Embarkation and Debarkation, *for embarkation and loading plan considerations.*

SECTION C. REHEARSALS

24. General

Rehearsal is the period during which the prospective operation is practiced for the following reasons:

a. Test adequacy of plans, timing of detailed operations, and combat readiness of participating forces.

b. Ensure that all echelons are familiar with the plan.

c. Test communications-information systems.

> "The projection of the 10th Mountain Division (Light) from the aircraft carrier USS America into Haiti in 1994 showed what can result when we break down traditional service walls in search of a new synergy. An Army official aboard the carrier during the operation affirmed the need for practice: "The key to this operation is combat rehearsals. You have to make it work before you show up in theater and are trying it for the first time."
>
> **Source: Joint Force Quarterly, Autumn/Winter 1998-99**
> **(Quote from interview with Rick Cantwell, December 31, 1996)**

25. Requirements

The rehearsal phase may be conducted concurrently with other phases of the amphibious operation but most often is associated with the movement to the operational area phase. During this period the AF, or elements of, conduct one or more rehearsal exercise(s), ideally under conditions approximating those encountered in the littorals and expected landing area. The objective during this phase will be to exercise as much of the force and the OPLAN as the situation permits, with OPSEC and time being limiting factors.

26. Rehearsal Plans

Responsibility for preparation of rehearsal plans is the same as for preparation of the OPLAN. Rehearsal plans will be issued separately from actual plans and require execution of the various tasks and functions paralleling those required during the operation.

a. The number, nature, and scope of rehearsals will be influenced by the following considerations:

(1) The complexity of the tasks.

(2) Time available for rehearsals.

(3) State of training.

(4) Suitability of available areas.

(5) Special or unusual problems to be faced in the actual operation.

(6) Intelligence.

(7) Adequacy of communications system.

(8) Logistic and CSS availability to replenish, replace, or repair assets used.

(9) OPSEC to prevent disclosure of timing, location, or intent to conduct an amphibious operation.

(10) Organic modeling and simulation ability.

b. Factors influencing the dates on which rehearsals are conducted and the time allocated for them include the following:

(1) Complete and careful execution of the entire rehearsal.

(2) Re-embarkation of all troops, equipment, and supplies.

(3) Replenishment, repair, or replacement of equipment and supplies used during rehearsals including landing craft, ships, or aircraft.

(4) Critiques at all levels of command for evaluation and correction of problems.

(5) Time to revise areas of the plan in which the rehearsal identified problems.

c. Selection of the rehearsal area is influenced by the following:

(1) Suitability.

(2) Similarity of the rehearsal area to the actual landing area.

(3) Feasibility of employing live ammunition.

(4) OPSEC.

(5) Susceptibility to enemy interference.

(6) Location of the rehearsal area in relation to the operational area and to points of embarkation.

(7) Health conditions at the rehearsal area.

(8) Activity of civilian personnel, vehicles, shipping, and small craft that may interfere with the rehearsal.

(9) Environmental and management restrictions.

d. Testing the effectiveness of communications-information systems plans will be influenced by the following:

(1) Level of training of communications-information systems personnel and training time available.

(2) Level of training of intelligence, maneuver, fires, logistics, and other functional area personnel regarding their use of communications-information systems resources.

(3) Status of communications-information systems equipment.

(4) OPSEC and information security (INFOSEC) restrictions.

SECTION D. MOVEMENT

27. General

The movement phase commences upon departure of ships from loading points in the embarkation areas, and concludes when ships arrive at assigned stations in the operational area. **During this phase, the AF is organized into movement groups, which execute movement in accordance with the movement plan on prescribed routes (with alternate routes designated for emergency use).** In amphibious operations, the movement plan is the naval plan providing for the movement of the ATF to the objective area. It includes information and instructions concerning departure of ships from embarkation points, the passage at sea, and the approach to and arrival in assigned positions in the objective area. Movement of the force to the operational area may be interrupted by rehearsals, stops at staging areas for logistic reasons, or pauses at rendezvous points. Execution of a postponement plan due to adverse weather or other unfavorable situations may necessitate a revised movement plan.

28. Echelons of the Landing Force

The echelons of the LF will include the AE, the MPF ships, afloat pre-positioning force (APF), AFOE, and follow-up transport ships and aircraft as described below. The Marine Corp's APF ships are identified first as they are the first assets from the APF to be called up.

a. **AE.** The AE is that element of a force that comprises tailored units and aircraft assigned to conduct the initial assault on the operational area. **The AE is normally embarked in amphibious ships, which include the following naval ship classes: the LHA, LHD, amphibious transport dock (LPD), and dock landing ship (LSD).** These ships, each with its internal dock, are designed to embark, deploy, and land elements of a LF in an assault by helicopters, landing craft, amphibious vehicles, and by combinations of these methods. The LHDs and LHAs are the Navy's largest amphibious ships. Their mission is to embark, deploy, and land elements of the landing force in an amphibious assault by helicopters, landing craft, amphibious vehicles, or by combinations of these methods. The LPD is designed to transport and land troops, equipment, and supplies by means of embarked landing craft, amphibious vehicles, and helicopters. The LSD is designed to transport and launch loaded amphibious craft and/or amphibian vehicles with their crews, embarked personnel, and equipment. It also has the ability to render limited docking and repair services to small ships and craft. The AE ships are combat loaded with troops, equipment, and supplies that typically provide at least 15 days of sustainment. Other elements included in the AE are LF elements of the advance force that deploy with sufficient supplies to accomplish their mission and sustain themselves until subsequent forces arrive.

b. **MPF and APF. MPF and APF operations that augment and reinforce the LF will normally occur before the arrival of the AFOE.** The pre-positioned force can provide equipment and supplies to a MEB or US Army maneuver unit at a permissive location in the operational area. These additional troops, supplies, and equipment can then be transported by ATF assets or other means to reinforce or augment the landing and support forces ashore.

c. **AFOE.** Information concerning AFOE is contained in Section E, "Action."

d. **Follow-up Ships and Aircraft.** In amphibious operations, follow-up is the landing of reinforcements and stores after the AEs and AFOEs have landed. Follow-up is carried by transport ships and aircraft not originally part of the AF.

29. Organization for Movement

Based on the landing plan, AF assets are organized for embarkation and deployment to support the amphibious operation. This organization is based on the time-phased force requirements of the AF in the operational area.

a. **Transport Groups.** Those elements that directly deploy and support the landing of the LF are functionally designated as transport groups in the ATF organization.

(1) Amphibious transport groups provide for embarkation, movement to the landing area, landing, and logistic support of the LF. An amphibious transport group is a subdivision of an amphibious task force composed primarily of transport ships. The size of the transport group will depend upon the scope of the operation. A transport unit will usually be formed to embark troops and equipment to be landed over a designated beach or to embark all helicopterborne troops and equipment. They are comprised of all the assets in which the LF is embarked, including lighterage and cargo offloading and discharge systems to be employed in ship-to-shore movement. The amphibious transport group can include ships from commercial and other sources that include the following:

(a) At present MSC has approximately 30 pre-positioned force vessels including 6 in reduced operating status laden with military equipment, supplies, and fuel. This force has three separate elements: maritime pre-positioned ships, afloat pre-positioning ships, and a collection of vessels that support the Navy, Air Force, and Defense Logistics Agency. The MPF(enhanced) represents an increased capability with an augmented ship for each squadron that carries an expeditionary medical facility and expeditionary airfield engineering equipment.

(b) MSC's surge sealift fleet consisting of large, medium speed roll-on/roll-off (RO/RO) ships capable of moving large amounts of heavy unit equipment such as tanks, large wheeled vehicles, and helicopters.

(c) Other MSC-provided ships, consisting of commercial ships (both US and foreign flag) acquired for specific lift requirements.

(d) Two MSC operated hospital ships.

(e) The Ready Reserve Force consisting of commercial or former military vessels of high military utility including commercial RO/RO and fast sealift ships, barge, container, tanker, crane, and breakbulk ships. Some of these vessels have had their military capabilities enhanced with the addition of systems such as the modular cargo delivery system and the offshore petroleum discharge system (OPDS). Some have been altered for specific missions such as aviation logistic support ships and auxiliary crane ships. The Maritime Administration maintains these vessels in a 4- or 5-day readiness status. When activated, these ships are under the operational control of MSC.

(f) Ships provided by allied and friendly governments.

(g) Additional detachments can add capabilities provided by the joint high speed vessel or Army watercraft such as the logistic support vessel or landing craft utility. These detachments may augment amphibious transport group task organizations when conditions permit Army land component command seaborne and beach landing capability integration.

(2) Airlift is used for amphibious operations involving the fly-in echelon to link up with equipment delivered by the MSC. Aircraft assigned can be organic military or commercial, to include:

(a) Aircraft activated/volunteered under Civil Reserve Air Fleet.

(b) Aircraft requisitioned by the US Government.

(c) Aircraft provided by allied and friendly governments.

b. **Multiple Transport Groups.** If more than one landing area is established in the operational area, additional transport groups (one for each landing area) are formed. Transport groups are combat loaded to support the landing plan of the assigned landing area. Each amphibious transport group is assigned assault ships and lighterage required by the LF in its assigned landing area.

c. **Movement Group(s).** The ATF may be task-organized into movement groups based on ports of embarkation (POEs), and individual ship speed, mission, and required arrival time in the operational area. Using the above criteria, all Navy forces, self-deploying LF aircraft, and self-deploying Air Force units should be task-organized into separate movement groups. A movement group will include all required screen and logistic support.

d. **Pre-D-day Groups.** The advance force, when used, usually proceeds to the landing

Essex Amphibious Ready Group steams in formation, in the Andaman Sea.

area as a single movement group. However, if there is a wide disparity of speed between various ships, or if part of the LF is required to capture nearby islands or other key terrain before the arrival of the main body of the AF, **it may be necessary to organize the advance force into two or more movement groups, each with a screen.**

(1) The main body of the AF should consist of the following groups: one or more transport groups, one or more combat logistic groups, and one or more support battle groups.

(2) Under certain conditions, it may be desirable to attach all or part of the combat logistic groups or support battle groups to the transport groups, in order to provide support and protection from attack while en route. Protection from attack while en route may also be provided by nonorganic forces.

(3) Elements of the AF may be phased into the operational area by echelons, instead of being brought in simultaneously.

e. **Post-D-day Groups.** Movement groups of the AF scheduled to arrive in the operational area after D-day will usually be assigned a screen for force protection.

f. **Follow-up.** The first follow-up elements may arrive in the operational area before unloading of the AE or AFOE ships is complete. In such cases, OPCON or TACON of these elements will normally be passed to the CATF at a designated point before their arrival in the operational area. The CATF retains OPCON or TACON of these elements until such time as the amphibious operation is terminated, the elements are detached from the AF, or another offload authority has been designated.

See JP 4-01.6, Joint Logistics Over-the-Shore (JLOTS), *and JP 4-01.5,* Joint Terminal Operations, *for further information.*

SECTION E. ACTION

30. General

In an amphibious operation, the action phase is the period of time between the arrival of the LF of the AF in the operational area and the accomplishment of their mission.

31. Organization and Command Relationships

Organization of forces, responsibilities for accomplishment of tasks, and command relationships during the action phase of all types of amphibious operations are essentially the same. Variations in responsibility and authority as required by the individual situation will be specified in the initiating directive.

a. **Organization for the action phase of an amphibious operation is based on the parallel organization of the ATF, LF, and other designated forces.** LF organization for landing is the specific tactical grouping of forces for accomplishment of the assigned mission. Tactical integrity of landing elements is maintained insofar as practicable during ship-to-shore movement. The ATF and LF organizations should parallel one another to facilitate execution of the landing plan and the LF scheme of maneuver ashore.

b. The organization of ATF forces for the action phase is as follows:

(1) ATF forces afloat provide the transport groups for the vertical and surface ship-to-shore movement and also provide the necessary landing craft, and AAV control organization.

(2) For the surface movement, the LF may be landed from ships by landing craft; AAVs, or small boats (e.g., combat rubber raiding craft).

(3) The amphibious shipping, landing craft, AAVs, and organic aviation are organized to correspond to the tactical organization of troops to ensure control and maneuverability. This organization includes boat waves, boat groups, and boat flotillas.

(4) A boat wave consists of the landing craft or AAVs within a boat group that carries the troops, equipment, or cargo requiring simultaneous landing.

(5) The boat group is the basic organization of landing craft. One boat group is organized for each surface landing force element within scheduled waves at a designated beach.

(6) The boat flotilla is an organization of two or more boat groups.

(7) Although LCACs are landing craft, their employment differs slightly from displacement landing craft. Operations conducted from 25 nautical miles (nms) offshore or more are usually considered OTH. Limited operations using one or more LCAC groups may be conducted from as far as 100 nms offshore. However, this distance approaches the maximum capability of the craft and requires careful planning.

c. The organization of the LF for the action phase will be different with each operation, but the general task organization remains the same. The LF is organized to execute the landing and to conduct initial operations ashore in accordance with the commander's CONOPS. The major **subordinate elements of the LF should be capable of independent operations during the initial stages of the landing and operations ashore**. For example, a regimental commander will need time to establish C2 over the separate battalions, which may have landed across different beaches and/or LZs. The organization for landing should also provide for:

(1) Maximum combat power at the point of landing.

(2) Depth to the assault to ensure flexibility and a sustained buildup of combat power.

(3) Dispersion of the force as consistent with other requirements.

(4) Sufficient flexibility to exploit weaknesses found in the adversary defenses.

(5) Timely establishment/employment of tactical and administrative support systems ashore.

(6) Closest possible resemblance to the organization for combat.

d. As discussed earlier, the Marine Corps will organize as a MAGTF to conduct LF operations, but will further organize into "landing teams" to facilitate the ship-to-shore movement and initial operations ashore. When Army forces are employed as the LF, they will generally consist of a ground combat division, brigade, or battalion that is task-organized with other combat, combat support, and CSS units. As with the MAGTF, the Army LF will also organize into "landing teams" that are based around ground maneuver units within the LF. The organization for the LF will be as follows:

(1) Divisions. Although smaller organizations may be employed in appropriate cases, the reinforced infantry division is the basic self-contained tactical organization for the conduct of amphibious assault operations. Landing support and aviation units are included in the LF organization for landing. Those specifically designated CSS and aviation units scheduled to land during the initial assault, and over the same beaches as the assault divisions, are included in the landing plans of the assault divisions.

(2) Regiments or Brigades. The regimental landing team or brigade landing team is a task-organized assault element consisting of an infantry regiment or brigade reinforced by those support elements required. This reinforcement usually includes subordinate BLTs, aviation, and CSS elements.

(3) Battalions. The BLT is the basic organization of the LF for ship-to-shore movement planning. The BLT consists of an infantry battalion or similar unit reinforced by such supporting and service units as may be attached for the movement. Because the BLT is a specific tactical organization for landing, it should be differentiated from the infantry battalion or similar organization. For ship-to-shore movement, the BLT is further organized for waterborne and/or helicopterborne movement.

(a) For movement by landing craft and amphibious vehicles, the BLTs are formed into boat flotillas, boat groups, boat waves, and boat teams. Insofar as practicable, the tactical integrity of troop units should be maintained within boat waves and boat teams. The ATF landing craft are also organized by boat flotillas, groups, and waves. A boat team consists of the LF personnel assigned to an individual landing craft.

(b) For movement by helicopter, the BLTs are formed into helicopter flights, waves, and teams.

(4) Task grouping of tanks, artillery, antitank, engineer, and other supporting arms or service units may be formed to support initial operations ashore, but not integrated into a BLT.

(5) Reserve forces are organized in a manner similar to their assault counterparts. Although not tailored for a specific beach or LZ, reserve forces are normally prepared to conduct an assault landing by either landing craft or helicopter movement.

e. Organization of Sea Areas. Sea areas in the vicinity of the objective area are selected and designated by the CATF or higher authority in order to minimize the possibility of interference between components of the AF and other supporting forces, and to maximize force defense and speed of the offensive. Those portions of the sea areas in the landing area in which the ship-to-shore movement is conducted are of particular concern to the LF. CATF, in coordination with the CLF, plans the necessary approach and retirement lanes, checkpoints, rendezvous points and aids to navigation to facilitate the control and coordination of ship-to-shore movement.

32. Control

a. **The CATF is responsible for overall control of both surface and air ship-to-shore movement.** Initially, ship-to-shore movement, both on the surface and through the air, is centrally controlled to permit coordination of support for LF elements. Later, as circumstances permit, control of surface movement is decentralized for efficient and rapid execution. However, VTOL aircraft movement remains under centralized control.

b. Control and coordination measures necessary for employment of airborne elements of the LF will be established by the CATF in conjunction with the CLF and other concerned commanders specified in the initiating directive or establishing directive, if appropriate.

c. **Control Organizations**

(1) **Movement control of landing ships, landing craft, amphibious vehicles, and helicopters from the transport and landing ship sea echelons areas to landing beaches and HLZs is exercised through a Navy control group.** A control group consists of personnel, ships, and craft designated to control the waterborne ship-to-shore movement. Organization of the control group is based on the arrangement and number of beaches on which the LF is to land. CATF, in collaboration with the CLF, will develop the OPTASK Amphib message. This overarching OPTASK specifies the ATF commander's intent, duties and responsibilities, all geographic areas (surface: inner transport areas, outer transport areas, beaches, CLZs, boatlanes, etc., air: ingress, egress routes, HLZs, etc; fires: fire support areas/stations, no fire areas, targets, etc;), the operational area (e.g. AOA or AO/HIDACZ), timelines for the assault, medical regulating instructions, force protection instructions, etc. The initial OPTASK Amphib message should be promulgated no later than 72 hours prior to the assault to allow sufficient time for the subordinate units to plan. Updates can then be promulgated as more information becomes available.

(2) **The Navy control group** keeps the CATF, CLF, and other designated commanders informed of the progress of the movement from ship-to-shore, including the actual landing of the waves and the visible progress of operations ashore. The CATF and transport group commanders designate control ships and control officers, as appropriate. The organization of the Navy control group is based on the arrangement and number of landing beaches used by the AF and is specifically designed to support the LF's organization for landing. The Navy control group uses control measures such as approach lanes, boat lanes, and transfer lines, to facilitate control of movement. The primary agencies of the Navy control group include the following:

(a) **Central Control Officer.** This Navy officer is normally located aboard the CATF's flagship to coordinate the overall ship-to-shore movement of surface assault units, including LCAC operations. The CCO is responsible for:

1. Planning and supervising the surface-borne ship-to-shore movement.

2. Organizing the Navy control group to best support the landing plan.

3. Maintaining liaison with the tactical action officer.

4. Maintaining liaison with the TACLOG group.

(b) **Primary Control Officer.** The PCO is embarked in a primary control ship assigned to control the movement of the landing craft and amphibious vehicles. A PCO is assigned for each landing beach and is responsible for the following:

1. Promulgate the primary control ship intentions message no later than 48 hours prior to the assault to allow sufficient time for the subordinate units to plan. Updates can then be promulgated as more information becomes available.

2. Maintaining the current location and status of ships, landing craft, and boats assigned to conduct a landing on a specific beach.

3. Monitoring surf and weather conditions, and recommending the termination of boat operations should conditions warrant.

4. Maintaining the status of debarkation or embarkation.

5. Landing scheduled waves at the correct beach at the specified time.

6. Arranging for fueling boats, and providing rest and food for boat crews.

7. Providing liaison to the surfaceborne TACLOG group detachment.

8. Conducting landing craft or amphibious vehicle salvage operations.

9. Coordinating landing craft operations within a designated area following the initial action.

(c) **LCAC Control Officer (LCO).** The LCO works for the PCO and is in charge of all ship-to-shore movement using LCACs. He is aboard the LCAC control ship (LCS) and is responsible for promulgating the LCS intentions message.

(d) **Secondary Control Officer (SCO).** When designated, the SCO embarks in the secondary control ship and is the principal assistant to the PCO. The SCO responsible for:

1. Maintaining duplicate control records and plots required of the PCO.

2. Monitoring PCO radio circuits.

3. Controlling surfaceborne ship-to-shore movement over a landing beach when two or more landing beaches are designated.

4. Assuming PCO duties in an emergency.

Detailed description and use of these control measures can be found in NTTP 3-02.1M/Marine Corps Warfighting Publication (MCWP) 3-31.5, Ship-to-Shore Movement.

(3) **LFSP** is a temporary, special category task organization of the AF that contains a shore party support element, a helicopter assault support element, and a Navy beach group element. **The primary mission of the LFSP is to facilitate the landing and movement of troops, equipment, and supplies across beaches and into LZs, ports, and airfields.**

See NTTP 3-02.1M/MCWP 3-31.5, Ship-to-Shore Movement, *for detailed discussion of the organization and functions of the Navy control group.*

(4) VTOL aircraft units employed in the ship-to-shore movement are subordinate elements of the LF. These units execute the ship-to-shore movement in accordance with the landing plan. Plans include provisions for shifting control of VTOL aircraft operations to the CLF when the situation ashore permits. **During the ship-to-shore movement, the CATF coordinates and controls air operations through the Navy TACC.** Within the Navy TACC, coordination of VTOL aircraft operations is accomplished by the helicopter/VTOL aircraft coordination section. Control of VTOL aircraft ship-to-shore movement is further delegated to the HDC, which is the primary direct control agency for the helicopter/VTOL aircraft transport unit. Once established ashore, the CLF coordinates and controls air operations through the Marine TACC.

See NTTP 3-02.1M/MCWP 3-31.5, Ship-to-Shore Movement, *for further detailed discussion of the organization and control of the VTOL assault.*

(5) **Tactical-Logistical Group.** The TACLOG group is a temporary agency, composed of landing force personnel, that advises the Navy control organization of LF requirements during ship-to-shore movement. TACLOG groups assist the Navy control organization in expediting the landing of personnel, equipment, and supplies in accordance with the LF landing plan. TACLOG groups also serve as the primary source of information to the CLF regarding the status of LF units during ship-to-shore movement. The TACLOG group provides the link between the LFSP and advises the LF operations center and the Navy control organizations on the status of the offload.

33. Supporting, Advance Force, and Preassault Operations

a. **General.** Prior to the execution of the decisive action phase of an amphibious operation, the AF commanders may seek to shape their operational environment through three complementary operations. Although these operations are usually referred to in the context of an amphibious assault or raid, they may be used to shape the operational environment for a NEO or humanitarian operation. The exact manner in which these operations are conducted will depend on the type of amphibious operation. **The force and the time period in which these operations are conducted typically define the operation.** These shaping operations usually occur sequentially, but may in some instances occur simultaneously. These operations are, in order of occurrence, supporting, advance force, and preassault operations.

(1) **Supporting operations** are conducted by forces other than the AF in support of the amphibious operation; are ordered by a higher authority, normally based on a request from the AF commanders; and may set the conditions for the advance force to move into the operational area.

(2) **Advance force operations** are conducted in the operational area by a task-organized element of the AF, prior to the arrival of the AF in the operational area.

(3) **Preassault operations** are conducted by the AF upon its arrival in the operational area and prior to the time of the assault or decisive action, normally delineated by H- and L-hour.

b. **Supporting Operations. Supporting operations conducted by forces other than the AF may establish the prerequisites for an amphibious operation (e.g., establishment of air and maritime superiority).** Supporting operations are ordered by the JFC or a designated commander and are to a large degree based on requests for certain actions from the amphibious commanders. These operations are normally conducted by naval, air, and SOF prior to the arrival of the advance force; however, they may occur at any time before or after H-hour.

(1) Supporting maritime operations may include establishing maritime superiority, the initiation of MCM operations, deception, and hydrographic survey of potential landing beaches. Meteorological and oceanographic (METOC) data, including tailored imagery, may be obtained directly from the Naval Oceanographic Office or via a joint or Service METOC forecast activity in support of naval forces.

(2) Sea- and land-based supporting air operations may include establishing air superiority, reconnaissance, and the attack of land targets that may impact the amphibious operation. Assault breaching efforts may also include aerial delivered weapons intended to destroy obstacles within the surf zone, such as mines and barriers.

(3) Supporting SOF operations may include but are not limited to: psychological operations, civil affairs, special reconnaissance, and direct action.

See JP 3-05, Doctrine for Joint Special Operations, *for more information.*

c. **Advance Force Operations**

(1) The advance force conducts operations within the AF operational area established by the initiating directive. However, based on the limited capabilities of the advance force, this operational area may not be activated until the arrival of the AF. Advanced force operations range from clandestine reconnaissance to bombardment of the landing area by air, naval surface fires, and even artillery if firing positions are available. Overt actions are usually meant to either shape the operational area or to deceive the enemy as to the real objectives. The advance force may be assigned a smaller operational area (AOA or AO) if it has sufficient assets to control it or an operational area may not be established. Advance forces are task-organized to perform tasks that may include, but are not limited to:

(a) MCM operations with emphasis on the clearance of mines in the transport areas, FSAs, and sea approaches to the landing beaches.

Navy Seals perform beach reconnaissance.

(b) Hydrographic reconnaissance of the landing beaches and seaward approaches.

(c) Reconnaissance and surveillance of AF objectives, LF objectives, landing beaches, LZs, DZs, and high speed avenues of approach into the landing area.

(d) Neutralization or destruction of adversary high-value assets.

(2) **Decision to Employ an Advance Force.** The JFC or other higher authority may restrict or preclude the use of an advance force based on the diplomatic or military situation. **If advance force operations are authorized, the decision to employ an advance force is made after weighing the advantages of operational and tactical surprise and the requirements for preparation of the landing area.** Knowledge of the operational area, the indigenous population, extent of adversary fixed defenses, air defenses, mines and obstacles, must be evaluated.

(a) **Surprise.** Complete surprise is difficult to attain against an alert adversary and the prospects of achieving it will decrease with efforts to isolate the AOA/AO. In any event, advance force operations should always cover areas that are not within the selected LZs. OPSEC is an important consideration to the success of any amphibious operation. Every effort must be made to conceal the landing areas and AF objectives from the enemy until the commencement of the ship-to-shore movement. When surprise is a principal consideration for success, but is not attained, the risk to the AF is increased.

(b) **Preparation of the Landing Area.** When the landing area is extensively organized for defense or the offshore areas are heavily mined, the AF commanders may elect to conduct advance force operations. In this case, the destruction or neutralization of the fixed defenses far outweighs the disadvantage of disclosing the selected landing area. Conversely, advance force operations may not be prudent when the landing area selected is lightly defended and the main defending force is held in reserve — waiting to employ against the AF's main effort.

(3) **Planning Advance Force Operations. Planning the advance force operation is an integral part of planning the overall amphibious operation.** The command relationships between commanders within the advance force must be specified in the initiating directive. **The LF CONOPS should never be based on the assumption that these forces will always be available for tasking by the CLF upon the arrival of the AF into the operational area.** The CATF designates the amphibious task group (ATG) commander for the advance force, provides forces, and ensures that the requisite command and information systems are available to conduct the operation. **CLF will evaluate the missions assigned to the advance force and assume the following additional planning responsibilities:**

(a) Form a landing group or subordinate task organization, designating the advance force landing and/or reconnaissance group commander and providing the requisite staff and forces to accomplish assigned LF tasks.

<u>1.</u> A landing group commander will be used when offensive landings or strikes are conducted by LF units of the advance force. In amphibious operations, a landing group commander is the officer designated by the CLF as the single tactical commander of a subordinate task organization capable of conducting landing operations against a position or group of positions.

<u>2.</u> A reconnaissance group commander is used when LF units conduct only reconnaissance and surveillance missions.

(b) Determine LF requirements for NSFS, priority intelligence requirements (PIRs), air support, space support, reconnaissance, etc. and submit to the CATF.

(c) Determine communications system requirements for the LF personnel who will accompany the advance force.

(d) Determine SOF support requirements and coordinate command relationships with the advance force commander.

(e) Designate FSCC and/or fires cell (FC) personnel to augment the advance force SACC.

(f) Modify embarkation and landing plans (cross deck equipment and personnel as required) to support the advance force operations.

(4) The decision on establishment of an advance force operational area must be made after considering the advance force's mission, forces, ability to control an assigned area, and the level of threat.

(5) Appropriate coordination measures are established to facilitate coordination and unity of effort. These measures are influenced by, among other things, the scope of the supporting operations taking place in the vicinity of the operational area, and the command relationships established between the advance force and other forces in the area.

(6) SOF employed during advance force operations will usually remain under the OPCON of the theater special operations command commander (acting as the commander, joint force special operations component command [JFSOCC]) and be assigned in support of the CATF and/or CLF depending on the location and nature of the mission. SOF may also be operating in or near the AOA on distinctly separate low-visibility or clandestine missions in support of the combatant commander. Coordination must occur between AF planners and the JFSOCC/joint special operations task force to maximize effectiveness.

(7) Upon arrival of the AF in the operational area, the advance force is usually disestablished and forces revert to control of CATF and CLF or other designated commanders. Certain tasks may dictate that the OPCON or TACON of SOF or reconnaissance teams remains with the advance force to minimize disruptions prior to the decisive action. It is important to maintain the SOF chain of command in order to preserve the C2 relationship(s) of SOF forces for the gaining commander.

d. **Preassault Operations.** Final preparations of the landing area are usually under the control of the CATF and CLF. These preparations are usually of a more overt nature. Assets used to conduct these operations may reduce the resources available for tasking at H- and L-hour. The CLF must ensure that inherent risks associated with preassault operations do not critically impair the CONOPS ashore. Some of the planning considerations may include the following:

(1) Demolition of visible obstacles, clearance of required mines, breaching of any remaining seaward minefields and barriers to and on the beach, overt marking of usable channels, direct action missions, target acquisition (TA) and spotting for NSFS, and initial terminal guidance for designated assault landings.

(2) Air operations in accordance with air support plans, including EW, and preplanned air strikes against adversary installations en route to and in the vicinity of beaches, DZs, LZs, targets of opportunity, and mines and obstacles in the SZ and on the beach.

(3) NSFS in accordance with the NSFS plan, including destruction or neutralization of adversary installations that might interfere with the approach and final deployment of the AF or otherwise interfere with the operation.

(4) Artillery support on landing areas in accordance with artillery fire support plans if artillery has been put in place during preassault operations.

(5) Ammunition (naval, aviation ordnance, artillery, etc.) expenditure and fuel consumption prior to the landing.

(6) Loss of equipment prior to D-day to include high demand, low density item losses due to maintenance and repair.

(7) Loss of personnel due to casualties, injuries, sickness, or required "down time" (such as recovery periods for long range reconnaissance teams, aircrews, etc.).

(8) Resupply and rearming schedule for the AF, or lack thereof.

(9) LF requirement to support other forces prior to and after D-day.

e. With the completion of preassault operations, the AF will conduct surface and/or vertical assaults into the landing area to accomplish the decisive action.

34. Final Preparations for the Ship-to-Shore Movement

In some cases units may need to be cross-decked prior to the assault. This should be kept to the minimum as there may be insufficient berthing for the troops that are cross-decked. Also, this means that the air or landing craft crews will be transferring personnel instead of making last minute preparations for the operation. Upon completion of any pre-execution operations the ATF starts the final approach to assigned positions for the landings. Ships prepare for the debarkation of the embarked troops, equipment, and supplies in accordance with previously prepared plans. The commencement of debarkation and the timing of the ship-to-shore movement depend on the designated H-hour. All elements must be prepared to modify plans on short notice to conform to changes in H-hour.

a. **Landing Force Operations**. LF operations ashore begin with the landing of the first scheduled wave, by surface means, vertical insertion, or airborne landing. Elements of the LF quickly transition from an organization for landing to an organization for combat in order to accomplish the LF missions ashore. Once fully established ashore, the LF conducts tactical operations similar to normal land operations but remains dependent on at-sea forces for support. As the operation progresses and support is established ashore, the degree of dependence is reduced.

b. The CLF is responsible for the overall planning and execution of LF operations ashore. **To guide LF operations ashore during the action phase, the CLF and his staff develop the LF plan for operations.** During the initial preparation of the plan, the LF staff will need to develop the essential items necessary to frame the overall OPLAN. The LF CONOPS ashore, the plan for fire support, and the concept for CSS are produced based on the CLF's guidance and intent.

(1) **CONOPS Ashore.** The development of the concept of LF operations ashore is an evolutionary process. The concept developed during detailed planning is a refinement of the initial concept developed during preliminary amphibious planning. Ultimately, the detailed concept is included in the OPLAN. The operational and logistic requirements of subordinate elements and changes in the adversary situation may necessitate modifications to this concept, but it must always provide additional clarity to the LF commander's intent. **The detailed CONOPS ashore amplifies CLF's decisions and indicates how he visualizes the operation.** Included in the CONOPS, the scheme of maneuver is a plan for the execution of a tactical COA. It **includes objectives, types of offensive maneuver** to be employed, **distribution of forces, and necessary control measures**. In formulating the scheme of maneuver for an amphibious operation, the principles of ground combat remain valid. However, variations of application may be necessary because of the character of the operation.

(2) **Plan of Supporting Fires.** Fire support has a major effect on the development of the LF plan for operations. Until the LF's organic artillery is ashore, NSFS and aviation assets (fixed- and rotary-wing) are normally the only means of fire support for

the LF. A portion of these assets may also be tasked to defend the AF as a whole, limiting their availability to the LF.

For additional information on supporting arms, see Chapter V, "Support to Amphibious Operations," Section B, "Fire Support."

(3) **Plan for the Employment of LF Aviation.** The plan for the employment of LF aviation to support operations ashore is integrated with the overall air plans of the CATF and AF commanders. Air operations performed by ATF and LF aviation elements, and other supporting air forces, complement one another and constitute a collective capability for support of the amphibious operation. When the LF is a MAGTF, the MAGTF commander retains OPCON of the organic aviation assets for use in support of the LF CONOPS and his overall mission. During the course of the operation, excess MAGTF sorties can be allocated by the JFC to other component commanders as appropriate. The MAGTF commander provides excess sorties and sorties for air defense, long-range interdiction, and long-range reconnaissance to the JFC in accordance with JP 1, *Doctrine for the Armed Forces of the United States.*

(4) **Plan for the Employment of the LF CSS.** The plan for the employment of the LF CSS is expressed in the concept for CSS. This document establishes the logistic support plan for the LF **from the embarkation phase through the termination of LF operations ashore.**

c. **Reserves.** The CLF will usually plan to withhold a portion of the force during the initial stages of the action phase. The LF reserve must be capable of landing when and where required in order to best influence the tactical situation as it develops ashore.

(1) Subordinate units of the LF will normally not have their own reserve due to the limited ship-to-shore movement assets and the need to commit all landing groups to maximize the combat power ashore. On-call waves are the normal means with which the ground commander can influence the action ashore. While afloat, certain units may be treated as a reserve for commitment as required by the situation.

(2) When keeping the reserve afloat is no longer any advantage, it is landed and positioned ashore to facilitate future employment. This action should not be undertaken until sufficient area has been seized ashore to permit adequate maneuver space.

35. Subsidiary Landings

In an amphibious operation, **a subsidiary landing is a landing, normally conducted by elements of the AF, usually made outside the designated landing area to support the main landing.** An amphibious operation may require one or more subsidiary landings conducted before, during, or after the main landing. If made before, the effect on the main landing must be considered in terms of possible loss of surprise. Subsidiary landings must be planned and executed by commanders with the same precision as the main landing. Division of forces to conduct subsidiary landings is justified only when such employment will be of greater value than commitment to the main landing. Forces employed in subsidiary landings that precede the main landing may be re-embarked and employed as a tactical reserve supporting the main landing. Subsidiary landings may be executed to accomplish one or more of the following specific purposes:

a. Seize specific areas to be used in support of the main landing; i.e., seizing islands or mainland areas adjacent to the main landing area for use as:

(1) Artillery, missile, and rocket firing positions.

(2) Airfields or vertical and short takeoff and landing aircraft-capable locations.

(3) Protected anchorage, temporary advanced naval bases, or logistics and CSS sites from which the main landing can be supported.

(4) Air warning and control system sites.

b. Seize an area to deny its use to the enemy in opposing the main landing.

c. Divert enemy attention and forces from the main landing or fix enemy defensive forces in place as part of a deception operation.

36. Joint Logistics Over-the-Shore

Joint logistics over-the-shore (JLOTS) are operations in which Navy and Army LOTS forces conduct LOTS operations together under a JFC. Traditionally, Navy LOTS includes the use of United States Marine Corps forces. **Generally, LOTS operations are joint in all but a few exceptions.** The scope of JLOTS operations extends from acceptance of ships for off-load through the arrival of equipment and cargo at inland staging and marshalling areas. **The JLOTS forces are normally organized along Service lines**, but can also follow functional lines, with Service elements integrated under the TACON of the JLOTS commander. **Geographic combatant commanders** have overall responsibility for JLOTS operations in their areas of responsibility. United States Transportation Command (USTRANSCOM) forces, when attached to the supported geographic combatant commander, will normally also be under TACON of the JLOTS commander. The geographic combatant commander may delegate authority to subordinate JFCs in the conduct of their assigned missions. Each **Service component** has personnel and equipment necessary for the conduct of LOTS operations. During the planning for and execution of JLOTS operations, each Service component will furnish such equipment and perform those tasks required by the OPLAN and OPORD or as directed by the JFC during OPORD execution. The JLOTS commander will accomplish detailed planning and execution of JLOTS operations through a central planning team composed of representatives from participating Service and USTRANSCOM components. **Principal responsibilities of the JLOTS commander include the following:**

a. **Publishing an OPORD or directive** that states responsibilities and describes procedures for the conduct of the JLOTS operation.

b. **Handling JLOTS execution**, beginning with acceptance of ships for off-load, through the arrival of equipment and cargo at inland staging and marshalling areas.

c. **Coordinating over-the-shore liquid cargo operations.** For the OPDS, responsibility includes acceptance of OPDS vessels and the installation and operation of OPDS to its termination point on the beach, where it interfaces with the inland petroleum distribution systems and the amphibious assault fuel system.

For additional information see JP 4-01.6, Joint Logistics Over-The-Shore (JLOTS).

SECTION F. SPECIFIC CONSIDERATIONS BY TYPE OF AMPHIBIOUS OPERATION

37. Assault

a. **Action.** The assault begins on order, after sufficient elements of the main body of the AF that are capable of beginning the ship-to-shore movement arrive in the operational area. For an assault, the action phase ends when conditions specified in the initiating directive are met, as recommended by the CATF and CLF and approved by the JFC or designated commander.

b. **Sequence.** The assault is the most difficult type of amphibious operation and one of the most difficult of all military operations. Many of the principles and procedures of the assault apply to other types of amphibious operations. The normal sequence during the action phase of the operation is depicted in Figure III-8.

c. **Planning Considerations for Assault**

(1) The LF mission is developed early in the planning process **after careful analysis of the AF mission and only after all specified and implied tasks are identified and understood**. The mission is translated into specific LF objectives by the CLF, objectives that serve as the primary basis for determining the LF scheme of maneuver, fire support, organization for combat, formation for landing, landing plan, and logistic support requirements. The mission developed by the commander, and as amplified by the CONOPS ashore, is the principal means by which the commander ensures that his intent is understood and accomplished in detailed planning and execution of the operation.

(2) **Projection of Combat Power Ashore.** In the amphibious assault, combat power is progressively phased ashore. **Initially, the LF is able to employ only a small fraction of its total potential power.** Tactical operations are initiated by small units that are normally only supported by NSFS and attack aircraft. Before long, the preponderance of the LF is ashore and functioning as a cohesive organization exerting its maximum

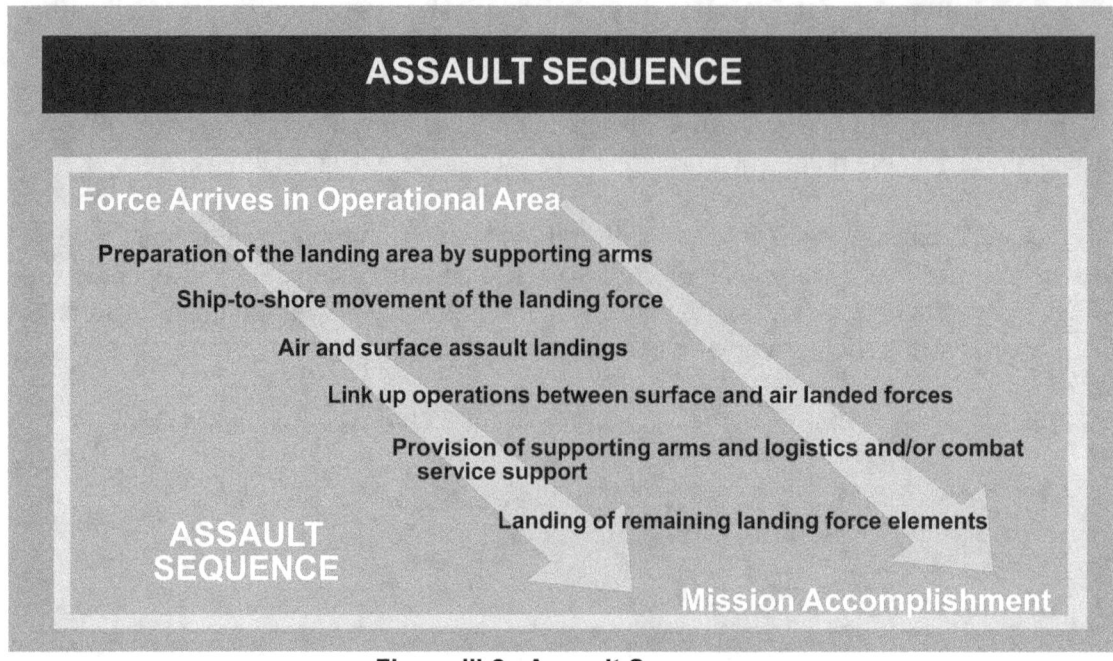

Figure III-8. Assault Sequence

combat power. The echelonment reflected in the organization for landing provides for the orderly progression and development of combat power.

For more information on LF echelons see Section D, "Movement."

(3) The time required to phase the LF's combat power ashore depends on many factors and the CATF and CLF must develop the OPORD based on best estimates. Some of those factors affecting the build up of combat power ashore include the following:

(a) Degree of adversary interference with the landing.

(b) Availability, by type and number, of ship-to-shore movement assets.

(c) Availability by type and number of amphibious ships.

(d) The location of the transport areas with respect to the beach.

(e) Capacity (including throughput considerations) of landing beaches and LZs.

(f) Extent of fire support available to the LF prior to establishing organic assets ashore.

(g) Terrain, weather, and sea conditions in the landing area.

(h) Available maneuver space, and trafficability considerations, in the landing area.

(4) **Phasing Ashore.** The LF will seldom be able to secure control of the landward section of the landing area in a single landing. Therefore, the CLF will have to phase his units and capabilities ashore during the execution of the OPORD. Intermediate objectives and phase lines may be used to coordinate and track the phases of LF operations ashore. Phasing can revolve around many mediums: time, (in relation to H-hour, L-hour, or D-day), distance (intermediate objectives or phase lines), terrain (crossing of obstacles), or event-driven (linkup with helicopterborne forces or seizure of an off shore fire support position). Regardless of the method used, the CLF must ensure that the plan is based on sound decisions and the capabilities of the LF as a whole. **Especially during the landing of scheduled waves, the action phase is characterized by decentralized execution of the plan by subordinate commanders.** The concept for phasing ashore the LF's combat power should plan for the reestablishment of centralized control of the LF. This **reestablishment of centralized control normally progresses from lower to higher echelons successively**.

(a) **Support Capabilities of Other Elements of the ATF.** In developing plans, the CLF must consider all elements of the AF, as well as other forces that will be able to support his CONOPS.

(b) **Other Plan Requirements.** This publication does not discuss, in detail, all the functional planning responsibilities normally associated with an OPLAN. Planning factors that do not differ significantly from land combat such as public affairs, civil-military operations, information operations, and offensive/defensive operations in general, remain valid and they will not be addressed in this chapter.

d. **Landing Force Scheme of Maneuver.** The formulation of the scheme of maneuver for an amphibious assault is based on the same fundamentals of warfare normally associated with all military operations. However, there are a few conditions and considerations that may require particular attention.

(1) **The fundamental goal is to introduce the LF ashore to accomplish the assigned mission.** Normally starting from a zero combat capability ashore, the LF seeks the early seizure of key objectives through aggressive offensive action to disrupt adversary defenses, permit the rapid landing of supporting units, and contribute to the rapid development of full combat power ashore.

(2) **The scheme of maneuver may support the rapid build up of combat power ashore vice the immediate seizure of AF objectives.** The scheme of maneuver may allow the engagement of the adversary on ground chosen by the CLF and at a time that gives the LF a marked advantage.

(3) **The landing of the force at separate locations can create problems in achievement of mass,** with attendant difficulties in C2, fire support, and other functional

areas. The CLF can overcome this obstacle by ensuring that the major elements of the LF fully understand the mission, commander's intent, and are task-organized to act independently during the early stages of the operation.

(4) The types of combat units in the LF task organization and their strength influence the scheme of maneuver.

(a) LFs that have organic or attached combat support and CSS capabilities are usually better suited for amphibious operations than LFs comprised of infantry units alone.

(b) Armored elements provide substantial combat power and mobility for the LF if landed early in the operation.

(c) Artillery in the AE may be either self-propelled or towed. All Marine Corps artillery is towed. The LF may contain Army self-propelled artillery, which is well suited for certain conditions and is landed in the same manner as armor. Towed artillery is best transported by helicopter until landing craft become available.

(d) Combat engineer units will normally be attached to infantry and mechanized units to provide immediate, responsive, and decentralized support. Later, engineer forces may be reorganized to provide direct or general support.

(e) Air defense units organic to the LF are established ashore early to provide for the landward extension of an air defense system. They will be part of the CATF's integrated air defense system until control is phased ashore.

(5) The LF scheme of maneuver should meet certain key requirements:

(a) Its primary purpose, should be the seizure of objectives requisite to the buildup and establishment of the LF ashore.

(b) Utilize all avenues of approach proximate to the selected beaches and LZs.

(c) Supportable by NSFS, missiles, and tactical air, especially prior to the landing of artillery.

(d) LF echelons should be capable of initial success without dependence on other assault units.

(e) Provide for the development of mutual support between units as the attack progresses.

(f) Provide for early establishment of combat service support areas (CSSAs) as required.

e. **Reserves**

(1) Commitment of the reserve in an amphibious assault may be more complex than in normal land operations.

(2) When afloat, the reserve may be delayed pending availability of landing craft, amphibious vehicles, or helicopters, plus the time required for debarkation and movement ashore.

(3) Employment of the reserves may delay the movement of other assault formations because all elements of the LF must share the same ship-to-shore movement assets.

(4) Landing of the reserve by surface means depends on the availability of landing craft as well as a suitable landing beach near the area of intended employment.

f. **Assault Follow-on Echelon Operations.** The AFOE is that echelon of the assault troops, vehicles, aircraft, equipment, and supplies which, although not needed to initiate the assault, are required to support and sustain the assault. **The AFOE is normally required in the operational area no later than 5 days after commencement of the assault landing.**

(1) The AFOE is divided into airlifted and sealifted forces and supplies. Required arrival time in theater, suitability of material for air and sea lift, and lift availability, in that order, will determine transportation mode.

(2) The AFOE is organized for landing and embarkation, respectively, based on anticipated requirements of operations ashore. Units, personnel, and material configured in shipload and planeload lots as dictated by landing and embarkation plans are then organized into movement groups. Embarkation plans are prepared by the LF and appropriate subordinate commanders containing instructions and information concerning the organization for embarkation, assignment to shipping, supplies and equipment to be embarked, location and assignment of embarkation areas, control and communication arrangements, movement schedules and embarkation sequence, and additional pertinent instructions relating to the embarkation of the LF.

(3) Units and their equipment are marshalled at their home stations and staged at POEs in accordance with their time-phased deployment schedules. Materiel arriving from logistic sources is assembled at POEs under LF supervision.

(4) **The requirement to containerize AFOE material cannot be overemphasized.**

(5) Although the CATF and CLF are responsible for planning and executing embarkation, civilian stevedores, contracted by the Military Surface Deployment and

Distribution Command at commercial ports and by the Navy and naval installations, are used to load common-user shipping provided by the Commander, USTRANSCOM. Because of the large number of foreign nationals employed by foreign flag shippers and port facilities, it may be necessary for commanders of amphibious transport groups to augment port and/or embarked security forces to protect against sabotage of equipment, either in port or while embarked.

(6) Ship unloading is directed by the normal ATF-LF ship-to-shore control and support activities (PCO, HDC, TACLOG group, LFSP, etc.). The size and organization of these agencies will change as the operation matures. Additional cargo handling battalion and amphibious construction battalion forces are required to support the offload of merchant ships. As they become accessible, developed seaports and aerial ports are used to supplement traditional beach operations, expanding the ship-to-shore organization accordingly. The CATF and CLF are responsible for debarkation and offload until termination of the amphibious operation. In the case of an amphibious assault, the amphibious operation would not normally be terminated until the entire AFOE is ashore. At that time, the responsibilities for offload of follow-up material may be passed to another offload organization designated by higher authority.

g. **Follow-Up Transport Ships and Aircraft.** Follow-up ships and aircraft carry reinforcements and stores for use after landing of the AE and AFOE. The CATF will assume control of follow-up ships and aircraft upon arrival in the operational area.

38. Raids

a. **Scope. An amphibious raid is an operation involving a swift incursion into or the temporary occupation of an objective to accomplish an assigned mission followed by a planned withdrawal.** Amphibious raids are conducted as independent operations or in support of other operations. Depending on the purpose of the raid, it may be conducted using covert insertion means, relying on stealth to approach the objective, or overtly with full fire support in a manner that may resemble the early stages of an amphibious assault. Generally, amphibious raids are conducted to:

(1) Destroy certain targets, particularly those that do not lend themselves to destruction by other means.

(2) Harass the enemy by attacks on isolated posts, patrols, or headquarters.

(3) Capture or kill key personnel.

(4) Support forces engaged with the enemy by attacking the enemy rear or flank positions on a seacoast.

(5) Obtain information on hydrography, terrain, enemy dispositions, strength, movements, and weapons.

(6) Create a diversion in connection with strategic deception operations.

(7) Evacuate individuals or materiel.

(8) Establish, support, or coordinate unconventional warfare activities.

b. **General.** Thorough, integrated rehearsals are essential to precision and speed in executing a raid. All participating forces must be drilled in every detail of debarkation, movement ashore, operations ashore, withdrawal, and reembarkation. An amphibious raid is planned and executed in the same general manner as an amphibious assault, except that a raid always includes a provision for withdrawal of the raiding force. The following factors must be considered when planning an amphibious raid:

(1) The size of the raid force is normally limited to the essential number of personnel required to accomplish the mission. This increases the chance of maintaining security, achieving surprise at the objective, and facilitates rapid withdrawal upon completion of the mission.

(2) It may be unnecessary for selected beaches or LZs to meet all the requirements of an amphibious assault. Beaches or LZs may be chosen to ensure tactical surprise or facilitate withdrawal.

(3) A raid will be of limited duration.

(4) The objective, and nature and duration of the operation may simplify logistic requirements.

c. **Planning Considerations.** The following must be considered when planning a raid:

(1) Surprise is an essential ingredient in the success of an amphibious raid and offsets the lack of logistic and fire support normally associated with amphibious operations.

(2) Security during the planning and execution of a raid must receive particular attention, to include full exploitation of deceptive measures. Such deceptive measures may take the form of elaborate cover plans or may be confined to simple ruses.

(3) The following factors will influence the choice of landing areas for the raid force.

(a) Enemy disposition.

(b) Sea approaches.

(c) Hydrographic and beach characteristics.

(d) Availability of LZs.

(e) Avenues of approach to the objective and beach exits.

(4) The estimated time that the raiding force will have to be ashore may influence the choice of H-hour and, consequently, the conditions of visibility under which the raiding force may be landed and withdrawn. It will likewise affect the scope of logistic arrangements.

(5) Purpose of the raid, including its relation to other concurrent or imminent operations that it may support, will influence the selection of D-day for the raid. In addition, these same factors may affect the availability of shipping, aircraft, and logistic and fire support means for the raid.

(6) Planning for the embarkation of forces assigned to participate in an amphibious raid is similar to preparation for the amphibious assault, including consideration of OPSEC measures.

(7) Fire support planning is similar to that for an amphibious assault, except that, where surprise is a major factor, supporting fires usually are withheld and EMCON is maintained until surprise is lost.

(8) Planning for ship-to-shore movement is generally similar to that for an amphibious assault except movement may be made entirely by rotary-wing or tilt-rotor aircraft, raiding craft, or LCACs.

(9) Withdrawal must be planned in detail, including provisions as to time and place for re-embarkation. If the landing point and withdrawal point are not the same, positive means of location and identification of the latter must be established. Special situations may permit planning for withdrawal of the raiding force directly into friendly territory without re-embarkation. Withdrawal by air may be possible when the area of the raid includes a usable airfield or terrain suitable for landing VTOL aircraft. Detailed planning must include provisions for an alternate extraction method in the event of inclement weather. One consideration may be to have the raid force remain ashore in a hiding position until extraction can be executed.

39. Demonstrations

a. **Scope. The amphibious demonstration is intended to confuse the enemy as to time, place, or strength of the main operation.** Amphibious demonstrations may be conducted in conjunction with other deception operations in order to delude or confuse the enemy. In the operational area, an amphibious demonstration may be conducted in or near the landing area in conjunction with an amphibious assault. In still other cases, a demonstration may be conducted outside the operational area by forces not attached to the main amphibious effort to divert or immobilize enemy strategic reserve forces that could threaten the amphibious assault. Likewise, the demonstration could be used to divert enemy attention from other operations.

b. **General.** Effectiveness of a demonstration increases in direct proportion to the degree of realism involved in its execution. The enemy must be convinced that a LF is preparing for an amphibious landing. All visible, audible, and electronic aspects of the demonstration must appear to be authentic. A demonstration normally includes the approach of forces to the demonstration area, at least a part of the ship-to-shore movement, and employment of supporting fires. A brief but intense preliminary bombardment will usually be more effective than deliberate harassing fire over longer periods of time. A communications deception plan will be used. SOF and tactical deception units may be employed.

c. **Demonstrations Within the Operational Area.** An amphibious demonstration may be conducted by a portion of the force within the operational area when it is intended to influence enemy action within that area. The intended purpose may be to cause the enemy to employ its reserves improperly, to disclose weapon positions by inducing premature firing, to distract attention, to place an early burden on communications system, to precipitate a general air or naval engagement, or to harass. The decision to conduct such a demonstration is made during the planning phase, in consultation with supporting commanders as appropriate.

d. **Demonstrations Outside the Operational Area.** An amphibious demonstration may be conducted outside the operational area to divert or immobilize enemy strategic reserves or other forces capable of affecting the amphibious operation, to distract hostile attention from such an operation, or to precipitate a general air or naval engagement. Such a demonstration may be executed as a supporting operation by a separate AF. The time and place of the demonstration is decided by the JFC or higher authority based on the recommendations by the CATF and CLF.

e. **Demonstrations in Support of Other Operations.** An amphibious demonstration may be conducted with the intent of supporting other operations in the theater or designated operational area. A demonstration conducted before, during, or after commencement of another operation may distract the attention of enemy commanders and induce the enemy to divert major resources.

f. **Planning Considerations.** In planning amphibious demonstrations, consideration must be given to the following:

(1) **Location.** The demonstration area must be near enough to the main effort to permit subsequent employment of the demonstration force if that force is required for subsequent operations. On the other hand, it will be sufficiently separated from the main effort to avoid interference and to ensure that the enemy will be materially delayed in repositioning forces. The demonstration area must be suitable for an actual landing, for only in such an area can the threat of landing be plausible. The demonstration area should appear to be a viable threat to the enemy; otherwise the enemy may not react. An alternate

landing area will often prove suitable for demonstration purposes. If the purpose of the demonstration is to cause the enemy to prematurely disclose its positions or for harassment, it may be conducted prior to execution.

AMPHIBIOUS OPERATIONS DURING THE GULF WAR

During the Gulf War, an additional dimension of deception activity, besides masking the stealthy relocation of the coalition line, was the demonstration of amphibious assault capabilities. As part of this ruse, an impressive amphibious assault task force was stationed conspicuously off the coast of Kuwait. This fleet was comprised of forty amphibious landing craft, the largest such force to be assembled since Inchon. The force contained the most up-to-date, equipment-laden amphibious ships, as well as aircraft, and helicopter airlift. Battleships provided offshore artillery support. For movement to the beach, these forces were equipped with new LVTP-7s (landing, vehicle, track, personnel), LCAC (landing craft, air cushion) hovercraft, and CH-53E Super Stallion helicopters. In short, this was a powerful and credible force stationed threateningly close to the Iraqi defenses along the coast.

To solidify what must have been the Iraqi military's predicted axis of attack, USCENTCOM [US Central Command] regularly made references to the press concerning the training capabilities and presence of the amphibious force in the Persian Gulf and, later, off the coast of Kuwait. On 1 February, *Newsweek* magazine carried a beach assault in the news about a large-scale amphibious invasion. To keep the idea of a beach assault in the news, large-scale amphibious rehearsals were conducted, including, notable, the one held during the last 10 days of January in which 8,000 US Marines landed on the coast of Oman. Moreover, during this period, Navy SEALs (sea-air-land teams) carried out numerous missions along the Kuwaiti coast to gather information on the beach gradients and firmness of the sand, the nature and location of minefields, and the disposition of enemy forces. Carrier air and naval artillery missions were also executed throughout the period to support suspicions of a major coalition amphibious assault.

So that Iraqi commanders would continue to anticipate an amphibious attack, US amphibious support vessels along the coast remained positioned as if threatening to attack, and the battleships *Missouri* and *Wisconsin* and carrier-based aircraft continued bombardments. The object was to fix the six Iraqi infantry divisions deployed along the shoreline, and this was achieved. Iraqi strategists made no early effort to withdraw their forces from the coastal defense works, with the consequence that those forces were rapidly pinned against the coast by the 1st and 2d Marine Divisions, which had broken through the lines in the south.

SOURCE: Deception: *Deceiving the Enemy in Operation DESERT STORM*, Thomas M. Huber, 1992

(2) **Timing.** The timing of a demonstration conducted in support of another operation must be coordinated to achieve the maximum desired level of reaction from the enemy force.

(a) **Prior to Main Operation.** A demonstration before the main operation is conducted to:

1. Draw enemy forces to the demonstration area and away from the area of the main operation.

2. Cause the enemy to disclose its positions.

3. Provide protracted and systematic harassment.

4. Divert the attention of the enemy from the main operation.

5. Cause premature commitment of enemy forces.

(b) **Simultaneously with Main Operation.** A demonstration may commence at the same time as the main operation if it is desired to prevent redeployment of enemy forces and delude the enemy as to the location of the main operation.

(c) **Subsequent to Main Operation.** A demonstration may be conducted subsequent to the main operation to divert enemy forces or fire from the point of the main effort. Successive demonstrations may be executed at a number of points after the main operation commences.

(3) **Forces.** The demonstration force must appear to be of such composition and size as to cause the desired reaction. When the demonstration force is constituted from within the AF, the LF reserve and the shipping in which it is embarked may be employed if the presence of the reserve is not required in the immediate area of the main landing.

(4) **Supporting Arms.** The demonstration force will execute supporting fires of a nature and scope that ensures credibility. Factors that may serve to limit the amount of supporting fires are the availability of NSFS ships, aircraft, and ammunition supply.

(5) **Rehearsals.** Sufficient rehearsals will be held to ensure that the demonstration will be realistic.

g. **Action.** The demonstration must occur over a long enough period to allow the enemy to react. The movement of waves toward the beach or LZs must be conducted as a normal ship-to-shore movement, except that boat waves normally do not actually beach and VTOL aircraft waves do not land. Empty landing craft must maintain sufficient distance from the beach to preclude close enemy observation. At a prearranged time or distance from the beach or VLZ, or on signal, the boat waves and VTOL aircraft waves withdraw.

On completion of the demonstration, the demonstration force is dissolved and its elements are reassigned in accordance with the OPORD or OPLAN.

40. Withdrawals

a. **Scope. Amphibious withdrawals are operations conducted to extract forces by sea in ships or craft from a hostile or potentially hostile shore.** They may be conducted under enemy pressure, under operational urgency to obtain forces needed elsewhere, or to remove forces whose mission is completed. Withdrawal begins with establishment of defensive measures in the embarkation area and ends when all elements of the force have been extracted and embarked on designated shipping.

b. **Characteristics.** While sharing many traits of the amphibious assault, the amphibious withdrawal embraces the following distinguishing characteristics:

(1) Except in the case of withdrawals associated with amphibious raids, planning processes will usually be abbreviated.

(2) Time available to execute will be limited when enemy action against the LF being withdrawn is substantial or when the requirement for forces elsewhere is urgent.

(3) Facilities and equipment for embarkation, available fire support means, and means for C2 of the withdrawal may be limited.

(4) The operation may be conducted under adverse weather conditions or unfavorable terrain or hydrographic features.

(5) The force to be withdrawn may not have been inserted by an amphibious operation and units may be unfamiliar with amphibious procedures, thus significantly complicating the operation.

(6) Additionally, there may be the requirement to evacuate significant numbers of foreign nationals for diplomatic/humanitarian needs.

c. **Execution.** The amphibious withdrawal is normally executed in the following general sequence of steps.

(1) Establish defense of the embarkation area by air, naval, and ground covering forces while organizing and embarking LF personnel, supplies, and equipment not required for support of operations ashore. It is important to maintain local air and maritime superiority to ensure the success of the withdrawal.

(2) Progressively reduce troop strength and quantity of materiel and equipment ashore under protection of air, naval, and ground covering forces. Depending on limitations in afloat cargo capacity and loading time, all usable military materiel is either evacuated or destroyed. During this phase, specific provisions are made for the evacuation of casualties.

(3) Withdraw the ground covering force. Consideration must be given to the difficulty of embarking heavy elements such as artillery and armor.

d. **Supporting Arms.** As in the amphibious assault, defense of an embarkation area on a hostile or potentially hostile shore requires closely coordinated employment of all available supporting arms. Procedures used in the coordination are essentially the same in both cases. The primary difference is that in the assault, supporting arms and control facilities are progressively built up ashore, whereas in a withdrawal, supporting arms and control facilities are progressively decreased ashore until all functions are performed afloat.

e. **Embarkation Procedures**

(1) If embarkation is preparatory to immediate reemployment of the force, planning for embarkation of forces is conducted in accordance with normal planning procedures, as set forth in JP 3-02.1, *Amphibious Embarkation and Debarkation.* Combat loading will be employed in preparation for a subsequent amphibious operation. Combat loading is the arrangement of personnel and the stowage of equipment and supplies in a manner designed to conform to the anticipated tactical operation of the organization embarked. Each individual item is stowed so that it can be unloaded at the required time. Embarkation for movement to base areas will normally employ administrative loading.

(2) Initial size of the embarkation area depends on several factors, such as:

(a) Terrain essential for defense in the event that the embarkation is conducted under enemy pressure.

(b) Number of personnel (potentially including friendly indigenous population) and amount of equipment and supplies to be embarked.

(c) Artillery, NSFS, and air support available for defense.

(d) Nature and extent of usable beaches.

(e) Time available for the embarkation.

41. Amphibious Support to Other Operations

Amphibious forces routinely contribute to conflict prevention and crisis mitigation. Although beyond the scope of this publication, these may include operations such as security cooperation, FHA, civil support, NEOs, peace operations, recovery operations, or disaster relief.

a. **Amphibious forces are particularly well suited to conduct many types of these operations.** Their ability to operate either OTH or within sight of land provides an ability to demonstrate a varying degree of US force presence. Task-organized elements, precisely tailored for specific missions, can be inserted, employed, and withdrawn to meet specific military or diplomatic objectives. The ability to operate from a sea base reduces the overall "footprint" ashore, thus reducing the potential diplomatic impact as well as reducing the potential threat to the force. The maneuverability of sea-based forces also allows them to conduct operations over a large area. Finally, the ship-to-shore movement capability and the ability to shelter, feed, and provide medical care provides maritime forces with a unique capability to conduct a NEO.

b. **The Afloat Pre-positioning Force.** Because of the large and varied quantity of supplies and equipment embarked, MSC's APF is particularly well suited to support FHA operations.

c. **Characteristics.** Amphibious forces must be prepared for involvement in a wide range of operations. In general, operations focus on deterring war, resolving conflict, promoting peace, and supporting civil authorities in response to domestic crises. In addition, these forces may be only one of many participating US and foreign government or nongovernmental organizations. As a result, these operations normally have more restrictive ROE. The goal is to achieve national objectives as quickly as possible and conclude operations on terms favorable to the United States and its allies.

CHAPTER IV
AMPHIBIOUS OPERATIONS AGAINST COASTAL DEFENSES

"A comparison of the several landings leads to the inescapable conclusion that landings should not be attempted in the face of organized resistance if, by any combination of march or maneuver, it is possible to land unopposed within striking distance of the objective."

Major General A.A. Vandegrift, US Marine Corps
Commanding General, 1st Marine Division, 1 July 1943

1. **General**

Coastal defenses against amphibious operations have become a military necessity for a number of countries considered a threat to regional stability and national interests. **Enemies often employ integrated antilanding capabilities that have evolved incorporating the use of land, sea, air, and, in some cases, space assets.** These capabilities involve integration of reconnaissance, long-range interdiction by air and sea forces, and a combined arms ground force at the beach. **Central to most antilanding defenses is the use of littoral mine warfare.** In most cases adversaries will employ mines as an economy of force defensive measure. In addition, some countries may base their coastal defense on the threatened employment of CBRN weapons or may integrate CBRN weapons into their existing coastal defense. **The preferred tactic for AFs operating against countries or organizations employing coastal defenses is to avoid, bypass, or exploit gaps in these defenses whenever possible.** However, operational limitations may preclude this tactic and a breach of these defenses may be required.

2. **Antilanding Doctrine**

Coastal defenses depend on the hydrography, terrain, resources, development time available, and ingenuity of the antagonists. **Antilanding doctrine usually focuses on the development of four layered barriers within the littorals.** These barriers are under observation and covered by shore-based fires. Because of the littoral nature of these barriers, they generally fall within the hydrographic description of shallow water (up to 200 feet in depth). The four barriers from the littorals to land are perimeter, main, engineer, and beach.

a. **Perimeter Barrier.** The first littoral barrier encountered is the perimeter minefield. **This minefield, located at the maximum range of ground-based covering fires, is intended to delay and break up the ATF.** Covering fire is used to protect defensive barriers from assault forces attempts to breach those barriers. Delay at the perimeter minefield could allow coastal defenses time for final preparation and movement of reserves to potential landing beaches. Antiship cruise missiles and coastal artillery may provide covering fires. Electric and diesel submarines and aircraft may attempt to attack the AF.

b. **Main Barrier. The main barrier holds the primary minefield.** The minefield may be approximately two (2) to three (3) nms off the coast and is intended to deny the

Minefields and obstacles are placed along avenues of egress off the beach and in front of defended positions.

maneuver of ATF ships and landing craft during ship-to-shore movement. Land-based artillery, air-defense systems, and possibly small boats and aircraft cover the main barrier.

c. **Engineer Barrier. The engineer barrier is located at or near the shoreline and contains both minefields and obstacles.** The engineer barrier is often laid in very shallow water (VSW) from 40 to 10 feet of water and the SZ from 10 feet of water to the high water mark. Installed by ground force engineers, the barrier targets landing craft and amphibious vehicles and attempts to deny access to the beach. Land-based artillery, air defense systems, and crew-served weapons cover the engineer barrier.

d. **Beach Barrier. The beach barrier canalizes the LF for counterattacks by tactical reserve forces.** Minefields and obstacles are placed along avenues of egress off the beach and in front of defended positions. Land-based artillery, air defense systems, and crew-served weapons all provide support to a counterattack by the reserve.

3. **Amphibious Breach of Coastal Defenses**

a. AFs should request national and theater collection assets to conduct reconnaissance and surveillance of the defended coastal area to determine the best landing area to conduct the breach. The collection request should focus on location of mines, obstacles, and enemy locations in the area, to include air, naval, and ground forces. Also key is the compatibility of the beach and the suitability of the area for available landing craft and vehicles, including maneuver area, tidal levels, and incline.

b. **Mine Threat.** Because adversaries proliferate the use of mines into which they have incorporated new technology, current information on a potential adversary's **mine resources** is crucial to planning. The types, characteristics, numbers, and storage locations of mines as well as the transportation assets and at-sea delivery capability are vital information.

c. **Operational Area Characteristics.** Efforts required to clear, remove, or sweep a minefield **depend significantly on the mined area's physical environment.** Water depth and beach characteristics are key factors. Significant ocean currents increase the difficulty of sweeping moored mines. Tidal ranges expose mines in VSW, making them easy to detect but placing a burden on clearing teams to finish their task within a prescribed time limit. Knowing their precise locations aid assault breaching efforts. Natural and man-made obstacles also hinder breaching operations. High densities of mine-like objects on the bottom complicate operations. Once the landing area is chosen, the coastal defenses in the vicinity are degraded to the desired level through supporting, advance force, and preassault operations conducted by AF and other forces, to include the full spectrum of MCM forces (if not part of advance forces) and the advance force.

Refer to Chapter V, "Support to Amphibious Operations," for information on supporting and advance force operations.

d. Local air and maritime superiority in the operational area is required in order for the MCM forces to commence operations. Supporting operations may also be conducted for proactive MCM and to wear down land forces.

e. **Proactive MCM.** If ROE permit, MCM is best accomplished by destruction of mines prior to their deployment. **Proactive MCM includes lethal and nonlethal attacks on production and storage facilities, transportation assets, and forces used to plant mines.** A key consideration in any potential littoral conflict is the establishment of ROE that allow for early, aggressive, and proactive MCM operations.

f. **MCM Forces.** The time required for MCM operations will usually require MCM forces to commence operations prior to the arrival of the AF and, potentially, the advance force. **MCM forces are extremely vulnerable and will require constant protection from hostile forces.** Due to the limited assets available for an MCM operation, the CATF will need to prioritize the MCM effort in the operational area. There should also be an awareness that MCM operations have the potential to compromise the OPSEC of the impending amphibious operation. Appropriate consideration or measures should be implemented to minimize the operational impact. Two primary MCM techniques are mine hunting and minesweeping.

(1) **Mine Hunting.** During mine hunting, the MCM platform uses its available assets to detect, classify, identify, and neutralize all mine-like contacts found. In favorable hydrographic conditions, mine hunting is the preferred method for conducting enabling MCM. Mine hunting does not require specific knowledge of the mine threat and provides a means to estimate the remaining risk to transiting vessels.

(2) **Minesweeping.** Minesweeping is the technique of clearing mines using either mechanical, explosive, or influence sweep equipment. Mechanical sweeping removes, disturbs, or otherwise neutralizes the mine; explosive sweeping causes sympathetic detonations in, damages, or displaces the mine; and influence sweeping produces either the acoustic and/or magnetic influence required to detonate the mine. It is performed at slightly faster speeds than hunting, but its success is largely a factor of environmental conditions and the intelligence data available. Minesweeping does not allow the MCM commander (MCMC) to accurately estimate the remaining risk.

See JP 3-15, Barriers, Obstacles, and Mine Warfare for Joint Operations.

4.   **Integrated Mine Countermeasures and Amphibious Breaching Operations**

a. **Responsibility**. The MCMC, who is usually subordinate to the CATF upon the arrival of the AF in the operational area, is responsible for planning all MCM and breaching operations and conducting MCM operations including breaching outer mine barriers from deep water, 200 feet and deeper, to the beginning of the SZ, the 10-foot contour depth. The CATF is responsible for conducting assault breaching operations from the SZ to the beach exit. The assault breaching mission is conducted and coordinated with the LF CONOPS through the SACC. Airspace synchronization and control procedures are provided by the Navy TACC. The CLF is responsible for conducting mine and obstacle breaching and clearing operations from the beach exit inland and follow-on clearance operations on the beach. **MCM and amphibious breaching operations must be synchronized.** Lane requirements of the landing force and mine or obstacle construction will dictate size and composition of the amphibious breach force. During assault breaching efforts involving munitions, large lane widths exponentially increase the number of weapons required to neutralize beach obstacles and mines. The CLF must carefully consider the SZ lane widths, the requirement for surprise, and the tactical needs of the landing force when relying upon delivered munitions.

b. **Fundamentals.** Suppression, obscuration, security, reduction, and deception are fundamentals that must be applied to amphibious breaching operations to ensure success.

(1) **Suppression.** Effective suppression is the mission-critical task during any breaching operation. Suppression protects forces reducing and maneuvering through the obstacle and fixes the enemy in position. Suppressive fires include the full range of lethal and nonlethal fires from NSFS and CAS to electronic attack (EA).

(2) **Obscuration.** Obscuration hampers enemy observation and TA, and conceals friendly activities and movement. EA prevents the enemy use of radar and radio signals to observe and report the operation.

(3) **Security.** Support forces prevent the enemy from interfering with obstacle reduction and the passage of the assault waves through the breach lanes. Security must be effective against coastal defenses and counterattack forces. Vertical assault forces may

seize and deny routes of ingress into the landing area to prevent the counterattack of the landing beaches.

(4) **Reduction.** Reduction forces, normally composed of ATF and LF elements, and supported by tactical aviation dropping precision guided assault breaching munitions, create lanes through the mines and obstacles, allowing the assault waves to pass. The location of lanes depends largely on identified weaknesses in the mine and obstacle belt. If the AF cannot find gaps or weak coverage in the obstacles, they will apply concentrated force at a designated point to rupture the defense and create a gap. Units reducing the obstacle mark the lane and report the obstacle type, location, and lane locations to higher headquarters. Lanes are handed over to follow-on forces who further reduce or clear the obstacles, if required.

(5) **Deception.** Deception operations are a necessity during assault breaching efforts. Large lane sizes demand large numbers of weapons and multiple aircraft passes to clear the SZ prior to the assault. This may draw immediate attention to the LF unless alternate lanes are brought under fire as well.

5. **Operations in Chemical, Biological, Radiological, and Nuclear Environments**

The employment or threat of use of CBRN weapons or the intentional release of toxic industrial materials (TIMs), pose unique challenges for AFs when planning and conducting amphibious operations. The CBRN threat occurs across the full range of military operations. Recent improvements in missile technology that have increased the range and precision of weapons capable of carrying bulk CBRN materials, together with the use of mines and barriers to canalize or impede the AFs, has amplified our potential vulnerability to a CBRN attack. These trends are requiring AF commanders to always consider the potential impact of enemy CBRN weapon employment when planning and conducting amphibious operations. Commanders must maintain a clear understanding of potential CBRN threats, and planning must include measures to minimize associated AF vulnerabilities.

Refer to JP 3-11, Operations in Chemical, Biological, Radiological, and Nuclear (CBRN) Environments.

a. **Responsibilities. The AF must be capable of efficiently and effectively continuing its operations in a CBRN threat environment.** Within the AF, the CATF is responsible for CBRN defense of the forces afloat, including the LF while embarked. The CLF is responsible for CBRN defense of the landing force once ashore.

b. **Planning Considerations.** AF commanders address potential CBRN threats during the planning phase.

(1) **Advanced CBRN Defense Planning.** CBRN defense plans include provisions for the following:

(a) Requesting supporting operations to eliminate or reduce an adversary's CBRN capabilities within the operational area prior to the arrival of the AF.

(b) Planning advance force operations to further degrade an adversary's CBRN capabilities and to detect contaminated areas that may interfere with the CONOPS.

(c) Planning offensive and defensive actions taken by the AF to minimize the vulnerability to and mitigate the effects of CBRN attacks, to include the development of branches and sequels.

(2) The AF's joint intelligence preparation of the operational environment (JIPOE) process must address the capabilities and limitations of an adversary's CBRN weapons and delivery systems; their C2 and release procedures; and indicators of intent to employ CBRN weapons. The AF commanders should provide target planning and execution guidance using the full extent of actions allowed by the ROE based on the desired effects needed against the adversary's CBRN weapons, delivery means, and C2 capabilities to support achievement of the objectives.

(3) The principles of CBRN defense must be factored into planning and specifically address the hazards created by CBRN weapons: avoidance of CBRN and TIM hazards, particularly contamination, protection of individuals and units from unavoidable CBRN and TIM hazards, and required decontamination in order to restore operational capability. Application of these principles (see Figure IV-1), helps to minimize vulnerabilities, protect the AF, and maintain the operational tempo in order to achieve the AF objectives.

(4) **CBRN Contamination Avoidance.** CBRN contamination avoidance prevents the disruption of the amphibious operation by eliminating unnecessary time in elevated protective postures (see JP 3-11, *Operations in Chemical, Biological, Radiological, and Nuclear (CBRN) Environments*) and minimizing decontamination requirements. Avoiding contamination requires the ability to recognize the presence or absence of CBRN and TIM hazards in the air, on water, land, personnel, equipment, and facilities, at both long and short range. Supporting and advance force operations should provide for long-range surveillance and detection capabilities focusing on such areas as the landing beaches, HLZs, LF objectives, and the AF objectives. Pre-assault operations and actions taken throughout the remainder of the amphibious operation should provide for short-range surveillance and detection capabilities in support of the LF units operating ashore and ATF ships within the sea echelon area.

(5) **CBRN Protection.** Specific actions required of the ATF and LF before, during, and after CBRN attacks should be clearly communicated and rehearsed. CBRN protection conserves the force by providing individual and collective protection capabilities essential to mitigating the effects of CBRN hazards. Protecting the force from CBRN hazards may include preventing or reducing individual and collective exposures, and applying medical prophylaxes. Individual protection also includes measures to protect equipment, vehicles and supplies.

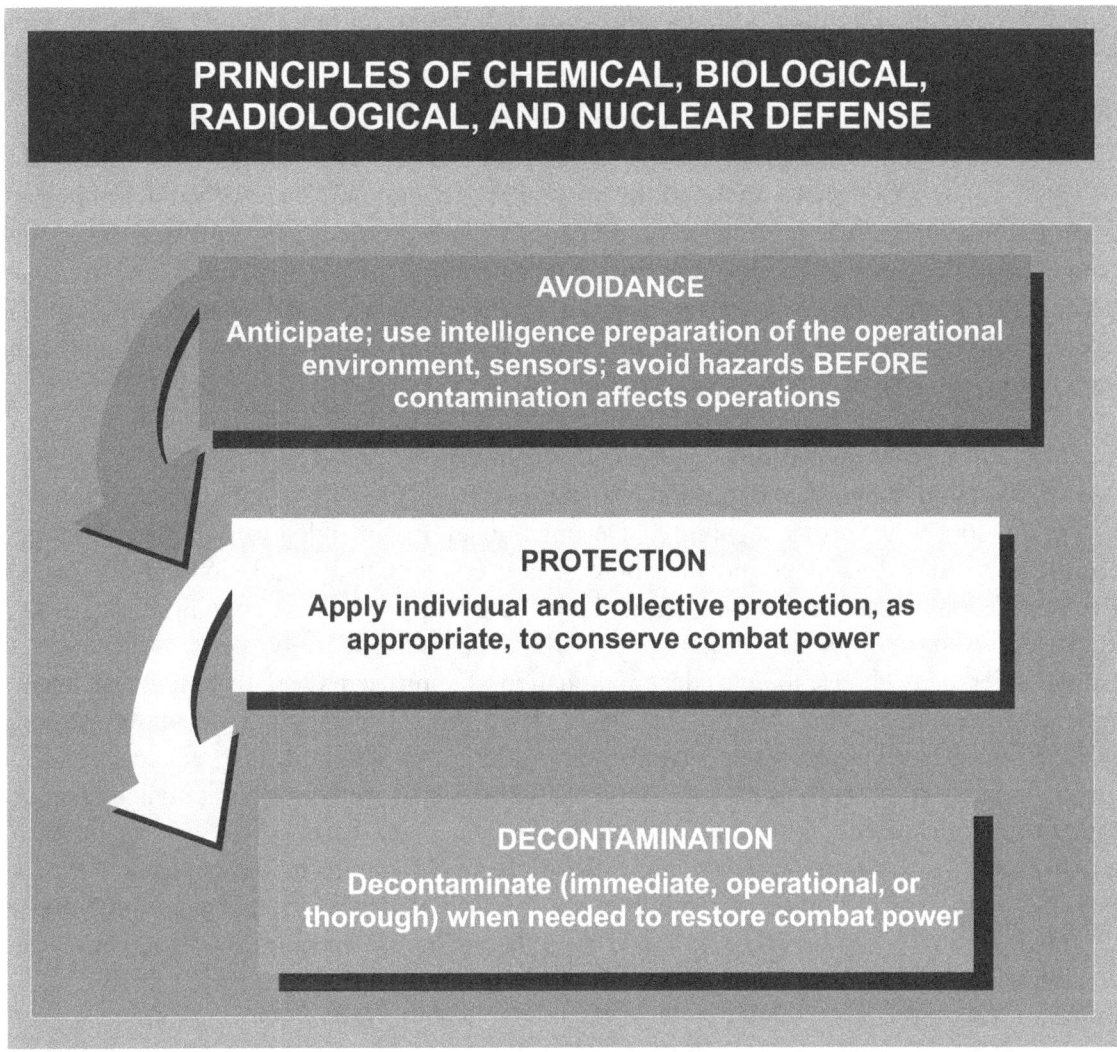

PRINCIPLES OF CHEMICAL, BIOLOGICAL, RADIOLOGICAL, AND NUCLEAR DEFENSE

AVOIDANCE

Anticipate; use intelligence preparation of the operational environment, sensors; avoid hazards BEFORE contamination affects operations

PROTECTION

Apply individual and collective protection, as appropriate, to conserve combat power

DECONTAMINATION

Decontaminate (immediate, operational, or thorough) when needed to restore combat power

Figure IV-1. Principles of Chemical, Biological, Radiological, and Nuclear Defense

(a) **Individual Protection.** Commanders must adopt a mission-oriented protective posture (MOPP) to establish flexible force readiness levels for individual CBRN protection, ensure the force has received pre-treatments and immunizations as required, and has available antidotes and other medical treatments to survive the effects of the CBRN threats. MOPP analysis (the process of determining a recommended MOPP) integrates CBRN protection requirements — derived from CBRN threat assessments — with mission requirements in light of the performance degradation caused by wearing protective equipment. The LF and ATF personnel manning flight decks, well decks, and landing craft, as well as operating ashore (such as beachmaster units), require individual protective equipment and must be capable of operating in MOPP-levels commensurate with the threat. Likewise, individual equipment, vehicles and supplies gain considerable protection from covers. These covers may be as simple as thick plastic sheathing, which should provide immediate protection against large-scale use of liquid chemical agents.

For additional information on individual protection see JP 3-11, Operations in Chemical, Biological, Radiological, and Nuclear (CBRN) Environments, *and Field Manual (FM) 3-11.21/Marine Corps Reference Publication (MCRP) 3-37.2C,* Multi-Service Tactics Techniques and Procedures for CBRN Consequence Management Operations.

(b) **Collective Protection.** Sustaining operations in CBRN environments may require collective protection equipment, which provides a toxic-free area for conducting operations and performing life support functions such as rest, relief, and medical treatment. When collective protection is not available ashore, plans must be developed, exercised, and evaluated to move personnel to alternative toxic-free areas afloat that are well away from contaminated areas ashore.

(6) **Decontamination.** When contamination avoidance is not possible, decontamination supports the post-attack restoration of the AF and the resumption of operations to a near-normal capability. Decontamination is intended to minimize the time required to return personnel and mission-essential equipment to a mission-capable state. Because decontamination may be labor and logistic intensive and assets are limited, the AF commanders must prioritize requirements and decontaminate only what is necessary. Commanders may choose to defer decontamination of some items and, depending on agent type and weather conditions, opt to either defer use of equipment or allow natural weathering effects (temperature, wind, salt water, and sunlight) to reduce hazards. Decontamination is organized into four categories that reflect operational urgency: immediate, operational, thorough, and clearance. In order to maintain the operational tempo, the AF uses immediate and operational decontamination to the maximum extent possible until the AF objectives are secured. During an operational pause, thorough decontamination is conducted. Clearance decontamination is accomplished following the cessation of hostilities in preparation for force reconstitution and return to garrison. For more information refer to JP 3-11, *Operations in Chemical, Biological, Radiological, and Nuclear (CBRN) Environments.* Service publications provide detailed tactics, techniques, and procedures for the technical aspects of decontamination.

"For the whole reason-for-being of all military intelligence personnel is to facilitate accomplishment of the mission, and to save lives. When they fail, all the wrong people are hurt."

Stedman Chandler and Robert W. Robb
Front-Line Intelligence

1. **General**

a. **Supporting operations** may set the conditions for the advance force to move into the operational area and are enablers that support the execution of the amphibious operation. These operations are conducted by forces other than the AF and need to be thoroughly coordinated. Examples of supporting operations are:

(1) Military deception operations to influence the actions of adversary forces.

(2) Interdiction operations to isolate the landing area.

(3) Destruction of specific targets ashore.

(4) Defensive counterair, undersea warfare, and surface warfare operations to gain local air and maritime superiority prior to combat operations in the operational area.

(5) Psychological operations.

(6) Mine hunting, minesweeping, or minelaying.

(7) Information operations.

(8) Irregular warfare.

b. Support for amphibious operations can be broken down into intelligence, fire support, communications, logistics, protection, and seabasing.

SECTION A. INTELLIGENCE

2. **Introduction**

a. Amphibious Operations Intelligence

(1) Amphibious operations involve extensive planning in all functional areas to ensure that ships, aircraft, landing craft, and supporting fires are synchronized to arrive at specific points at specific times to take advantage of enemy critical vulnerabilities and expedite combat power build-up and sustainment ashore. **This requires comprehensive**

JIPOE, including harmonization of intelligence and operational planners to ensure that COAs are feasible and that enemy capabilities, vulnerabilities, and COGs are identified and taken into consideration.

(2) Amphibious operations have been characterized as the most complex and difficult of military operations; however, **the basic nature of intelligence, surveillance, and reconnaissance (ISR) does not change in amphibious operations**. Depending on the size and duration of the operation, the AF commander may direct either a joint intelligence support element (JISE) or an operational level joint intelligence operations center (JIOC) be established to support the AF. The JISE or JIOC will be the central node in securing theater and/or national level intelligence support for the AF, and provide direct intelligence support to AF components. Amphibious operations differ from other military operations because of the significant challenges posed by relatively fewer AF ISR assets in the operational area during the planning phase, a heavy initial reliance on national and theater collection assets, the transition to shore, and the ability to provide predictive analysis to compensate for relatively longer periods of uncertainty.

For more information, see JP 2-01, Joint and National Intelligence Support to Military Operations.

b. Required ISR Capabilities. The following intelligence capabilities are required to support amphibious operations:

(1) Detailed terrain and hydrographic analysis to identify suitable zones of entry (e.g., beaches, HLZs, DZs).

(2) Interoperable information systems that provide timely dissemination of information for amphibious planning and rehearsals.

(3) Standoff collection assets capable of satisfying ATF and LF requirements from OTH.

(4) Intelligence dissemination systems linking widely dispersed forces afloat and ashore.

(5) Flexible intelligence assets capable of rapidly transitioning ashore with minimal degradation of support.

c. Intelligence Process

(1) **Planning and Direction.** There are a number of unique intelligence considerations for amphibious operations. During the embarked planning phase, the ATF and LF intelligence officers direct their personnel from the intelligence center established aboard amphibious shipping to support the intelligence needs of the entire AF. The intelligence center brings together all AF intelligence-related activities. While personnel

and material remain organic to their respective commands, they may task-organize to perform intelligence work necessary for completion of the mission.

(2) **Collection.** AF intelligence requirements are serviced by all available assets (national to organic). These assets collect information in denied and remote areas without compromising OPSEC and perform missions at significant distances from embarked forces. The small number of these systems and their inherent limitations often result in an incomplete intelligence picture. **Advance force or pre-assault collection operations are often required to confirm and further develop the operational picture.** An aggressive pre-assault intelligence effort will provide support for target selection however, the effort must ensure that collection operations do not expose the commander's intent.

(3) **Processing and Exploitation.** Individual intelligence sections will normally concentrate on their particular areas of expertise, satisfying their units' requirements while contributing a broad-scope product to the general intelligence production effort. For example, LF intelligence could analyze the land operational environment, to include the enemy's C2, ground forces, logistics, and reserves, while ATF intelligence could analyze enemy maritime forces and coastal defense threats. Air threats could be analyzed from a combined AF perspective.

(4) **Analysis and Production.** During the analysis and production phase, all available processed information is integrated, analyzed, evaluated, and interpreted to create products that will satisfy the AF commanders' requirements. Intelligence products are generally placed in one of eight categories: JIPOE; indications and warning; current intelligence; general military intelligence; target intelligence; scientific and technical intelligence; counterintelligence; and estimative intelligence.

(5) **Dissemination and Integration.** Intelligence dissemination and integration during amphibious operations presents significant challenges. AF and supporting forces can be widely dispersed and may not assemble until late in the planning phase, if at all. Advances in technology have improved intelligence dissemination between afloat forces, but limitations still exist in the quantity and quality of intelligence exchanged. The immense volume of data required overtaxes communications and intelligence systems, to include critical graphic products that must be distributed during the planning phase. Intelligence officers at all levels, working in coordination with unit operations and communications-information systems officers, must develop plans that provide dissemination of actionable intelligence in a timely manner to all elements of the AF. Units located on ships not equipped with the latest C2, communications, or intelligence systems will be a high priority. Rather than an end of a process, the integration of intelligence is a continuous dialogue between the user and the producer.

(6) **Evaluation and Feedback.** During the evaluation and feedback phase, intelligence personnel at all levels assess how each phase of the intelligence process is being performed. Commanders and staffs throughout the AF provide feedback if they are not receiving timely, accurate, usable, complete, and relevant information to support the

operation. Within the intelligence center, the AF intelligence officers are also evaluating the intelligence process to improve performance.

    d. Key Intelligence Activities

       (1) **Mission Analysis**

        (a) **The AF will develop preliminary intelligence studies and estimates upon receipt of the initiating directive or on being alerted for the potential operation.** Preliminary planning may include an analysis of the operational area and the possible impact of terrain, hydrography, weather, traffic patterns of the local populations, and cultural features on the proposed operation. The most favorable areas for executing the landing are determined and additional intelligence requirements defined. Studies of beaches, ports, communications networks, existing air facilities, and terrain provide an initial basis for determining the number and types of LF elements that can be accommodated and supported within possible landing areas. These studies assist in the initial engineering and other service support requirements.

        (b) **Many of the ten primary decisions made during the amphibious planning process are based on the initial intelligence estimate.** The initial estimate serves to orient the AF commanders and their staffs to the operational environment including the nature of the threat; aids in the development of the commander's intent by outlining what is operationally possible and most advantageous; and formulating the commander's guidance to help shape intelligence operations. As a minimum, the initial estimate should provide the commander with information on the general weather conditions expected in the objective area; key terrain and man-made features and avenues of approach; the location, nature, and extent of available beaches including their respective operational constraints; and the general composition, strength, and disposition of adversary forces in the area, including all chemical, biological, radiological, nuclear, and high-yield explosive capabilities.

       (2) **COA Development.** Intelligence operations support COA development in several ways.

        (a) Defining operational possibilities through the joint intelligence preparation of the operational environment (JIPOE) process. Certain products from the JIPOE process may be included as an annex or distributed as separate studies and reports, such as:

           1. Weather studies.

           2. Astronomical and tidal data.

           3. Beach, LZ, and DZ studies.

           4. Trafficability studies.

<u>5.</u> Airfield and potential airfield studies.

<u>6.</u> Special studies on adversary forces.

<u>7.</u> Surveys of the civilian populace and cultural resources.

<u>8.</u> Studies on the terrain impact on communications systems.

(b) Continuously updating the view of the operational environment and estimates of adversary capabilities, intentions, and activities.

(c) Providing focus on the adversary through identification of adversary COGs, critical vulnerabilities, and potential COAs, with emphasis on the most likely and most dangerous COAs.

(d) Assisting in the prioritization of targets of interest.

(3) **COA Analysis.** Intelligence operations assist COA analysis by:

(a) Identifying and refining likely and dangerous adversary COAs and their potential impact on the LF and actions and/or reactions to friendly COAs under consideration.

(b) Wargaming the adversary's role.

(c) Developing an independent evaluation of each friendly COA based upon an understanding of the operational situation and the potential adversary response as well as on the ability to provide intelligence support to that COA.

(d) Helping to focus commanders and their staffs on the adversary and environment, with emphasis on the degree of uncertainty and resulting risk associated with each friendly COA.

e. **Plans and Orders Development.** Once the AF COA has been mutually selected, intelligence operations are focused in order to collect against specific PIRs and update relevant intelligence. **This detailed intelligence becomes the intelligence annex to the LF OPLAN/OPORD.** It prescribes the conduct of intelligence operations and activities and is a medium through which information and intelligence may be disseminated, reconnaissance and surveillance missions assigned, and other intelligence tasks and procedures stated. Drafts of the intelligence annex should normally be distributed to other commanders in advance of the OPLAN/OPORD for use as planning studies. The volume and complexity of the material in the intelligence annex dictates the use of appendixes.

f. Intelligence Support to Landing Force Operations Ashore

(1) Intelligence operations must ensure a continuous flow of timely, pertinent, and tailored intelligence throughout the LF to maintain a common operational picture of the operational environment while rapidly identifying new intelligence requirements (IRs) of commanders and the operating forces. **Intelligence support operations involve the satisfaction of a much larger body of IRs, involving a significantly greater degree of detail.** Additionally, time is a greater factor during the execution of operations than it was during planning. While days, weeks, and longer periods often are available during planning, **intelligence support to current operations must be planned, executed, and the resulting intelligence products provided in hours, minutes, and even seconds.** Finally, the uncertainty and disorder inherent in the initial stages of LF operations are significant, and the clash of opposing forces normally result in significant and fundamental changes in the situation that existed prior to landing.

(2) **Intelligence Focus During Execution.** Intelligence support provided to the LF during operations ashore focuses on furnishing information that provides an exploitable advantage over the adversary. Accordingly, intelligence operations focus on providing information necessary to build situational awareness, identifying the latest adversary activities and friendly opportunities, aiding friendly maneuver and targeting, and supporting force protection — all while continuing to support future operations planning. Two key factors for ensuring effective intelligence support during these operations are:

(a) As IRs usually exceed available intelligence resources, intelligence operations must be focused where they can have the greatest impact and value. **A detailed, well thought out concept of intelligence support in accordance with the CLF's intent and synchronized to LF CONOPS will lead to the best allocation of intelligence capabilities.**

(b) Intelligence collection, production, and dissemination plans are developed to support the execution of LF tactical operations, the engagement of targets, the protection of the force, and the selection of branches and sequels. **Close and continuous coordination between intelligence and LF operations personnel is essential to maintain common situational awareness of ongoing and planned future operations, monitor potential adversary reactions, identify new opportunities, and assess the impact of friendly actions on the adversary.**

(c) **By satisfying the CLF's critical information requirements and supporting the LF's main effort,** intelligence operations help generate operational tempo. They also facilitate tempo by supporting the decision making process through accurate situational awareness and by recognizing emerging patterns that enable the CLF and subordinate commanders to rapidly make decisions.

SECTION B. FIRE SUPPORT

3. General

a. Properly planned and executed supporting fires are critical to the success of an amphibious operation. Since the availability and employment of one supporting weapon system influences the requirements for the others, the fire support requirements of all components of the AF must be considered together in planning the employment of fire support means. **Fire support planning** and **coordination** in amphibious operations are continuous processes seeking timely and appropriate application of force to achieve the objectives within the operational area. **Maneuver** and **fires** are complementary functions. Fire support planning **integrates** and **synchronizes** the AF organic fires with nonorganic supporting fires to achieve the commander's intent.

b. Both the ATF and the LF will require fire support during the amphibious assault.

(1) AFs in the AOA/AO normally require fire support for operations such as beach reconnaissance, hydrographic survey, removal of beach and underwater obstacles, and MCM. In addition, aircraft and ships capable of providing fire support must be allocated to protect the force from air, surface, or subsurface attack.

(2) The LF normally requires fire support against shore targets before, during, and after the initial landings. Once sufficient area is seized ashore, artillery can be landed to provide additional fire support. Until ground fire support means (e.g., mortars, rockets, and cannon artillery) of the LF are landed and ready to provide support, fire support is provided by CAS, NSFS, and in limited cases direct and indirect fires from adjacent friendly forces.

4. Responsibilities

Commanders at each level of the LF have certain fire support responsibilities.

a. **Establishing a fire support coordination agency at each appropriate level of the LF** for accomplishment of fire support coordination responsibilities during planning and execution of the operation.

(1) Detailed integration of the fire support agencies of the ATF and LF.

(2) Flexible, parallel C2 architecture that allows for decentralized fire support control, when applicable.

b. Determining requirements for air, NSFS, and artillery fire support.

c. Coordinating requests for fire support.

d. Presenting the coordinated requests for NSFS and air support to the CATF.

e. Developing the **LF concept of fires to support the scheme of maneuver**.

f. Conducting target analysis and selection.

g. Establishing FSCMs, as required.

5. Systems

a. **Overview of Systems. Fires in support of amphibious operations (amphibious fire support) is the synergistic product of three subsystems: TA, C2, and attack resources.** TA systems and equipment perform the key tasks of target detection, location, tracking, identification, and classification in sufficient detail to permit the effective attack of the target. C2 systems bring all information together for collation and decision making. Vertical and horizontal coordination is essential, requiring a hierarchy of mutually supporting fire support coordinators and agencies. Attack systems include fires delivered from air, surface, land, and subsurface attack systems. Navy, Marine Corps, Army, and Air Force aircraft may perform air-to-surface attack, including EW, within the operational area. Land-based attack systems typically include Marine Corps and Army artillery, mortars, rockets, missiles, and EW systems. Sea-based attack systems include Navy guns, missiles, and EW systems.

b. **Target Acquisition**

(1) **Organic.** The typical AF has numerous organic TA assets, such as reconnaissance units, UAS shipboard and artillery counterfire radars, naval aviation, and ground sensors, as well as other observers, spotters, and controllers.

(2) **Nonorganic.** The typical AF has the capability to exploit the information provided from non-organic ISR systems (manned and unmanned), subsurface, surface (ground and sea), military space systems, and national systems. Fire support information could be from SOF, interagency, multinational, and other nonorganic sources.

(3) **Intelligence Integration.** The intelligence center established within the AF supports the TA system by coordinating the use of limited collection assets throughout the operational area.

See Section A, "Intelligence," *for more information.*

c. **Command and Control Agencies**

(1) **Overview.** The initiating directive should identify responsibilities for fire support planning and coordination among the commanders of the AF. For the purposes of this chapter, the term **"designated commander"** will refer to the commander who has been delegated the command authority to plan and coordinate fires either for the entire amphibious operation or a particular phase of it. The effectiveness of fire support in

amphibious operations is predicated on the designated commander providing clear and coordinated guidance to the forces involved, since unity of effort is essential.

See Chapter II, "Command and Control," for more information.

(2) **Supporting Arms Coordination Center.** Upon initiation of planning, a SACC is established. **The SACC plans, coordinates, and controls all organic and nonorganic fires within the operational area in support of the AF.** It is located aboard an amphibious ship or appropriate ship configured with the requisite C2 facilities, enabling coordination of all forms of supporting fires (land, air, and sea based). The designated commander may choose either the ATF's supporting arms coordinator (SAC), the LF's force fires coordinator (FFC) (if US Marine Corps) or fire support coordinator (FSC) (if US Army) to supervise the SACC. Whether the SAC, FFC, or FSC supervises the SACC, **fire support personnel from both the ATF and LF operate the SACC.** The organization of the SACC is typically the same for any size amphibious operation; however, variations in operations may require specific needs. The organization described below is therefore to be used only as a guide.

(a) **Naval Surface Fire Support Section.** The ATF staff mans the NSFS section. This section monitors the naval gunfire control net, support net, and other gunfire nets as appropriate. The LF staff provides liaison to the section.

(b) **Air Support Section.** This section is manned by members of a Navy air control agency (e.g., tactical air control squadron or tactical air control group) and directed by the air support coordinator who reports to the tactical air officer. The tactical air officer is the equivalent of the CCO and is in charge of ship-to-shore movement by air. Until control is passed ashore, this officer exercises control over all operations of the Navy TACC and is charged with the following: a. control of all aircraft in the objective area assigned for tactical air operations, including offensive and defensive air; b. control of all other aircraft entering or passing through the objective area; and c. control of all air warning facilities in the objective area. This section supports the Navy TACC by controlling, supporting, or transferring control to subsidiary tactical air direction controllers afloat or ashore. The section is located in the SACC and coordinates with the Navy TACC to assist in the deconfliction of air missions, routes, and requests for fires. The LF staff provides liaison to the section.

(c) **Target Information Center (TIC).** The TIC is the agency or activity responsible for collecting, displaying, evaluating, and disseminating information pertaining to potential targets. The TIC is responsible for targeting information and intelligence. It is manned by the ATF target intelligence officer, ATF air intelligence officer, LF target information officer, and other personnel, as required. TIC members will normally operate in the SACC. The ATF target intelligence officer supervises the TIC and maintains close liaison with ATF and LF intelligence and operations staff. The LF target information officer normally works in the intelligence center of the AF.

(3) **Force Fires Coordination Center.** When the responsibility for fire support planning and coordination is passed ashore, **the FFCC is the Marine Corps' senior fire support coordination agency and is responsible for the planning, execution, and coordination of all fires within the operational area**. Prior to control being passed ashore, the FFCC incrementally assumes responsibility for fire support planning and coordination from the SACC. The FFCC is organized and supervised at the MAGTF-level by the FFC who is responsible to the LF operations officer for MAGTF fires. The organization operates at both the tactical and operational level addressing current and future fire support issues.

For further information, refer to JP 3-09, Joint Fire Support.

(4) **Fire Support Coordination Center.** The FSCC is the fire support coordination agency within the LF GCE. FSCCs are established at the battalion, regiment, and division level. The FSCC is responsible for the planning, execution, and coordination of all forms of fire support within the GCE's area of operations. The FSCC is organized and supervised by the fire support coordinator who is responsible to the appropriate level GCE operations officer for GCE fires. FSCCs are initially subordinate to the SACC and, if the FFCC is established ashore, subordinate to that agency.

d. **Attack Resources**

(1) **Organic.** The AF's organic attack resources are capable of delivering lethal and nonlethal fires, and include naval aviation, NSFS, EW systems, artillery, rockets, and mortars.

(2) **Nonorganic.** The SACC and the FFCC are able to coordinate and control nonorganic attack resources in support of the amphibious operation. Aircraft (manned and unmanned), ship-launched missiles, SOF, and nonlethal systems attacking targets within the operational area must be coordinated through the senior fire support coordination agency.

6. **Planning and Coordination**

a. **Fire Support Planning.** The purpose of fire support planning is to **optimize the employment of fire support to achieve the designated commander's intent by shaping the operational area and providing support to maneuver forces**. Fire support planning is the continuous and concurrent process of analyzing, allocating, and scheduling of fire support to integrate it with the forces to maximize combat power.

(1) **Commander's Guidance.** Commanders determine how to shape the operational area with fires to assist both maritime and land maneuver forces and how to use maritime and land maneuver forces to exploit fires. **When developing the fire support plan, the designated commander will formulate the "commander's guidance for fires."** It is from this guidance that supporting and subordinate commanders and fire support personnel begin to frame the role of fire support in the plan. The commander's guidance for fires should articulate the desired effects against the enemy's capabilities and how these

effects will contribute to the overall success of the operation. The designated commander identifies targets that are critical to the success of the operation (high-payoff targets), force protection issues, and any prohibitions or restrictions on fire support. A clear determination of the enemy's COGs, decisive points, and critical vulnerabilities is central to fire support planning.

(2) **Apportionment and Allocation.** In order to develop the fire support plan, attack resources may be considered for apportionment and allocation to the AF. In the general sense, apportionment is the distribution of resources among competing requirements. Specific apportionments are described as apportionment of air sorties and forces for planning. For example, air apportionment is a determination and assignment of the total expected air effort by percentage and/or priority that should be devoted to the various air operations and/or geographic areas for a given period of time. The AF could use this to influence and shape the conduct of the operation. Allocation, in a general sense, is the distribution of limited resources among competing requirements for employment. For example, air allocation is the translation of the air apportionment decision into total numbers of sorties by aircraft type available for each operation or task. The apportionment and allocation process requires input from the subordinate commands within the AF to ensure that their requirements are addressed.

(a) Direct support air requirements and any excess sorties are identified to the establishing authority for further tasking.

(b) Normally, the JFC will apportion assigned air assets (by priority or percentage) to support the AF. The JFC may also task supporting commands for air support as required.

b. **Targeting**

Refer to JP 3-0, Joint Operations, *JP 3-09,* Joint Fire Support, *and JP 3-60,* Joint Targeting.

(1) **Targeting Board for the AF. The AF normally conducts an integrated targeting board to provide broad fire support and targeting oversight functions.** Depending on the command relationships that the establishing authority promulgates in the initiating directive, the designated commander coordinates the targeting process for the AF through preparation and submission of target nominations and FSCMs. The designated commander during the period within which the targets are attacked has final approval authority over the fire support plan and target list. Those targets to be serviced by organic assets are passed to the appropriate agencies for servicing. Targets identified for servicing by nonorganic attack systems are forwarded to the next higher-level targeting board for consideration. The AF will provide, at a minimum, liaison officers to this targeting board (i.e., component-level) and may provide liaison officers to the senior joint targeting board (i.e., the JFC's joint targeting coordination board), if established. AF targeting timelines are normally out to 72-96 hours in order to match the targeting timelines and planning cycle of the JFC.

(2) **Submission of target nominations for supporting operations.** The AF may seek to shape their designated (but not activated) operational area prior to the arrival of AFs through target nominations for attack by other components' forces. Restrictions on the attack of certain targets may also be requested, if the designated AF commander desires to exploit them at a future time, such as certain enemy communications sites or bridges.

c. **Fire Support Coordination.** From the beginning of the action phase until a short time after the first waves land, the LF is normally supported by scheduled fires. Once control agencies (e.g., forward observers and NSFS spotters) are ashore, the LF will normally begin calling for fires to support operations. Coordination is accomplished at the lowest echelon possible. This same principle applies in the planning of subsequent planned fires. Planning is accomplished as required at each level of the LF before daily fire support plans are transmitted to the next higher level for similar action.

For more details, see JP 3-09, Joint Fire Support.

d. **Air Support Planning Responsibilities**

(1) **CATF responsibilities** include the determination of overall requirements of the AF, determination of air support capabilities, coordination of all air support requests, and preparation of an air plan.

(2) **CLF responsibilities** include the determination of LF air support requirements, determination of LF air support capabilities, submission of plans for deployment of aviation elements ashore, and preparation of an air plan.

(3) **Air Force component commander responsibilities** include providing for Air Force representation, determining Air Force air support capabilities, submission of deployment plans, and preparation of supporting air plans.

See JP 3-09, Joint Fire Support, *and JP 3-60,* Joint Targeting, *for more information.*

(4) **Air Support Planning Considerations**

(a) **Centralized Control System.** All aircraft operating within the objective area must be under centralized control. A tactical air control system capable of providing the requisite centralized control is organized. A combination of positive and procedural control measures may be required.

(b) **Early Seizure of Airfields.** Plans will usually provide for rapid seizure of existing airfields, airfield capable sites, and sites for early warning and air control. This enables the early deployment ashore of aviation elements and extends the radius of warning and control.

(5) **LF Air Support Planning.** The LF plans for the employment of LF aviation to support the ship-to-shore movement and scheme of maneuver ashore. Basic planning

also establishes requirements for air support from the other elements of the AF and joint force. Any adversary facilities to be captured intact must be specified and exempted from destruction.

(a) Recommendations and requests from subordinate echelons of the LF are evaluated and consolidated with overall LF requirements into a comprehensive request for air support. When determining overall requirements, pre-D-day should be separated from D-day and post-D-day requirements.

(b) LF requests for **pre-D-day air operations** concern primary intelligence needs and offensive air operations to reduce adversary forces and defensive installations in the landing area. The scope of pre-D-day operations may be limited by the need for surprise. The standard joint tactical air strike request is used for air support requests.

(c) LF requests for **air support of operations ashore commencing on D-day** include identification of targets to be attacked, their priority, timing of attacks, and desired effects. The request may be in the form of an air schedule with amplifying instructions appended. During the ship-to-shore movement, preplanned air strikes assist in creating exploitable gaps within the landing area. During the critical period when landing craft, amphibious vehicles, and helicopters are making the final run to the beach or LZ, aircraft integrated with NSFS to support maneuver assist in neutralizing the beaches, LZs, approach routes, and adjacent key terrain features as the LF comes ashore.

(d) **Post-D-day air support** can only be planned in general because requirements will depend on the tactical situation ashore and will not be fully known in advance. Applicable pre-D-day and D-day air operations are continued.

(6) **Air Support During the Assault**

(a) **Before Air Support Control Agencies are Established Ashore.** Until the TACPs arriving with assault units are established ashore, CAS missions are executed under the direction of the tactical air coordinators (airborne) (TAC[A]s) and the terminal control of the forward air controllers (airborne). When the TACPs are established ashore, they request CAS from the Navy TACC. The Navy TACC assigns aircraft to missions as requests are received, and in accordance with the commander's guidance for priority of fires. As the landing progresses, air control elements to be established ashore land and prepare to operate shore-based facilities for control of air operations.

(b) **Air Support Control Agencies Established Ashore.** As air support control agencies are established ashore, they function initially under the Navy TACC. These agencies subsequently operate under the designated authority when control of CAS has been passed ashore by the CATF. In any case, requests are sent by the TACP directly to the air control agency, which assigns aircraft to CAS missions. TACP requests are monitored by the SACC and FSCC/FC.

(c) **Terminal Phase.** The terminal phase of a CAS strike is executed under the control of a joint terminal attack controller or forward air controller (ground and/or airborne). CAS missions are executed only on the approval authority granted by the commander of the supported LF.

7. Naval Surface Fire Support

a. The CATF is responsible for preparation of the overall NSFS plan, based on the CLF and Navy requirements. The plan includes allocation of gunfire support ships and facilities. The CATF is also responsible for the general policy on targeting priorities. The CLF is responsible for determination of LF requirements for NSFS, including selection of targets to be attacked in preassault operations, those to be fired on in support of the LF assault, and the timing of these fires in relation to the LF scheme of maneuver. When designated the supported commander, the CLF coordinates the timing, priorities, and desired effects of fires within the operational area.

Arleigh Burke-class guided missile destroyers are equipped with a 5-inch (127 mm) gun.

b. As a general rule there will be one NSFS ship in direct support for each battalion and one NSFS ship in general support for each regiment.

c. Control of NSFS is exercised by, and passes to, different commands and agencies as the operation progresses. Arrangements must be made to provide appropriate commanders the proper facilities for control of NSFS.

(1) **Advance Force Commander.** The advance force commander has control of NSFS during advance force operations. Control is normally exercised through the advance force SACC.

(2) **CATF.** Upon arrival in the objective area, the CATF exercises control of the NSFS through the SACC.

(3) **Subordinate ATGs.** When subordinate ATGs are formed and separate landing areas are designated, the CATF may delegate to each attack group commander control of NSFS in the landing area.

(4) **CLF.** Control may be passed to the CLF once he establishes the necessary control facilities ashore. He then has the authority to assign NSFS missions directly to the fire support ships. The CATF or his designated subordinate retains responsibility for allocation of available fire support ships. He also retains responsibility for logistic support and OPCON functions other than control of fires.

d. **NSFS Organization**

(1) **Naval Organization.** Briefly, the naval echelons involved in surface fire support are as follows:

(a) **AF.** The AF is the highest echelon directly concerned with the NSFS of the amphibious operation.

(b) **Fire Support Group.** The fire support group is usually subdivided into fire support units and/or elements for efficient and effective delivery of gunfire support.

(c) **Fire Support Unit.** When necessary for flexibility in organization, an echelon called the fire support unit may be interposed between the fire support group and fire support element. The fire support unit will function similarly to the fire support group. Fire support unit commanders normally do not deal directly with LF agencies.

(d) **Fire Support Element.** Each fire support group (unit) is divided into smaller task elements of fire support ships, regardless of type operating in the same general locality.

(e) **Individual Fire Support Ship.** The individual fire support ship is the basic echelon in NSFS. Its function is to deliver gunfire support under the control or direction of the agency to which assigned. The ship deals directly with the LF agencies.

(2) **LF Organization.** The LF organization for control and employment of NSFS provides special staff or liaison representation at every level from and including the infantry battalion or comparable troop unit to the highest troop echelon present.

(a) **LF NSFS Section.** If established, the LF NSFS section provides NSFS communications and facilities for LF headquarters, performs NSFS special staff functions, and directs fires of assigned general support ships.

(b) **Division NSFS Section or Team.** The division NSFS section or team provides NSFS communications and facilities for division headquarters, performs NSFS special staff functions, and directs employment of assigned support ships.

(c) **Regimental or Brigade NSFS Liaison Team.** The regimental or brigade NSFS liaison team provides communications, liaison, and direction of NSFS in support of an infantry regiment or comparable unit. In addition, the team directs the fire of assigned general support ships.

(d) **Battalion Shore Fire Control Party (SFCP).** The battalion SFCP includes a NSFS liaison team and a NSFS spotting team. The NSFS liaison team is specifically organized to handle NSFS liaison matters for the supported commander, while the spotting team is charged with requesting and adjusting fires of assigned direct support ships and general support ships.

e. **NSFS Plans**

(1) **Pre-D-Day NSFS Plans.** The primary objective of pre-D-day NSFS is preparation of the landing area for the assault. The plan usually includes the following elements:

(a) Assignment of ships to FSAs and zones of fire.

(b) Announcement of ammunition allowances and plans for replenishment.

(c) Communications instructions.

(d) Designation of targets, provision for damage assessments, and acquisition of target intelligence.

(e) Provision for availability of spotting aircraft (manned or unmanned) and reference to appropriate air support plans, to include potential CAS operations.

(f) Provision for coordinating with MCM, underwater demolition, and air operations.

(g) Provision for recording target information and reporting latest intelligence data to the CATF.

(2) **D-Day NSFS Plans.** Essential elements of the plan for NSFS operations on D-day include:

(a) Assignment of ships to FSAs, zones of fire, and in direct and general support of specific LF units.

(b) Announcement of ammunition allowances and plans for replenishment.

(c) Location when required, of landing craft approach and retirement lanes, aircraft ingress/egress routes and necessary coordinating instructions. These same instructions will be found in the appropriate portions of the related air support plan.

(d) Communication instructions and procedures for transfer of control.

(e) Designation of targets, target areas, deep support areas, and probable routes of approach of adversary reinforcements.

(f) Provisions for spotting aircraft.

(g) Instructions for massing fires of several ships.

(h) Provisions for coordination with the ship-to-shore movement, MCM, underwater demolition, artillery, and air operations.

(i) Closely timed neutralization of remaining adversary defenses to cover the waterborne and helicopterborne ship-to-shore movements, and support of the landing, deployment, and advance of troops.

(j) Prompt and effective delivery in direct support of LF units.

(k) Disruption of adversary systems of command, communication, and observation by destruction, neutralization, interdiction, and harassment.

(l) Isolation of the landing area and defense against adversary counteroffensive action by massed fires on probable routes of approach with particular provisions for countermechanized programs.

(3) **Post D-Day.** Post D-day NSFS plans provide for:

(a) Fires on the flanks of the landing area and fires against targets of opportunity.

(b) Defensive targets, night fires, illumination, countermechanized fires, and any special fires utilizing the inherent capability of gunfire ships and available munitions as required.

f. **NSFS Support During the Landing**

(1) **Final Preparation of the Landing Area.** This fire support is designed to destroy or neutralize adversary defense installations that might interfere with the approach and final deployment of the AF and to assist in isolation of the landing area. NSFS is used to support underwater demolition and MCM operations. Immediately before H-hour, major emphasis is placed on the destruction and neutralization of adversary defenses most dangerous to the successful landing of LF teams.

(2) **Fires in Close Support of the Initial Assault.** NSFS is continued on those adversary installations that could prevent the landing until the safety of the leading waves requires these fires to be lifted. The final approach of the leading waves of assault craft, amphibious vehicles, or helicopters necessitates a shift of the scheduled fires inland from the landing beaches or outward from the LZs. The major portion of the fires delivered in close support of the landings consists of prearranged fires delivered on a closely fixed schedule in the assault landing team's zone of action. Because the actual rate of advance and the estimated rate of advance may not coincide, the CATF, through the SACC, retards or accelerates the movement of scheduled fires as requested by the CLF. Close supporting fires continue until the SFCP with the assault landing teams are in a position to conduct the fires of the assigned direct support ships. At this time, the SFCPs begin adjusting fires.

(3) **Deep Support Fires.** Deep support fires usually are delivered by ships assigned in general support. Each such ship is assigned a zone of responsibility that it covers by fire and observation. Within assigned zones of responsibility and on a prearranged schedule, ships neutralize known adversary targets, interdict adversary LOCs, attack targets of opportunity, execute counterbattery fire, reinforce fires of direct support ships as directed, and conduct missions assigned by the supported unit.

For more details, see JP 3-09, Joint Fire Support.

g. **Other Planning and Coordination Considerations**

(1) **Air Defense.** The CATF usually assigns an ADC, normally on the most capable air defense platform, to carry out air defense operations. The ADC coordinates with the Navy TACC to maintain situational awareness. A coherent air defense plan also requires coordinated planning with the SACC to ensure the physical location of air defense weapons systems afloat, ashore, and aloft. The procedures for identifying aircraft and other relevant information are shared.

(2) **Advance Force SACC.** Although normally only one SACC is active at any one time, advance force operations may require the establishment of a fire support agency to coordinate fires in support of the neutralization or destruction of enemy high value assets or the emergency extraction of SOF or reconnaissance units. The advance force SACC must maintain situational awareness on the insertions and extractions of teams, locations of teams ashore, and mine warfare operations within the area, to include sea and air assets. The AF SACC assumes responsibility as the primary fire support agency from the advance force SACC, upon its arrival in the operational area.

(3) **Assault Breaching Operations.** Assault breaching, a part of amphibious breaching, is a preplanned fire support mission using precision guided munitions to neutralize mines and obstacles in the surf zone and on the beach (10 foot depth contour to high water mark [HWM] and HWM to beach exit, respectively). Assault breaching must be coordinated and synchronized with the maneuver of troops going ashore, other D-day fires, and ongoing MCM operations, in particular, underwater MCM operations being conducted in the very shallow water (10-40 foot depth contours) region. JDAM [Joint Direct Attack Munition] JABS [Assault Breaching System] is the only capability currently available for breaching mines and obstacles from the 10-foot depth contour to the beach exit. The MCMC, in coordination with the CATF and CLF, is responsible for planning the breach and determination of individual weapon aim points, fuze settings, and priority of effort for the CATF to forward an air support request (ASR) to the appropriate air component. As with all other ASRs within the operational area, Air Force and US Marine Corps tactical air support is planned and tasked in accordance with the established air tasking process. The breach is conducted by the CATF through the SACC and the Navy TACC.

Additional information on assault breaching is provided in Chapter IV, "Amphibious Operations Against Coastal Defenses."

SECTION C. COMMUNICATIONS

8.   Overview/Considerations

Amphibious operations require a flexible C2 system capable of supporting rapid decision making and execution to maintain a high tempo of operations. These systems must be robust, flexible, sustainable, survivable, and as expeditionary as the AF. Communications system architecture must provide strategic and tactical connectivity to a variety of tailored AFs. The AF must have the ability to plan for, provide C2 for, and support all functional areas (fires, aviation, intelligence, and CSS, etc.) afloat and ashore. Communications support requirements in amphibious operations are summarized in Figure V-1.

Communications system support functions will be performed in accordance with JP 6-0, Joint Communications System, *and CJCSM 6231 series,* Manual for Employing Joint Tactical Communications System.

9.   Identifying Requirements

a. An effective communications system support plan:

(1) Provides an EMCON plan and INFOSEC posture that balances OPSEC versus operational requirements.

(2) Provides transmission and cryptographic security. Avoid cryptographic code changes where possible during initial phases of amphibious assaults.

COMMUNICATIONS SUPPORT REQUIREMENTS

A reliable, secure, rapid, flexible, and interoperable command and control, communications and information, system is required in both planning and execution

- Support planning
- Control ship-to-shore movement
- Coordinate protection of the amphibious force
- Control tactical air operations
- Control assault vehicles and craft
- Monitor command and control of advance force operations

- Coordinate supporting arms
- Coordinate logistic support and combat service support
- Coordinate support provided by other forces
- Medical regulation
- Coordinate use of communications and electronic warfare

Figure V-1. Communications Support Requirements

(3) Provides information assurance.

(4) Avoids mutual interference throughout the electromagnetic spectrum. Communications system support plans of the AF must be integrated into the JFC's joint communications-electronics operating instructions.

(5) Deconflicts friendly EA with other friendly frequency use in accordance with the joint restricted frequency list.

(6) Provides monitoring and defense of tactical and non-tactical computer networks.

(7) Provides friendly forces' position reporting to the Global Command and Control System-Maritime common operational picture.

(8) Uses common agencies and alternate means of communications to assist in reducing mutual interference and decreasing frequency requirements.

(9) Provides access to meteorological and oceanographic forecasts and information impacting amphibious planning and execution.

(10) Incorporates coalition or multinational forces into communications plans.

b. Each major command of the force must have compatible and interoperable communications that will support the tactics and techniques employed by that force. **Circuits provided must assure effective exercise of command and coordination of supporting fires.**

c. Subordinate commands of the AF may operate in widely separated areas during some phases of the amphibious operation. **The communications plan must permit rapid integration of the force without undue interference between elements.**

d. Local frequencies and communications standards in use in the landing area must be considered to ensure compatibility and to prevent interference.

e. Communications system connectivity must be established among all major participating commands at commencement of the planning phase.

10. Responsibilities

a. CATF and CLF are responsible for communications system support planning, with the designated commander consolidating the requirements. The communications system support plan must reflect the coordinated communications system requirements of the AF. The requirements may include radio and weapon guidance and control frequencies, call signs, compatible cryptographic and authentication systems, and special communications equipment, computer equipment and systems, or support. These responsibilities are very closely tied to both commanders and are best described as mutual as depicted in Figure V-2.

(1) The communication systems support plan fulfills communication systems requirements of the AF in terms of circuits, channels and systems required, and policies and procedures governing the operation and coordination of the overall system. The plan includes the items listed in Figure V-2.

(2) The plan is prepared in detail to facilitate use by commanders at all echelons.

b. Specific CATF responsibilities normally include the following:

(1) Preparation and promulgation of a coordinated plan for employment of AF communications during the operation.

(2) Acquisition and assignment of necessary communications assets to subordinate elements of the force.

COMMUNICATIONS SYSTEM SUPPORT PLAN

- General coverage of the communications situation, including assumptions, guiding principles, and the concept of operational communications employment

- Announcement of the communications mission

- Delegation of communications tasks and responsibilities to major elements of the force

- Detailed instructions for organization, installation, operation, coordination, and maintenance of the communications system

- Assignment and employment of call signs, frequencies, cryptographic aids, and authentication systems

- Instructions on countermeasures, operations security, military deception, and communications security

- Interoperability of computer systems, to include hardware and software

- Logistic support for communications and electronics

Figure V-2. Communications System Support Plan

(3) Preparation of appropriate OPSEC and military deception guidance.

(4) Preparation and promulgation of a coordinated EW plan for the force.

(5) Providing necessary shipboard communications system and services in support of the embarked LF.

(6) Development of a coordinated communications plan for the ATF for inclusion in the overall communications system support plan.

(7) Development and promulgation of a plan for communications connectivity with other maritime forces.

c. Specific communications system support planning responsibilities of CLF include the following:

(1) Development of a coordinated communications plan for the LF component of the AF for inclusion in the overall force communications system support plan.

(2) Development and promulgation of a plan for communications connectivity with other ground forces ashore.

(3) Establishment of computer and network requirements while embarked.

(4) Identification of connectivity requirements prior to movement ashore for follow-on operations, if required.

(5) Development of a LF EW plan based on the CATF's appropriate OPSEC and military deception guidance and coordinated EW plan for the force.

d. Due to the limited availability of AF communication assets, commanders of other embarked forces need to expeditiously determine and submit their communication requirements for inclusion into the communications system support plans.

11. Landing Force Communications Plan

The LF communications plan is normally issued as an annex to the OPLAN or OPORD and must be compatible with the overall communications plan of the AF. The actual drafting of the communications plan is the staff responsibility of the LF assistant chief of staff for communications (G-6). Throughout the preparation of the plan, the G-6 must coordinate with each staff section of the LF as well as his equivalent staff officers at parallel and subordinate commands. The G-6 counterpart on the ATF staff is the communications officer, or the Navy component communications staff officer (N-6). The G-6 and N-6 conduct concurrent and parallel planning addressing items such as:

a. Allocation of shipboard radio equipment, spaces, and personnel to support LF operations.

b. Assignment of call signs, coordinated with the CATF to facilitate handling of LF traffic over naval circuits during the movement phase.

c. Identification of cryptographic and authentication systems that must be used by ATF and LF units.

d. Development of communications security (COMSEC) procedures.

e. Evaluation of assigned radio frequencies for optimal performance, to prevent mutual interference, and ensure adequacy of support for LF operations.

f. Use of LF personnel to support the ships' communications personnel during the movement to the objective and during the initial stages of the action phase.

g. Development of computer networks that support the LF while embarked, including procedures for the receipt and distribution of message traffic.

12. Landing Force Communications System

The LF will embark in functionally operational spaces normally built on a Navy C2 infrastructure. These spaces will be complete with permanent access to voice, data, and video systems necessary for the LF's situational awareness. They will form the LF operational spaces, which are collectively known as the LF operations center. The infrastructure is based on joint standards and architectures and allows units, to draw upon a baseline of communications system capabilities, regardless of their Service.

13. Landing Force Communications System Support by Phase

a. **Planning Phase.** Communications system connectivity between the CLF, CATF, and AF commanders and staffs must be established immediately at commencement of the planning phase. Units of the LF must ensure preservation of COMSEC even though great distances may separate the various planning headquarters. The worldwide Defense Message System, supplemented by SECRET Internet Protocol Router Network (SIPRNET) electronic mail and secure telephone, provides the major communications means during this phase.

b. **Embarkation Phase.** Before embarkation, commanders must provide for adequate communications system support between the AF and any external agencies involved in transportation. **The CLF is normally responsible for planning and providing LF communications systems at the piers and/or beaches within the embarkation areas, to include coordinating the use of established facilities (military or civilian).** A significant portion of the LF's organic communications equipment will be packed and ready for embarkation so the CLF should make arrangements with the area's local commander to provide communications support. Specifically, the plan should establish:

(1) Ship-to-shore circuits for the control of loading (closely coordinated with the CATF).

(2) Convoy control for serials moving from point of origin to seaport of embarkation.

(3) Communications between the port of embarkation and the embarkation area, including the contracted use of commercial assets if feasible.

(4) Communications between control points within the embarkation area.

(5) Communications center and/or switching center operations within the embarkation area.

c. **Rehearsal Phase.** The rehearsal phase of the amphibious operation gives the CLF the opportunity to test the LF communications plan. Under ideal conditions, the rehearsal will involve all elements of the force and attempt to fully test the communications systems involved without violating COMSEC procedures. By having a full-scale rehearsal, the CLF can further refine his communications requirements and identify critical vulnerabilities, thus allowing for appropriate adjustments to the OPLAN or OPORD before execution. Specific considerations during the rehearsal phase include:

(1) Maximum use of secure voice equipment and use of minimum power on electronic emitters for COMSEC reasons.

(2) Use of call signs and frequencies for rehearsal use only.

(3) Plan to repair or replace communications equipment damaged during the rehearsal.

(4) Plan for, allocate, and embark expendable items (such as wire and batteries) for use during the rehearsal.

(5) Allocate enough time to conduct an objective critique of the communications plan after the rehearsal and to modify portions of the plan as necessary.

d. **Movement Phase.** As discussed earlier, the CATF provides functionally operational spaces built on a Navy C2 infrastructure to the LF. During the movement phase, however, the CATF normally restricts the use of equipment, particularly transmitters and emitters, to prevent disclosure of locations, movements, and intentions of the force. The LF plan must address how the commander will communicate with LF units embarked on different ships, and possibly even separate movement groups, during these periods of radio silence. Some potential alternate means are helicopter messenger, visual signals, or line-of-sight radio if permitted by the emission control condition. Other LF communications considerations during movement include ensuring:

(1) Embarkation information is accurate and reflects the communications guard situation for all elements of the LF.

(2) Communications officers with the ATF have an accurate list of appropriate LF units (e.g., next senior and immediate subordinate) and their assigned shipping location.

(3) ATF communications officers have an accurate listing of LF personnel who have message release authorities.

(4) ATF communications officers have an accurate listing of LF communications personnel embarked in their respective ships. The list should also contain clearance and access information of these LF personnel.

(5) Establishment of LF communications centers, or equivalents, on all ships when major LF units are embarked.

e. **Action Phase.** During the action phase, both the ATF and LF rely primarily on radio communications as the means for exercising C2. Accordingly, radio silence is usually lifted by the CATF prior to H-hour in order to test all circuits before the ship-to-shore movement begins. During the initial portion of this phase, when the major LF headquarters are still afloat, LF circuits are provided by facilities specifically installed in amphibious shipping for use by LF personnel. LF communications must be complementary and generally parallel to those established by the ATF. These parallel systems usually terminate at each significant control center aboard the amphibious ships; (e.g., SACC, Navy TACC, HDC, and TACLOG group). The LF communications plan must address the many operational aspects of the action phase.

(1) **Waterborne Movement.** Communications for control and coordination of landing ships, landing craft, and other waterborne vehicles moving from the transport area to landing areas are provided primarily by the CATF through a Navy control group. However, LF radio nets must be integrated into the group's plan so that LF commanders can properly monitor and control the movements of the LF, especially important when the ship-to-shore movement includes LF organic AAVs.

(2) **Helicopterborne Movement.** Communication nets for the control and coordination of the assault support helicopters are established and maintained by the CATF through his Navy TACC and HDC. LF personnel will augment the HDC and integrate LF communications into the overall aviation C2 systems. Helicopterborne movement normally generates additional, long-range communications requirements for the LF because of the inherent distances associated with helicopter operations.

(3) **Supporting Arms Coordination.** Whether supervised by the ATF's SAC or the LF's FFC, the SACC coordinates and controls all organic and nonorganic fires in support of the AF until the LF establishes adequate control and communications facilities ashore. The LF communications must include nets that integrate all agencies that interface with the SACC. These include, but are not limited to, the NSFS, the air support section, the TIC, the FFCC/FSCC/FC of the LF, fire support observers, TACPs, forward air controller (airborne) and TAC(A), and artillery fire direction centers.

Note: Consideration must be given to shipboard hazards of electromagnetic radiation to ordnance conditions/limitations that shut down or severely limit high frequency (HF) communication capabilities (e.g., loading of ordnance on aircraft requires securing HF communications on most naval vessels).

For further information on shipboard hazards of electromagnetic radiation, see JP 3-04, Joint Shipboard Helicopter Operations.

(4) **CSS.** Selected units and agencies of the LF are required to assist the CATF in controlling and coordinating logistics during the action phase. LF communications must provide a means for the control of medical evacuation, EPW collection, foot and vehicular traffic ashore, as well as the means to control the movement of supplies and equipment. Landing support units are required to establish communications within the CSS area. This communications network must include the Navy beach parties, TACLOG group, supported

LF units, HSTs and transport aircraft (if applicable), SACC, DASC (once established ashore), and other key agencies within the ATF and LF.

f. Transition of Landing Force Command Posts Ashore

(1) The command post (CP) movement from ship-to-shore must be accomplished in a manner that provides for communications continuity during the entire action phase. LF units are almost entirely dependent on netted radios during the early stages before they can gradually transition to wire, wire-multichannel radio, computer network systems (SIPRNET), messengers, or other means. The conduct of this transition governs the development of the LF communications system and is crucial to the seamless transition of effective C2 from the agencies afloat to those established ashore.

(2) A CP movement from ship-to-shore is normally made in two or more echelons, depending on the type and size of the headquarters. In any case, each echelon requires a near equal communications capability which must be planned out in detail by the CLF and his staff. Furthermore, the commander, staff, and supporting personnel that make up a particular CP may be embarked on separate ships. In that case, radio communications must be established between the two or more groups of the CP as soon as practical.

(3) When an advance party (or reconnaissance party) is sent ashore before the major echelons of a CP, direct radio communications are required between the advance party and the CP afloat. The type and quantity of communications equipment and personnel assigned to the advance party must be weighed against the need for those assets back at the CP during the action phase.

(4) When in transit from ship-to-shore, the CLF and appropriate staff members will require communications with LF units already ashore (including the CP advance party if employed), LF units also in transit, LF units remaining on shipping, and appropriate ATF agencies afloat. The communications facilities normally available to the CLF (e.g., C2 configured helicopter or AAV) will usually not be able to satisfy the total communications requirement. Therefore, the communications facilities should be allocated to only the most essential circuits.

SECTION D. LOGISTICS

"The logistical effort required to sustain the seizure of Iwo Jima was enormous, complex, largely improvised on lessons learned in earlier . . . operations in the Pacific. . . . Clearly, no other element of the emerging art of amphibious warfare had improved so greatly by the winter of 1945. Marines may have had the heart and firepower to tackle a fortress-like Iwo Jima earlier in the war, but they would have been crippled in the doing of it by limitations in amphibious logistical support capabilities. These concepts, procedures, organizations, and special materials took years to develop. . . ."

**From Closing In: Marines in the Seizure of Iwo Jima,
Joseph Alexander**

14. General

The CATF is normally responsible for determining overall logistic requirements for the AF. Those requirements that cannot be supported from resources available within the ATF are directed to the applicable Service component through the chain of command as established in the initiating directive.

Additional guidance for joint logistic operations in support of amphibious operations is contained in JP 4-0, Joint Logistics, *and JP 4-01.6,* Joint Logistics Over-the-Shore (JLOTS).

15. Responsibilities

AF commanders have specific and often complementary logistics planning responsibilities as listed below.

a. CATF is responsible for the following:

(1) Coordination of logistic requirements for all elements of the ATF.

(2) Determination of requirements that can be met by internal resources. Those which cannot are directed to a higher authority or the appropriate Service through the chain of command.

(3) Establishing priorities and allocating resources to meet the logistic requirements of the ATF.

(4) Notification of appropriate responsible agencies early in the planning phase of any unusual requirements or special supplies or equipment required.

(5) Providing the means required for the establishment and operation of a logistic system in the designated amphibious objective area.

(6) Development of plans for handling EPWs and civilian evacuees and internees.

(7) Development of the overall plan for HSS, including evacuation of casualties.

(8) Preparation of the logistics annex to the OPLAN.

b. For forces assigned, the CATF is responsible for the following:

(1) Determination of the overall logistic requirements of the forces assigned.

(2) Determination and allocation of the means to meet the logistic requirements of the forces assigned.

(3) Ensuring the promulgation of the overall schedule to include plans for the assembly of shipping at points of embarkation.

(4) Review and approval of embarkation and loading plans.

(5) Ensuring the organization of assigned shipping into echelons as necessary for continued support of the LF OPLAN.

c. The CLF is responsible for the following:

(1) Determination of overall logistic requirements of the LF, including units, special equipment, and shipping.

(2) Determination and allocation of the means to meet logistic requirements of the LF.

(3) Determination of logistic requirements that cannot be met by the LF and submission of these requirements to the supported commander, CATF, or designated commander as appropriate.

(4) Development of plans for the assembly of supplies and equipment to be embarked, including the supplies and equipment of other assigned forces for which the LF is responsible.

(5) Preparation of the LF embarkation and ship loading plans and orders, in coordination with the CATF.

(6) Planning for the coordination of logistics required by all elements of the LF.

(7) Planning for the conveyance and distribution of logistics required by the LF.

(8) Preparation of the logistics annex to the LF OPLAN.

d. Other designated commanders of the AF are responsible for determining their logistic requirements and submitting to the CATF or appropriate commander those requirements that cannot be met internally.

16. Considerations and Factors

The requirement for afloat forces to provide seamless support to the LF during the period in which its logistic system is primarily seabased has a significant influence on logistic planning for an amphibious operation. Like all logistic systems, **the AF logistic systems must be responsive, simple, flexible, economical, attainable, sustainable, and survivable**. Development of effective logistic systems must take into account the planning considerations and factors listed below.

a. **Planning Considerations**

(1) Orderly assembly and embarkation of personnel and materiel based on anticipated requirements of the LF scheme of maneuver ashore.

(2) Establishment and maintenance of a logistic system in the operational area that will ensure adequate support to all elements of the AF, and subsequent support of base development and garrison forces as directed.

(3) Impetus of logistic support from sea, or the rear, and directed forward to the point of application at the using unit.

(4) Preservation of OPSEC during logistic planning. Nonsecure logistic planning can compromise tactical surprise and landing location.

b. **Planning Factors.** Logistic planning factors are as follows:

(1) Character, size, and duration of the operation.

(2) Target date.

(3) Objective area characteristics:

(a) Terrain and hydrography.

(b) Climate and weather.

(c) Distance from support bases.

(d) Indigenous support.

(e) Facilities available.

(f) Transportation systems.

(g) Local resources.

(h) Throughput capacity.

(4) Enemy capabilities:

(a) Freedom from interference.

(b) Vulnerability to enemy.

(5) Strength and composition of LF.

(6) Distribution means.

(7) LOCs and transportation networks.

(8) Support base resupply.

(9) Progressive increase in level and form of logistics.

(10) Support required for EPWs.

(11) Availability of logistic means.

(12) Compatibility and capability of support systems.

(13) Communications means.

(14) Base defense and garrison plans.

(15) Requirements for rehabilitation or construction of airfields.

(16) Impact of CBRN effects (for more information about logistics planning factors in CBRN environments see JP 3-11, *Operations in Chemical, Biological, Radiological, and Nuclear (CBRN) Environments*).

(17) Availability of AE and AFOE shipping.

(18) Indigenous health risks and diseases prevalent.

17. Combat Service Support Plans

See Figure V-3.

a. The necessity to provide continuing and coordinated logistics to the LF when its logistic system is primarily sea-based requires coordination between the AF commanders to develop a control and delivery system that will ensure that the LF is provided the necessary support from embarkation through rehearsal, movement, execution, and continued operations ashore. **Wherever possible, sustainment planning should encompass the concept of direct ship-to-user delivery.**

b. Logistic planning is accomplished under two major categories: initial supply and sustainment.

(1) **Initial Supply.** Initial supply comprises the logistic levels carried as accompanying supplies in assault shipping, both AE and AFOE to provide required initial

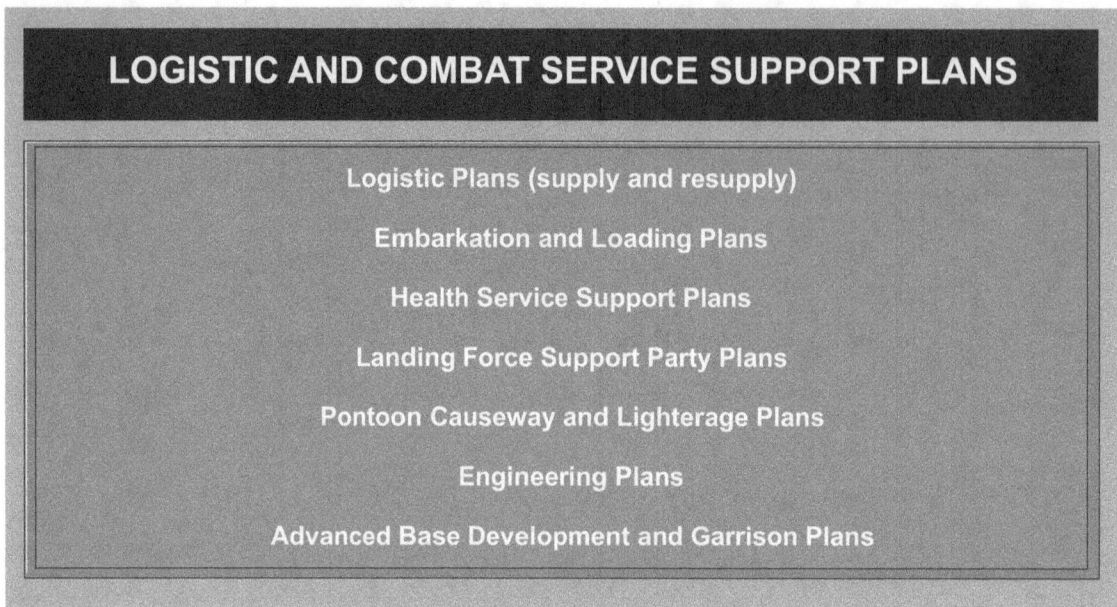

Figure V-3. Logistic and Combat Service Support Plans

support for the assault landing and initial operations ashore. Plans for initial supply include the following:

(a) ATF provision for:

<u>1.</u> Loading ships with supplies to prescribed levels as much as practicable considering the embarkation of troops.

<u>2.</u> Rations for LF while embarked.

<u>3.</u> Special facilities required for refueling and maintenance of aircraft, landing craft, amphibious vehicles, and other equipment as well as fuel for boat pools, beach groups, transportation pools, and other shore components.

<u>4.</u> Water for the LF ashore until supply from sources ashore is available.

(b) LF provision for:

<u>1.</u> Assembly and loading of supplies to be landed with the LF in such a manner as to ensure availability for issue before and during debarkation.

<u>2.</u> Establishment of pre-positioned emergency supplies (floating dumps) containing limited amounts of selected supplies for emergency issue. A floating dump consists of emergency supplies preloaded in landing craft, amphibious vehicles, or in landing ships. Floating dumps are located in the vicinity of the appropriate control officer, who directs their landing as requested by the troop commander concerned.

3. Establishment of selected pre-staged supplies for ship-to-shore movement by VTOL aircraft (pre-staged VTOL-lifted supplies).

4. Selective discharge of required supplies in accordance with the landing plan.

5. Positive and efficient control of the movement of supplies from ship to desired locations ashore.

6. Establishment of logistic heads ashore (if required) and the distribution of those supplies to forward units.

(2) **Sustainment.** Sustainment comprises logistic support transported to the landing area in follow-up shipping and aircraft to support tactical operations ashore.

(a) Sustainment is provided through either one or a combination of the following systems:

1. Maintaining shipping and aircraft in an on-call status to be ordered into the landing area by the CATF, as requested by the CLF.

2. Establishing fixed schedules for bringing shipping or aircraft into the landing area automatically as planned by the CLF.

(b) Factors affecting decisions in this regard depend primarily on:

1. Distance between the landing area and loading points.

2. Availability of forward sheltered ports or anchorages for use as regulating stations.

3. Requirement for convoy escort.

4. Availability of aircraft dedicated for sustainment lift.

5. Hostile activity on LOCs.

6. Plans for general engineering support, including facilities required to accommodate supplies and the phase-in of LF units to handle supplies.

7. Availability of manpower, materials handling equipment, and lighterage to off load shipping.

8. Availability of LOTS resources.

c. Logistic plans are prepared by the CATF, CLF, and other designated commanders of the AF and include the following:

(1) Primary source(s) of supply and responsibilities.

(2) Levels of supply to be carried in AE, AFOE, and follow-up shipping.

(3) Control and distribution of supplies.

(4) Plan for landing supplies.

(5) Resupply responsibilities, schedules, and sources.

(6) Air delivery responsibility, procedures.

(7) Captured material disposition instructions.

(8) Salvage instructions.

(9) Retrograde.

(10) Casualties.

18. Key Constructs

a. **Selective and General Unloading.** From the CSS standpoint, the ship-to-shore movement is divided into two clearly distinguishable time periods:

(1) **Selective Unloading.** The selective unloading period is primarily tactical in character and must be responsive to the requirements of LF units. During the early part of the ship-to-shore movement, CSS is provided on a selective basis from sources afloat. Movement of CSS elements to the landing beaches or LZs closely follows the combat elements. As the assault progresses, CSS units are established ashore, and support is provided both from within the beach support area (BSA) and from sources afloat.

(2) **General Unloading.** Normally, general unloading is undertaken when sufficient troops and supplies have been landed to sustain the momentum of the attack and when areas are adequate to handle the incoming volume of supplies. When adequate assault supplies are ashore, and the BSA is organized and operating satisfactorily, the CLF recommends to the CATF that general unloading begin.

b. **BSA and CSSA.** As the operation progresses and CSS units are phased ashore, the initial landing support organization is disestablished and its functions are assumed by the LFSP. BSAs, initially developed by the landing support elements, may be consolidated or expanded into CSSAs to provide continued support to the LF. The need for CSSAs and their number, size, and capabilities are situation dependent, but they are primarily influenced by the scope and duration of the operation.

c. **BSA/CSSA Defense.** The CLF normally assigns the mission of defending the BSA or CSSA to the senior tactical commander ashore. To clarify responsibility, the LF OPORD will specify the security commander and the task organization designated to perform this mission.

d. **Critical Early Requirements.** CSS in the initial stages of the amphibious operation is principally concerned with the provision of combat essential supplies such as rations, water, ammunition, and fuel. These critical items are normally drawn from LF stocks transported by AE and AFOE shipping. Other essential services, including medical support, are provided within the capabilities of the AF. Other CSS functions are of secondary importance during the early stages of the ship-to-shore movement and will normally not be involved in the scheduled waves.

e. **TACLOG Groups and the LFSP.** The CLF places special emphasis on the importance of CSS coordination during the ship-to-shore movement by establishing TACLOG groups and the LFSP.

f. **Seabasing and the Sea Echelon Level**

(1) **Seabasing.** In some cases, it may be undesirable or unnecessary to transfer substantial LF supplies and CSS organizations ashore. Seabasing allows for the majority of CSS assets to remain at sea and be sent ashore only when needed. In such cases, additional consideration must be devoted during the planning phase to ensure that CSS capabilities are balanced aboard those amphibious ships best suited to provide support.

(2) **Sea Echelon Level.** The sea echelon level plan normally reduces the concentration of amphibious ships in areas near the beach. The majority of shipping will remain in distant sea operating areas until called forward in accordance with established priorities. In such cases, the **out-of-sequence landing of supplies and equipment will cause delays in the established schedule**. Specific provisions may be required to ensure rapid evacuation of casualties to more distant primary casualty receiving and treatment ships (CRTSs).

g. **Embarkation, Movement, and Rehearsal Support.** Although the primary emphasis of CSS planning is to develop a CSS system to support the LF, the force must also be supported while en route. Support required in the embarkation areas may include the operation of camps and mess facilities in staging areas, road maintenance, and equipment maintenance. LF CSS requirements during the movement phase are primarily provided by the ATF but the LF must plan for administrative and maintenance requirements. CSS requirements during and after rehearsals may be extensive (especially if equipment repairs are necessary) and must be incorporated into the plan.

h. **LF Aviation.** During amphibious operations, fixed-wing aviation elements may be located outside the landing area, requiring a task-organized CSS detachment for support. When LF aviation is phased ashore into the AOA/AO, the CSS requirements (especially engineering and transportation) will be extensive.

19. Health Service Support Plan

a. The HSS plan is usually issued as annex Q (Medical Services) to the OPLAN and provides for HSS to all elements of the AF in accordance with the foregoing responsibilities. Likewise the LF HSS plan will be issued as annex Q (Medical Services) to the LF OPLAN. Both include the items listed in Figure V-4. The fleet surgical team, when assigned, should be included in operation planning to provide input into the medical logistic support plan. Additional HSS planning considerations are detailed in Figure V-5.

b. **Planning Responsibilities**

(1) The designated commander is responsible for overall preparation of plans, taking into account the following:

(a) Coordinating, with the JFC or establishing authority, patient movement by sea or air from the operational area to HSS facilities outside the area.

(b) Air transport of HSS supplies and equipment, which may involve intratheater airlift assets.

(c) Coordination with supporting commanders for HSS assets requiring intratheater transportation.

(d) Formulation, in conjunction with AF commanders, of a recommended patient movement policy for the operation.

(e) Establishment of HSS requirements and standards for the civilian population in the operational area, when not prescribed by higher authority.

(f) Development of procedures for regulating movement of casualties and patients within the landing area in conjunction with AF commanders.

For more information, see JP 4-02, Health Service Support, and JP 3-11, Operations in Chemical, Biological, Radiological, and Nuclear (CBRN) Environments.

(2) The CATF is responsible for the following:

(a) Provision for HSS for all embarked personnel between points of embarkation and the objective area.

CONTENTS OF THE HEALTH SERVICE SUPPORT PLAN

- Statement of the health service support (HSS) situation

- Statement of patient movement policy

- Clear delineation of HSS responsibilities, organization, and employment of the several elements, with particular emphasis on shifts in responsibility during several phases of the operation and measures necessary to ensure coordinated HSS action by all elements of the amphibious force

- Provision for delivery and regulation of HSS in the objective area

- HSS medical logistics, including operation of HSS supply stocks afloat and provision for pre-planned replenishment, repair, and exchange of supplies and medical equipment

- Procedures and responsibilities for keeping necessary records and reports on the flow of casualties

- Provision for HSS to patients while afloat

- Provision for obtaining medical intelligence

- Measures for preventive medicine, hygiene, and sanitation

- Procedures for distribution of whole blood and colloids

- Organization and operation of the patient movement system

- Development of preventive and environmental health plans and annex coordinated with the engineer environmental management plans and annex

Figure V-4. Contents of the Health Service Support Plan

(b) Provision for HSS personnel, supplies, and equipment for all units based ashore and not attached to the LF.

(c) In conjunction with the CLF, development of a procedure for movement of patients within the landing area.

(d) Seaward evacuation from the beach, including communications to support movement of patients, receipt of patients, hospitalization afloat within the operational area, and initial casualty reporting for the ATF, LF, and other forces assigned.

(e) Establishment of HSS requirements for the civilian population in the objective area, when not prescribed by higher authority.

(f) Coordination of HSS for the civilian population with nongovernmental organizations and coalition forces.

(g) Positioning and employment of hospital ships within the operational area.

(3) The CLF identifies and coordinates LF HSS requirements with the CATF. Once command is passed ashore, close coordination with the CATF is still required. See Figure V-5 for LF HSS planning considerations. The CLF is responsible for preparation of plans, taking into account the following:

(a) Providing HSS to LF personnel before embarkation.

(b) Assistance to ship's HSS department by providing HSS personnel to care for LF personnel while embarked.

(c) Development, in conjunction with the CATF, of the evacuation policy for the operation.

(d) Execution of the patient movement plan to the rear and from the operational area as directed.

(e) Providing HSS to all personnel ashore in the operational area who are not otherwise provided for.

(f) Determination of the HSS requirements of the LF that cannot be met by the LF capabilities.

See JP 4-02, Health Service Support, *for additional information regarding HSS.*

c. **Patient Movement**

(1) **Patient Movement Policy.** Patient movement policy is a command decision establishing the maximum number of days that patients may be held within the command for treatment. Patients who, in the opinion of responsible medical officers, cannot be returned to a duty status within the period prescribed are evacuated by the first available means, provided the travel involved will not aggravate their disabilities. The policy will be

HEALTH SERVICE SUPPORT PLANNING CONSIDERATIONS

GOAL
Providing for the health of the command and evacuation and hospitalization of sick and wounded

Planning Must Consider:

- Overall mission of the force and the supporting medical mission
- Policies of higher commanders
- Landing area characteristics
- Physical, biological, and psychological threats to personnel
- Lines of communications and evacuation
- Evacuation policies and procedures
- Medical supplies required
- Blood and colloid requirements
- Casualty estimates
- Medical personnel available and status of their training

- Supporting medical facilities and forces outside the objective area
- Medical needs for civilian population and enemy prisoners of war, if authorized
- Need for service medical unit augmentation
- Requirements for casualty receiving and treatment ships
- Aircraft and landing craft to provide ambulance facilities
- Medical augmentation requirements for common-user shipping
- Other medical facilities available within the objective area

Figure V-5. Health Service Support Planning Considerations

established for the theater by the combatant commander and is further defined by the CATF in conjunction with the CLF for the AOA. The use of any specific patient movement policy for the AOA serves only as a guide for medical planning, and must remain flexible to meet the changes in demand placed on the limited medical treatment capability initially available.

(2) **Patient Movement Plan.** Plans for patient movement must be well defined and widely disseminated. These plans must include at a minimum:

(a) Identification of CRTS or other medical treatment capabilities.

(b) Locations of medical treatment facilities ashore.

(c) Communications procedures for patient movement coordination.

(d) Provisions for mass patient movement.

(3) As a matter of policy, **the preferred mode of patient movement is via aircraft**. The speed, range, and flexibility of aircraft serve to enhance the medical support capability of the LF. However, patient movement plans must not be aircraft-dependent and must include provisions for maximum use of ground and surface means.

(4) **Chain of Patient Movement.** Patient movement experience during LF operations has demonstrated that there is no normal or typical chain of patient movement through which a casualty is moved from the place where wounded or injured to the medical treatment facility best suited to meet specific treatment needs. Past experience in no way eliminates the need for a functioning and coordinated patient movement using available transportation means to enhance the patient's chances for survival and to effectively employ available transportation means. In planning patient movement, the guiding principles include:

(a) Each successive echelon of HSS of care in the medical support system has greater treatment capability than the preceding echelon.

(b) Each casualty should advance through the system only as far as needed to meet the specific treatment need.

(c) Medical vehicles should be used for transportation at the earliest possible opportunity.

(d) The arrangement of patient movement between medical treatment facilities is usually administrative in nature and can be preplanned.

d. **Medical Regulating.** The actions and coordination necessary to arrange for the movement of patients through the levels of care. This process matches patients with a medical treatment facility that has the necessary HSS capabilities and available bed space

(1) **Medical Regulating Plan.** This plan contains policies and procedures for evacuation and primary medical regulation of patients to designated CRTSs in the landing area, and provides for medical services. It also provides for secondary medical regulating evacuation of patients by air to medical treatment facilities outside the operational area or following medical or surgical treatment onboard the CRTSs.

(2) **Medical Regulating Agency.** The functions of the medical regulating agency include:

(a) Maintaining inventory of locations and availability of operating rooms, beds, and medical/surgical specialty teams on various treatment ships.

(b) Maintaining inventory of locations and capabilities of treatment facilities established ashore.

(c) Directing or recommending destinations for the patients.

(d) Monitoring medical materiel, blood and blood products, and medical personnel replacement requirements.

(e) Consolidating patient movement requests for patients requiring onward evacuation.

e. **Hospitalization**

(1) **Initial Hospital Support.** Hospitalization support of LF operations is provided initially in CRTSs of the ATF and later by applicable appropriate medical units of the LF when they are established ashore. In most cases, however, the staff and equipment of LF medical units limit their capabilities to patient holding. Overloading is avoided to ensure that the capability to support current and future operations is not degraded.

(2) **Follow-on Hospital Support.** Follow-on hospitalization and treatment

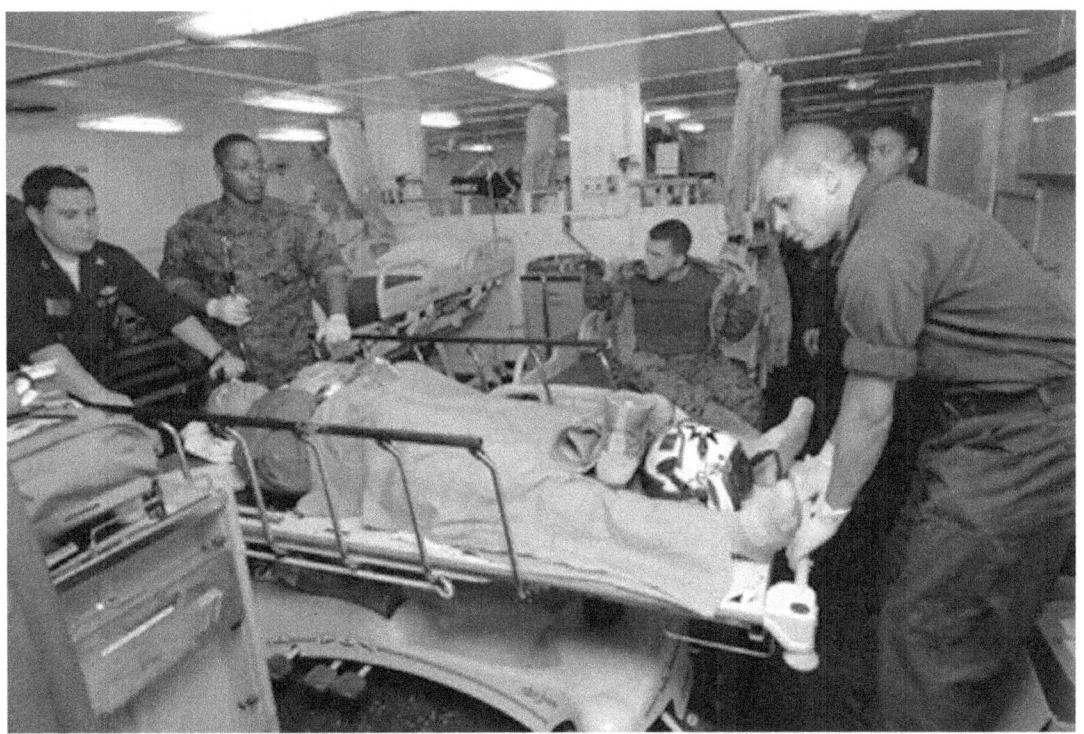

Sailors of Fleet Surgical Team 2 simulate mass casualty procedures aboard the USS Nassau (LHA-4).

support of the LF may be provided by Navy, Army, or Air Force medical units, such as fleet hospitals and hospital ships, combat support hospitals, or expeditionary medical support units, respectively. These units may or may not be considered part of the AF.

20. Landing Force Support Party Plan

a. **The LFSP is a temporary LF organization, composed of ATF and LF elements, that facilitates the ship-to-shore movement and provides initial combat support and CSS to the LF.** The CLF is responsible for organizing a system to accomplish this mission and other specific support functions within the landing area. Other missions of the LFSP are as follows:

(1) Facilitate the landing and movement of personnel, supplies, and equipment across the beach, into an LZ or through a port.

(2) Evacuate casualties and EPWs from the beach.

(3) Beach, retract, and salvage landing ships and craft.

(4) Facilitate the establishment of the LCE, ACE, and naval beach group. A naval beach group is a permanently organized naval command within an AF composed of a commander and staff, a beachmaster unit, an amphibious construction battalion, and assault craft units, designed to provide ship-to-shore interface support to the CLF. Its specific organization depends on the number of beaches or zones through which the LF will land and the size of the units using the beaches or zones. For planning purposes, the basic LFSP structure consists of the LFSP commander, the shore party, the beach party, special attachments, and ships' platoons.

(a) **LFSP Commander.** The designated commander of the LFSP controls landing support operations within the landing area. The LFSP commander ensures effective landing support through close coordination with subordinate units, timely reinforcement, and consolidation of shore party and beach party elements. Initially, LFSP operations are decentralized to the shore party and beach party teams per established code (Green Beach, Red Beach 1, etc.). TACON for landing support operations on these beaches resides with the shore party team commander. When the shore party and beach party groups are established ashore, they assume TACON of their respective teams. TACON for landing support operations on each coded beach resides with the shore party group commander. When the shore party and beach party are established ashore and the shore party commander has consolidated command of the shore party groups, TACON of the shore party and beach party groups transitions to the shore party and beach party commanders respectively. Concurrent with this transition, the LFSP is established ashore and the LFSP commander assumes TACON of the shore party, beach party, special attachments, and all other LFSP units ashore. If the LFSP is not established ashore concurrently with the beach party and shore party, TACON for landing support operations resides with the shore party commander until the LFSP commander assumes TACON. The LFSP personnel and equipment landed are minimal as the shore party and beach party form the predominant part of the LFSP.

(b) **Shore Party.** The shore party is the LF component of the LFSP. The nucleus for the shore party is the transportation support battalion, augmented with personnel and equipment from the GCE, ACE, and other LCE units.

(c) **Beach Party.** The beach party is the Navy component of the LFSP and is under the TACON of the LFSP commander. Personnel and equipment for the beach party comes from the naval beach group and/or elements from a Navy cargo handling battalion, as required by the JFC/CATF.

(d) **Special Attachments.** Special attachments are made to the LFSP for defense of the beach support area, to provide liaison personnel, and for specialized tasks.

(e) **Ships' Platoons.** A ship's platoon consists of assigned LF personnel responsible for loading, stowing, and offloading LF equipment and supplies. When a ship carries equipment and supplies that belong only to LF units embarked on that ship, the ship's platoon is sourced from the ship's embarked troops at the direction of the commanding officer of troops.

Detailed information about the LFSP is contained in NTTP 3-02.1M/MCWP 3-31.5, Ship-to-Shore Movement, *and NTTP 3-02.14,* The Naval Beach Group.

For further information, refer to JP 4-01.6, Joint Logistics Over-the-Shore (JLOTS).

b. **LFSP Plan**

(1) The CLF and appropriate subordinate commanders prepare LFSP plans containing instructions for the functioning of the LFSP, including the beach party and helicopter/VTOL aircraft support team, and air mobile support party requirements.

(2) The LFSP plan includes the following:

(a) Organization and mission of the LFSP.

(b) Instructions to all subordinate elements.

(c) LFSP communications instructions.

(d) Beach, DZ, and LZ defense instructions.

(e) Administrative instructions.

c. **LFSP Planning Considerations.** In developing the LFSP plans, consideration must be accorded the factors shown in Figure V-6 and the below:

(1) Early detailed analysis of the landing area.

(2) Detailed planning for organization of BSAs and LZ support areas.

(3) Adequate communications between tactical units, control elements, and landing support elements.

(4) Composition of the AE and AFOE.

(5) Plans after seizure of the force beachhead line.

LANDING FORCE SUPPORT PARTY PLANNING CONSIDERATIONS

- Landing force scheme of maneuver and related landing plan
- Enemy disposition in the landing area
- Mine and obstacle clearance in the landing area
- Landing area weather, terrain, and hydrographic conditions
- Requirements for multiple, separate logistic installations to provide for passive defense against weapons of mass destruction
- Requirement for beach development and clearance of landing zones
- Amounts and types of supplies and equipment to be landed
- Types of ships (amphibious and commercial), landing craft (displacement or air-cushion), and aircraft to be unloaded
- Availability of personnel and equipment for landing force support party operations
- Policy concerning method of handling and disposition of enemy prisoners of war
- Casualty evacuation and health service support regulating policies
- Coordination required with other agencies
- Provision for inter-Service support

Figure V-6. Landing Force Support Party Planning Considerations

(6) Concept of CSS.

(7) Environmental management requirements.

Build-up of beach support area at Inchon, Korea September 15, 1950.

d. **LFSP Planning Responsibilities**

(1) **The CLF is responsible for the timely activation of the LFSP and the conduct of LFSP operations**; however, AF elements participate in and contribute to the development of plans for its organization and employment. The CLF is responsible for the tactical employment and security ashore of all elements of the LFSP, and will integrate requirements into the fire support plan. **The CLF determines and presents requirements for support of LFSP operations to the CATF.** These requirements will be presented as early as possible in the planning phase.

(2) **The CATF is responsible for preparation of related plans that provide facilities and means to ensure effective support of LFSP operations.** Examples of such plans are the pontoon causeway and lighterage plan, unloading plan, casualty evacuation plan, and EPW evacuation plan. Integrated training of shore party and beach party elements will be conducted before embarkation begins.

e. **Employment.** The responsibility for embarking and landing the landing support units rests with the tactical unit supported. For this reason, the landing support units are attached to the tactical unit supported for embarkation and landing purposes only. The buildup of the LFSP ashore parallels the tactical buildup ashore. Landing support operations begin with the landing of the advance parties and continue until the operation is completed or until the parties are relieved. Throughout the operation, the landing support task organization changes as required to meet the situation until the operation is terminated or the LFSP is relieved of its responsibilities.

21. Pontoon Causeway and Lighterage Plans

a. The CLF is responsible for presenting to the CATF requirements on which plans for pontoon causeways and lighterage support for the operation are based. The CATF prepares the pontoon causeway and lighterage plan in consultation with the CLF considering the following:

(1) LF requirements.

(2) Hydrographic conditions.

(3) Availability of required types of sealift.

b. The plan should include details on loading, transportation, launching, initial operational assignment, and provisions for maintenance and salvage of the causeway and lighterage equipment. It also contains specific instructions for transition of control. The plan will include provisions for retaining lighterage in the area after the assault shipping departs, for use in unloading follow-up shipping, and for other support of tactical operations. The plan is published as an annex to the CATF's logistic plan.

22. Engineer Plan

Engineer operations support the development of the operational environment for maneuver, enhance strategic and operational movement, and provide infrastructure for force protection. In addition to normal engineer operations (i.e., combat, general, and topographic), special considerations must be made for MCM and amphibious breaching, joint reception, staging, onward movement, and integration, OPDSs, and amphibious bulk liquid transfer system connectivity. Involvement of the engineer staff is essential in the planning and execution of all phases of amphibious operations.

a. **Engineer Planning**. The nature of engineer support for the LF in amphibious operations ranges from combat engineer support of a pioneer nature for the assault units to general engineer and CSS functions for the LF. The normal engineer tasks (mobility, countermobility, survivability, and general engineering) are applicable.

(1) **Combat Engineers.** Combat engineer elements will normally be attached to the assault infantry units to perform a variety of tasks such as engineer reconnaissance, obstacle breaching and installation, development of BSAs, helicopter landing and VTOL site preparation, construction of beach exits, combat trails and pioneer roads, tactical bridging, integration of environmental planning issues, and water and bath services.

(2) **General Support Engineers.** General support engineer elements will normally perform these tasks: deliberate clearing of obstacles, explosive ordnance disposal, vertical and horizontal construction, provision of utilities (including potable water and mobile electric power), installation and operation of bulk fuel systems ashore, maintenance and repair of routes of communication, topographic support, environmental management support, advanced airfield preparation, and bridge construction/maintenance. It is desirable for general support engineer elements to relieve combat engineer elements of responsibilities in rear areas as early as possible.

b. **Naval Construction Force (NCF).** The NCF is the combined construction units of the Navy, including primarily the mobile construction battalions and the amphibious construction battalions. These units are part of the operating forces and represent the Navy's capability for advanced base construction.

(1) **Naval Construction Regiment (NCR).** When multiple naval mobile construction battalions (NMCBs) are deployed, an accompanying NCR will be deployed to serve as the C2 coordinator for the CATF/CLF and assigned naval construction support units.

(2) **NMCB.** The NMCB provides construction support to Navy, Marine Corps, and other forces in military operations and conducts protection as required by the circumstances of the deployment situation. The NMCB provides a major deliberate construction capability and is employed to provide facilities that require extensive technical control and construction capability. The NMCB can be employed in expanding or constructing airfield complexes, constructing forward operating bases, repairing or developing ports, constructing major temporary or semi-permanent camps, extensively repairing or rebuilding principal bridges, and installing large-scale utilities systems (i.e., well drilling, water distribution systems). When NMCBs are assigned to the LF, these units will normally be attached to the CSS element.

(3) **Amphibious Construction Battalion (PHIBCB).** The PHIBCB provides designated elements to CATF, supports the naval beach group during the initial assault and early phases of an amphibious operation, and assists the landing support element in operations that do not interfere with the PHIBCB's primary mission.

(4) **NCF Planning Considerations.** Engineer planning proceeds concurrently with tactical planning and other CSS planning. The organization for engineer support is based on the tasks to be accomplished and the priority established for principal tasks. The engineer appendix to the OPLAN or OPORD will include priorities for construction, road and bridge repairs, airfield development, concept of engineer operations, and control of Class IV engineer material. Planning considerations include the following:

(a) Capabilities of assigned engineer units.

(b) Requirements for new construction.

(c) Requirements for repair, maintenance, and improvement of facilities such as ports, roads, and airfields.

(d) Transportation and support requirements of engineer support equipment and Class IV construction materials.

(e) Limited beach trafficability of engineer support equipment.

(f) Requirements for the repair, rehabilitation, and operation of existing utilities systems.

(g) Announced priorities for semi-permanent construction.

(h) Requirements for base development as established by higher authority.

Further guidance can be found in JP 3-34, Joint Engineer Operations.

SECTION E. PROTECTION

23. General

Protection of the AF is essential for all operations, but especially during ship-to-shore movement. Prior to commencing combat operations, Navy will normally conduct operations (e.g., air defense, undersea warfare, surface warfare, mine warfare) to gain local maritime and air superiority. Maritime superiority permits the conduct of amphibious operations without prohibitive interference by the opposing force. These operations are normally conducted by forces other than the AF, and may involve aircraft carriers, surface combatants, submarines, mine warfare ships, naval air forces, and other assets. These operations are conducted to counter and neutralize enemy aircraft, submarines, surface combatants, small boats, land-based anti-ship missiles, mines, and other potential threats to the AF. SOF and other naval and joint forces may also be used in the operations. During the planning phase of an amphibious operation, the protection of the ATF and LF is one of the most important considerations.

24. Rehearsal and Movement Security

In formulating plans for movement to the operational area, sea routes and rendezvous points must be carefully selected. Sea routes through mineable waters, or close to enemy shore installations from which the enemy can carry out air, surface, or subsurface attacks, are to be avoided if possible. To minimize probability of detection, routes will be planned to avoid known or probable areas of enemy surveillance. Flexibility must be given in allocation of transit time to permit evasive courses to be steered by movement groups if it becomes necessary to avoid surface or subsurface threats.

a. **Because of similarity between the rehearsal and the actual operation, strict security measures must be enforced during rehearsals.** The reconnaissance for, selection of, and arrangements for the use of the areas in which rehearsal(s) are to be held must be accomplished carefully. Deception measures may be necessary to ensure the security of the rehearsal.

b. Unauthorized observation of the AF or unauthorized communications with external agencies must be prevented. The primary means of limiting unauthorized observation are restricting movements of personnel and ships, and establishing security perimeter patrols around the rehearsal area, both at sea and ashore. Special precautions must be taken to achieve communications security.

c. **The threat of reconnaissance satellites cannot be ignored.** Execution of the rehearsal may have to be timed to coincide with those time periods when satellites cannot observe the rehearsal area, which may or may not coincide with planned execution times. Adjustment to the rehearsal (e.g., selection of misleading terrain, decentralized rehearsals, subordinate rehearsals separated by time and distance, and deliberately executed deception operations) may also be used to mask the purpose, location, and timing of the amphibious operation.

d. In order to avoid detection of rehearsal activities, maximum use of wargaming and simulation will be considered. There are many events that take place in an amphibious operation that lend themselves to simulations. Denying observations of intentions is critical.

25. Communications Security

COMSEC is essential and must be maintained throughout planning.

See JP 6-0, Joint Communications System.

26. Deception

The scope of employment of communications deception and countermeasures will normally be specified in the initiating directive. Additional AF requirements for employment of these techniques will be made known to and coordinated with higher authority during planning.

See JP 3-13.4, Military Deception.

27. Protective Measures

The LF must arrive in the landing area without critical reduction of its combat power. Measures necessary for protection of the LF elements in transit from the sea include all measures taken by any ATF organization operating at sea.

28. Defensive Counterair Operations

Defensive counterair includes all measures designed to detect, identify, intercept, and destroy or negate enemy air and missile forces attempting to attack or penetrate the friendly air environment. These operations employ both active and passive measures to protect US or multinational forces, assets, population centers, and interests.

29. Mine Countermeasures and Mine Warfare

a. **General.** Mining may interfere with the AF's ability to maneuver within the AO, at sea, and on the beach. It may affect advance force operations and ship-to-shore operations through general unloading, and possibly hinder or preclude unloading of the AFOE. Planning for operational timelines, allocation of intelligence collection assets, AF task organization, the rate at which forces are established ashore, and deception operations can be affected by a mine threat. In a mined environment, available organic, national, and theater intelligence assets are obtained and used as soon as possible to gather information. Accomplishing this will enhance the ability of AF units to achieve surprise and rapidly project combat power or build up troops, equipment, and supplies ashore and into objectives located deeper inland.

An MH-53E Sea Dragon conducts mine countermeasure training using the MK-105 sled.

b. **Considerations.** The capability to counter mines and obstacles is essential to the conduct of amphibious operations, particularly ship-to-shore movement. The integration of MCM operations into the overall strategy of a landing plan is a responsibility shared by the ATF and LF commanders. In short, the ATF commander has primary responsibility for MCM operations in the water, and the LF commander is responsible for MCM operations ashore. To facilitate planning, participating commanders should provide detailed requirements for amphibious operations to the ATF commander, or MCMC, if assigned, as early as possible. Considerations should include location and size of the AO in comparison to available MCM assets, slow MCM transit times to the AO, rate of MCM operations to meet established deadlines, and requirements for protecting assets involved in the MCM effort.

Refer to Chapter IV "Amphibious Operations Against Coastal Defenses," for more information on MCM operations and mines.

SECTION F. SEABASING

30. General

Seabasing is the deployment, assembly, command, projection, reconstitution, and re-employment of joint combat power from the sea without reliance on land bases within the JOA. Seabasing can increase the maneuver options for elements ashore by reducing the need to protect elements such as C2 and logistic supplies. The duration of seabasing depends on the tactical situation and the size and intensity of the operation.

For more information on seabasing see NWP 3-62M/MCWP 3-31.7, Seabasing.

31. Components

Depending on the assigned mission, a JFC can select and task-organize a wide range of naval, joint, or multinational forces. The elements comprising the sea base will be chosen based on the mission assigned to a JFC. Employing the seabasing construct provides a JFC with options for closing, assembling, employing, sustaining, and reconstituting forces for amphibious operations. Units that could constitute a sea base should possess a wide range of capabilities that complement each other.

32. Planning Considerations

a. Seabasing provides operational maneuver for ship-to-shore movement and assured access to the joint force during the action phase of amphibious operations while significantly reducing the footprint ashore, and minimizing the permissions required to operate from host nations.

b. The situation on the ground may require the CATF and CLF to minimize the forces ashore. The seabasing construct allows certain LF and ATF support functions to remain aboard ship.

c. With a sustainable logistics tail safely at sea, it leverages the ATF's ability to operate from international waters, while providing support for the LF ashore.

d. Seabasing also increases the maneuver options for LF ashore by reducing the need to protect elements such as C2 and logistic supplies.

e. Continuous sustainment of the sea base and supported forces ashore requires logistic operations and plans personnel to operate across the range of logistics. Limited logistic support will be available to support other forces ashore that arrived in the operational area via means other than the sea base. Planning considerations for sea base logistic support are as follows:

(1) Infrastructure — the physical requirements and facilities needed to support and sustain force capability.

(2) Capacity — the measure of how much force capability can be supported.

(3) Rate — how fast things can be accomplished to support force capability over a given time under standard sets of conditions.

(4) Interoperability — the degree to which seabasing can seamlessly integrate and support force capability.

(5) Survivability — the ability to defend the sea base.

(6) Accessibility — the flexibility to bypass or operate within the physical constraints presented by terrain, hydrography, weather, depth of operations, and level of threat.

APPENDIX A
LANDING FORCE LOGISTICS PLANNING

1. Landing Force Supply Planning

The types and quantities of supplies taken into the AOA/AO directly affect the requirement for air and surface transportation. For ease of control and planning for an amphibious operation, requirements for supply support are stated under two major categories — LF supplies and resupply.

a. **Determination of Requirements.** Overall requirements for supply support of the LF indicate the total tonnage to be moved into the AOA/AO during a given period. Based on the statement of overall requirements for supply support, general requirements for the logistic support of the LF, including requirements for assault shipping and aerial resupply, are reported to higher authority.

(1) **Days of Supply (DOS).** The first step in estimating overall requirements for supply support is to determine the DOS. The DOS is based on standard Service planning factors and logistics planning factors for the operation. In calculating the DOS, the requirements for each separate class of supply are considered.

(2) **Stockage Objective.** The second step is to calculate the stockage objective for each class of supply. In operations of limited scope, limiting the stockage objective to 30 DOS may be desirable. However, even the limited objective may not be reached until the latter stages of the assault.

(3) **Factors Influencing Stockage Objective.** The amounts and types of supplies carried in the assault shipping must be compatible with the shipping space available and must meet the minimum requirements for support of the LF until termination of the amphibious operation. Before the stockage objective can be finally determined, the following factors must be carefully considered:

(a) Adversary capabilities.

(b) Availability of fixed-wing cargo aircraft.

(c) Availability of shipping and distances involved.

(d) Availability of ports and airfields.

(4) **Landing force operational reserve material (LFORM)/mission load allowance** is a package of contingency supplies pre-positioned in amphibious ships to reduce loading time in contingencies. The LFORM package comprises Classes I (packaged operational rations), III(A) and III(W) (petroleum, oils, and lubricants), IV (field fortification material), and V(A) and V(W) (ammunition). However, other selected items

can be included to support specific deployments and/or contingency operations at the discretion of the CLF.

b. **The Plan for Landing Supplies.** In coordination with the CATF, the CLF develops plans for selective unloading of supplies in the objective area. The CATF allocates landing ships and craft required to carry supplies from ship to shore and to establish floating dumps. Together, in the plan for landing supplies, the CLF and CATF plan the ship-to-shore movement of supplies and equipment so that it is responsive to LF requirements. TACLOG groups are established to ensure that responsiveness is achieved. In developing the plan for landing supplies, the following factors are considered:

(1) Types and amounts of supplies to be carried ashore by LF units as prescribed loads.

(2) Types and amounts of supplies to be established in floating dumps and pre-staged helicopter-lifted supplies.

(3) Levels of supply to be established ashore.

(4) Techniques that ensure the orderly, rapid buildup of supply levels ashore, such as:

(a) Use of landing craft and vehicles carrying assault troops to ferry designated types and amounts of supplies ashore on each trip.

US Marine MV-22 Osprey's provide lift for resupply and replacements for the landing force ashore.

(b) Provision for the mobile loading of each vehicle of the LF not involved in the lift of the assault elements ashore.

(c) Means for facilitating the transfer of supplies from ship to shore, including the most efficient use of such items as pallets, containers, cargo nets, and slings.

c. **Supply Operations Ashore.** During the early stages of the attack, the ATF ships are the primary supply source for the LF. Prior to the establishment of landing support ashore, critical supplies are furnished directly to the requesting unit by the CSS element, through the TACLOG group, from amphibious shipping. Subsequent to the establishment of landing support units ashore, combat elements are supplied through shore-based CSS facilities. As the operation progresses, several supply installations may be established within the beachhead by other CSS units of the LF. When adequate supply levels have been attained in installations ashore and transportation means are available, supply support of LF units will be provided from these areas. Supply sources may be augmented by the aerial delivery of supplies by fixed-wing aircraft operating from bases outside of landing area. The ships of the ATF continue as the primary source of immediate resupply for the LF.

(1) **Supply control and distribution** are accomplished at both the LF level and at the lowest levels that have an organic supply capability; e.g., battalion. These levels are most important within the overall function of supply, especially during the critical transition from sea-based to shore-based supply support during an amphibious operation. Adherence to the following principles during the transitional and ashore stages of the operation will result in a control and distribution system that is reliable, flexible, and responsive.

(a) **Control.** The flow of supply should be direct from source to consumer; supplies should be rehandled as infrequently as possible.

(b) **Distribution.** The distribution system may provide either supply point distribution, wherein the unit draws supplies from a central location, or unit distribution, wherein the supplying agency delivers supplies to the unit. During the initial stages of the amphibious assault, unit distribution is normally required and is effected through the organization for landing support in conjunction with the TACLOG group and consists of delivery of pre-positioned emergency supplies. During later stages of the operation, as additional CSS units phase ashore and supplies are built up, supply point distribution may be employed.

(2) **Salvage** is the term applied to materiel that has become unserviceable, lost, abandoned, or discarded, but which is recoverable. It includes captured adversary equipment. Unit commanders at all levels are responsible for salvage collection and evacuation within their respective unit areas. Designated salvage organizations receive and process salvage received from combat units.

2. Landing Force Maintenance Planning

Maintenance operations support the administrative and functional needs of the LF units at the organizational (unit) and intermediate levels. LF commanders, the senior CSS unit commander, and the LF logistics staff officer and staff share responsibilities for maintenance planning.

a. **Planning Considerations.** The LF maintenance plan should be based on an assumption that initial capabilities in the AOA/AO, especially once ashore, will be limited. The maintenance plan should provide for:

(1) Clearly defined maintenance capabilities and responsibilities during each phase of the operation.

(2) Early landing of maintenance personnel and critical repair parts.

(3) Simple and responsive maintenance request procedures, including use of floating dumps if applicable.

(4) Decentralized execution of maintenance action through contact teams and mobile repair facilities.

(5) Executing repairs as rapidly and as close to the using unit as possible.

(6) Coordinated employment of maintenance support with other CSS functions.

(7) Provisions for battlefield salvage of large combat systems or vehicles via maintenance channels.

b. **Planning Requirements.** All LF units must determine their maintenance requirements and compare them against their organic (unit level) capabilities. Shortfalls must be identified during the planning process and forwarded to higher and/or supporting unit commands. An estimate of maintenance requirements includes an in-depth examination of each of the following:

(1) Available personnel; required skills and quantity.

(2) Repair parts; consumables and secondary repairable items.

(3) Tools and equipment; by type, quantity, and location.

(4) Facilities support requirements during embarkation, movement, rehearsal, and action (including BSAs and CSSAs).

(5) Requesting and reporting procedures, including data requirements, routing, distribution, and means of transmission.

(6) Transportation requirements for equipment recovery and salvage, contact teams, and distribution of repair parts and materials.

(7) External maintenance units or agencies available for support.

(8) Assistance/coordination with other subordinate CSS elements.

3. Landing Force Transportation Planning

Transportation consists of movement of personnel, supplies, and equipment by water, air, or surface means. Transportation requirements are mainly based on **two factors — the character of the operation and the types and quantities of supplies required in the objective area**. Transportation tasks may include unloading and transfer of supplies ashore, forwarding of LF supplies and materials from the landing site(s), and operating the land transportation system (marking of routes, convoy control, etc.) within the AO.

a. Transportation Requirements

(1) Requirements are normally stated in tons of supplies and equipment, gallons of fuel, or number of personnel to be moved during a particular period. The estimated distances of these movements will also play a key role in the planning estimate.

(2) Detailed requirements state the specific numbers, types, and capacities of vehicles, bulk fuel facilities, and aircraft required at specific times and places. They also state the schedules of operation and routes to be traversed.

(3) Plans for the employment of engineer, maintenance, service, and control personnel can be developed. Particular consideration must be given to the supply of aviation fuel. Although initiating air operations ashore through the use of packaged fuel is possible, continuing supply of aviation fuel requires the installation of bulk fuel systems and a high-capacity mobile liquid fuel transport capability ashore as soon as possible.

(4) The demarkation line between ATF and LF responsibilities for bulk petroleum, oils, and lubricants supply is normally the high water mark. Delivering and transporting fuel to internal storage distribution areas is an LF responsibility.

b. Planning Considerations. Transportation planning is influenced by:

(1) The adequacy of the LOCs in the landing area (roads, rail, and waterway).

(2) The extent of degradation of LOCs by weather, adversary action, and use.

(3) The requirements for handling bulk fuel and water.

(4) The availability of helicopters for transportation.

c. Transportation in the AO

(1) The CLF, in coordination with the CATF, develops plans to sustain LF operations ashore.

(2) The CLF establishes priorities for movement and ensures adequate movement and traffic control within the LF operational area, optimizing the use of assets and facilities.

(3) The LF CSS plan makes provision for:

(a) Transportation assets scheduled for landing during the initial landing and unloading period.

(b) Combat loads prescribed for each vehicle prior to landing and once ashore.

(c) Attachment of transportation units to combat, combat support, or CSS elements of the LF.

(d) LF traffic control measures employed ashore.

APPENDIX B
REFERENCES

The development of JP 3-02 is based upon the following primary references:

1. **Chairman of the Joint Chiefs of Staff**

    a. CJCSM 3500.04E, *Universal Joint Task List.*

    b. CJCSM 6231 Series, *Manual for Employing Joint Tactical Communications System.*

2. **Joint Publications**

    a. JP 1, *Doctrine for the Armed Forces of the United States.*

    b. JP 1-02, *Department of Defense Dictionary of Military and Associated Terms.*

    c. JP 2-0, *Joint Intelligence.*

    d. JP 2-01.3, *Joint Intelligence Preparation of the Operational Environment (JIPOE).*

    e. JP 3-0, *Joint Operations.*

    f. JP 3-01, *Countering Air and Missile Threats.*

    g. JP 3-04, *Joint Shipboard Helicopter Operations.*

    h. JP 3-05, *Doctrine for Joint Special Operations.*

    i. JP 3-09, *Joint Fire Support.*

    j. JP 3-11, *Operations in Chemical, Biological, Radiological, and Nuclear (CBRN) Environments.*

    k. JP 3-15, *Barriers, Obstacles, and Mine Warfare for Joint Operations.*

    l. JP 3-18, *Joint Forcible Entry Operations.*

    m. JP 3-30, *Command and Control for Joint Air Operations.*

    n. JP 3-31, *Command and Control for Joint Land Operations.*

    o. JP 3-32, *Command and Control for Joint Maritime Operations.*

    p. JP 3-52, *Joint Airspace Control in the Combat Zone.*

q. JP 4-0, *Joint Logistics.*

r. JP 4-02, *Health Service Support.*

s. JP 5-0, *Joint Operation Planning.*

t. JP 6-0, *Joint Communications System.*

3. **Service Publications**

   a. Naval Doctrine Publication 1, *Naval Warfare.*

   b. FM 3-0, *Operations.*

   c. FM 100-7, *Decisive Force: The Army in Theater Operations.*

   d. FM 100-17, *Mobilization, Deployment, Redeployment, Demobilization.*

   e. FM 100-26, *The Air/Ground Operations Systems.*

   f. NTTP 3-02.1.3, *Amphibious/Expeditionary Operations Air Control.*

   g. NTTP 3-02.14, *The Naval Beach Group.*

   h. NWP 3-02.21, *MSC Support of Amphibious Operations.*

   i. Marine Corps Doctrine Publication (MCDP) 1, *Warfighting.*

   j. MCDP-6, *Command and Control.*

   k. MCWP 3-13, *Employment of Amphibious Assault Vehicles.*

   l. MCWP 3-25.10, *Low Altitude Air Defense Handbook.*

   m. MCWP 3-23, *Offensive Air Support.*

4. **Multi-Service Publications**

   a. MCWP 3-31.5/NTTP 3-02.1M, *Ship to Shore Movement.*

   b. MCWP 3-31.6/NTTP 3-02.2, *Supporting Arms Coordination in Amphibious Operations.*

APPENDIX C
ADMINISTRATIVE INSTRUCTIONS

1. User Comments

Users in the field are highly encouraged to submit comments on this publication to: Commander, United States Joint Forces Command, Joint Warfighting Center, ATTN: Joint Doctrine Group, 116 Lake View Parkway, Suffolk, VA 23435-2697. These comments should address content (accuracy, usefulness, consistency, and organization), writing, and appearance.

2. Authorship

The lead agent for this publication is the US Navy. The Joint Staff doctrine sponsor for this publication is the Director for Operational Plans and Joint Force Development (J-7).

3. Supersession

This publication supersedes JP 3-02, 19 September 2001, *Joint Doctrine for Amphibious Operations*.

4. Change Recommendations

a. Recommendations for urgent changes to this publication should be submitted:

```
TO:       CNO WASHINGTON DC//N511//
INFO:     JOINT STAFF WASHINGTON DC//J7-JEDD//
          CDRUSJFCOM SUFFOLK VA//JT10//
```

Routine changes should be submitted electronically to Commander, Joint Warfighting Center, Joint Doctrine Group and info the Lead Agent and the Director for Operational Plans and Joint Force Development J-7/JEDD via the CJCS JEL at http://www.dtic.mil/doctrine.

b. When a Joint Staff directorate submits a proposal to the Chairman of the Joint Chiefs of Staff that would change source document information reflected in this publication, that directorate will include a proposed change to this publication as an enclosure to its proposal. The Military Services and other organizations are requested to notify the Joint Staff J-7 when changes to source documents reflected in this publication are initiated.

c. Record of Changes:

CHANGE NUMBER	COPY NUMBER	DATE OF CHANGE	DATE ENTERED	POSTED BY	REMARKS

5. Distribution of Publications

Local reproduction is authorized and access to unclassified publications is unrestricted. However, access to and reproduction authorization for classified joint publications must be in accordance with DOD Regulation 5200.1-R, *Information Security Program*.

6. Distribution of Electronic Publications

a. Joint Staff J-7 will not print copies of JPs for distribution. Electronic versions are available on JDEIS at https://jdeis.js.mil (NIPRNET), and https://jdeis.js.smil.mil (SIPRNET) and on the JEL at http://www.dtic.mil/doctrine (NIPRNET).

b. Only approved joint publications and joint test publications are releasable outside the combatant commands, Services, and Joint Staff. Release of any classified joint publication to foreign governments or foreign nationals must be requested through the local embassy (Defense Attaché Office) to DIA Foreign Liaison Office, PO-FL, Room 1E811, 7400 Pentagon, Washington, DC 20301-7400.

c. CD-ROM. Upon request of a JDDC member, the Joint Staff J-7 will produce and deliver one CD-ROM with current joint publications.

GLOSSARY
PART I — ABBREVIATIONS AND ACRONYMS

AADC	area air defense commander
AATCC	amphibious air traffic control center
AAV	amphibious assault vehicle
ACA	airspace control authority
ACE	aviation combat element (MAGTF)
ACM	airspace coordinating measure
ACO	airspace control order
ACP	airspace control plan
ADC	air defense commander
ADS	air defense section
ADZ	amphibious defense zone
AE	assault echelon
AF	amphibious force
AFOE	assault follow-on echelon
ALLOREQ	air allocation request
AO	area of operations
AOA	amphibious objective area
APF	afloat pre-positioning force
ASCS	air support coordination section
ASR	air support request
ATCS	air traffic control section
ATF	amphibious task force
ATG	amphibious task group
ATO	air tasking order
BLT	battalion landing team
BSA	beach support area
C2	command and control
CAP	crisis action planning
CAS	close air support
CATF	commander, amphibious task force
CBRN	chemical, biological, radiological, and nuclear
CCO	central control officer
CE	command element (MAGTF)
CJCSM	Chairman of the Joint Chiefs of Staff manual
CLA	landing craft air cushion launch area
CLF	commander, landing force
CLZ	landing craft air cushion landing zone
CO	commanding officer
COA	course of action
COG	center of gravity
COMSEC	communications security

CONOPS	concept of operations
CP	command post
CRTS	casualty receiving and treatment ship
CSS	combat service support
CSSA	combat service support area
CWC	composite warfare commander
DASC	direct air support center
DOS	days of supply
DZ	drop zone
EA	electronic attack
EMCON	emission control
EPW	enemy prisoner of war
EW	electronic warfare
FC	fires cell
FFC	force fires coordinator
FFCC	force fires coordination center
FHA	foreign humanitarian assistance
FM	field manual (Army)
FSA	fire support area
FSC	fire support coordinator
FSCC	fire support coordination center
FSCL	fire support coordination line
FSCM	fire support coordination measure
G-6	assistant chief of staff for communications
GCE	ground combat element (MAGTF)
HCS	helicopter coordination section
HDC	helicopter direction center
HF	high frequency
HIDACZ	high-density airspace control zone
HLZ	helicopter landing zone
HSS	health service support
HST	helicopter support team
HWM	high water mark
INFOSEC	information security
IR	intelligence requirement
ISR	intelligence, surveillance, and reconnaissance
JFACC	joint force air component commander
JFC	joint force commander
JFSOCC	joint force special operations component command

JIOC	joint intelligence operations center
JIPOE	joint intelligence preparation of the operational environment
JISE	joint intelligence support element
JLOTS	joint logistics over-the-shore
JOA	joint operations area
JOPES	Joint Operation Planning and Execution System
JP	joint publication
JTF	joint task force
LCAC	landing craft, air cushion
LCE	logistics combat element (MAGTF)
LCO	landing craft air cushion control officer
LCS	landing craft air cushion control ship
LF	landing force
LFORM	landing force operational reserve material
LFSP	landing force support party
LHA	amphibious assault ship (general purpose)
LHD	amphibious assault ship (multipurpose)
LOC	line of communications
LOD	line of departure
LOTS	logistics over-the-shore
LPD	amphibious transport dock
LSD	dock landing ship
LZ	landing zone
MACCS	Marine air command and control system
MAGTF	Marine air-ground task force
MCDP	Marine Corps doctrine publication
MCM	mine countermeasures
MCMC	mine countermeasures commander
MCRP	Marine Corps reference publication
MCWP	Marine Corps warfighting publication
MEB	Marine expeditionary brigade
MEF	Marine expeditionary force
METOC	meteorological and oceanographic
MEU	Marine expeditionary unit
MOE	measure of effectiveness
MOPP	mission-oriented protective posture
MPF	maritime pre-positioning force
MSC	Military Sealift Command
MSOC	Marine special operations company
N-6	Navy component communications staff officer
NCF	naval construction force
NCR	naval construction regiment
NEO	noncombatant evacuation operation

nm	nautical mile
NMCB	naval mobile construction battalion
NSFS	naval surface fire support
NTTP	Navy tactics, techniques, and procedures
NWP	Navy warfare publication
OPCON	operational control
OPDS	offshore petroleum discharge system
OPGEN	operation general matter
OPLAN	operation plan
OPORD	operation order
OPSEC	operations security
OPTASK	operation task
OTH	over the horizon
PCO	primary control officer
PHIBCB	amphibious construction battalion
PIR	priority intelligence requirement
POE	port of embarkation
RADC	regional air defense commander
ROE	rules of engagement
RO/RO	roll-on/roll-off
SAC	supporting arms coordinator
SACC	supporting arms coordination center
SADC	sector air defense commander
SCO	secondary control officer
SFCP	shore fire control party
SIPRNET	SECRET Internet Protocol Router Network
SOF	special operations forces
SPINS	special instructions
SPMAGTF	special purpose Marine air-ground task force
SZ	surf zone
TA	target acquisition
TAC(A)	tactical air coordinator (airborne)
TACC	tactical air command center (Marine Corps); tactical air control center (Navy)
TACLOG	tactical-logistical
TACON	tactical control
TACP	tactical air control party
TADC	tactical air direction center
TAO	tactical air officer
TAOC	tactical air operations center (Marine Corps)
TIC	target information center

TIM	toxic industrial material
UAS	unmanned aircraft system
USTRANSCOM	United States Transportation Command
VLZ	vertical landing zone
VSW	very shallow water
VTOL	vertical takeoff and landing

PART II — TERMS AND DEFINITIONS

Unless otherwise annotated, this publication is the proponent for all terms and definitions found in the glossary. Upon approval, JP 1-02, *Department of Defense Dictionary of Military and Associated Terms*, will reflect this publication as the source document for these terms and definitions.

action phase. In amphibious operations, the period of time between the arrival of the landing forces of the amphibious force in the operational area and the accomplishment of their mission. (This term and its definition modify the existing term and its definition and are approved for inclusion in JP 1-02.)

advance force. A temporary organization within the amphibious task force, which precedes the main body to the objective area, for preparing the objective for the main assault by conducting such operations as reconnaissance, seizure of supporting positions, mine countermeasures, preliminary bombardment, underwater demolitions, and air support. (This term and its definition modify the existing term and its definition and are approved for inclusion in JP 1-02.)

afloat pre-positioning force. Shipping maintained in full operational status to afloat pre-position military equipment and supplies in support of combatant commanders' operation plans. The afloat pre-positioning force consists of the three maritime pre-positioning ships squadrons, the Army's afloat pre-positioning stocks-3 ships, and the Navy, Defense Logistics Agency, and Air Force ships. Also called APF. (This term and its definition modify the existing term and its definition and are approved for inclusion in JP 1-02.)

airspace control area. Airspace that is laterally defined by the boundaries of the operational area, and may be subdivided into airspace control sectors. (JP 1-02. SOURCE: JP 3-01)

airspace control authority. The commander designated to assume overall responsibility for the operation of the airspace control system in the airspace control area. Also called ACA. (JP 1-02. SOURCE: JP 3-01)

air support coordination section. In amphibious operations, the section of the Navy tactical air control center designated to coordinate, control, and integrate all direct support aircraft (i.e., close air support) and assault support operations. Also called ASCS. (Approved for inclusion in JP 1-02.)

air traffic control section. In amphibious operations, the section of the Navy tactical air control center designed to provide initial safe passage, radar control, and surveillance for close air support aircraft in the operational area. Also called ATCS. (Approved for inclusion in JP 1-02.)

air transport group. None. (Approved for removal from JP 1-02.)

amphibious assault. The principal type of amphibious operation that involves establishing a force on a hostile or potentially hostile shore. (JP 1-02. SOURCE: JP 3-02)

amphibious assault area. None. (Approved for removal from JP 1-02.)

amphibious assault landing. None. (Approved for removal from JP 1-02.)

amphibious assault ship (general purpose). A naval ship designed to embark, deploy, and land elements of a landing force in an assault by helicopters, landing craft, amphibious vehicles, and by combinations of these methods. Also called LHA. (JP 1-02. SOURCE: JP 3-04)

amphibious assault ship (multipurpose). A naval ship designed to embark, deploy, and land elements of a landing force in an assault by helicopters, landing craft, amphibious vehicles, and by combinations of these methods. Also called LHD. (This term and its definition modify the existing term "amphibious assault ship (dock)" and its definition and are approved for inclusion in JP 1-02.)

amphibious breaching. The conduct of a deliberate breaching operation specifically designed to overcome antilanding defenses in order to conduct an amphibious assault. (Approved for inclusion in JP 1-02.)

amphibious chart. None. (Approved for removal from JP 1-02.)

amphibious command ship. None. (Approved for removal from JP 1-02.)

amphibious construction battalion. A permanently commissioned naval unit, subordinate to the commander, naval beach group, designed to provide an administrative unit from which personnel and equipment are formed in tactical elements and made available to appropriate commanders to operate pontoon causeways, transfer barges, warping tugs, and assault bulk fuel systems, and to meet salvage requirements of the naval beach party. Also called PHIBCB. (This term and its definition modify the existing term and its definition and are approved for inclusion in JP 1-02.)

amphibious control group. None. (Approved for removal from JP 1-02.)

amphibious defense zone. The area encompassing the amphibious objective area and the adjoining airspace required by accompanying naval forces for the purpose of air defense. Also called an ADZ. (Approved for inclusion in JP 1-02.)

amphibious demonstration. A type of amphibious operation conducted for the purpose of deceiving the enemy by a show of force with the expectation of deluding the enemy into a course of action unfavorable to him. (JP 1-02. SOURCE: JP 3-02)

amphibious force. An amphibious task force and a landing force together with other forces that are trained, organized, and equipped for amphibious operations. Also called AF. (JP 1-02. SOURCE: JP 3-02)

amphibious group. None. (Approved for removal from JP 1-02.)

amphibious lift. The total capacity of assault shipping utilized in an amphibious operation, expressed in terms of personnel, vehicles, and measurement or weight tons of supplies. (JP 1-02. SOURCE: JP 3-02)

amphibious objective area. A geographical area (delineated for command and control purposes in the initiating directive) within which is located the objective(s) to be secured by the amphibious force. This area must be of sufficient size to ensure accomplishment of the amphibious force's mission and must provide sufficient area for conducting necessary sea, air, and land operations. Also called AOA. (This term and its definition modify the existing term and its definition and are approved for inclusion in JP 1-02.)

amphibious objective study. None. (Approved for removal from JP 1-02.)

amphibious operation. A military operation launched from the sea by an amphibious force, embarked in ships or craft with the primary purpose of introducing a landing force ashore to accomplish the assigned mission. (JP 1-02. SOURCE: JP 3-02)

amphibious planning. The process of planning for an amphibious operation, distinguished by the necessity for concurrent, parallel, and detailed planning by all participating forces. The planning pattern is cyclical in nature, composed of a series of analyses and judgments of operational situations, each stemming from those that have preceded. (JP 1-02. SOURCE: JP 3-02)

amphibious raid. A type of amphibious operation involving swift incursion into or temporary occupation of an objective followed by a planned withdrawal. (JP 1-02. SOURCE: JP 3-02)

amphibious reconnaissance. None. (Approved for removal from JP 1-02.)

amphibious reconnaissance unit. None. (Approved for removal from JP 1-02.)

amphibious shipping. Organic Navy ships specifically designed to transport, land, and support landing forces in amphibious assault operations and capable of being loaded or unloaded by naval personnel without external assistance in the amphibious objective area. (JP 1-02. SOURCE: JP 3-02)

amphibious squadron. A tactical and administrative organization composed of amphibious assault shipping to transport troops and their equipment for an amphibious assault operation. Also called PHIBRON. (JP 1-02. SOURCE: JP 3-02)

amphibious striking forces. None. (Approved for removal from JP 1-02.)

amphibious task force. A Navy task organization formed to conduct amphibious operations. The amphibious task force, together with the landing force and other forces, constitutes the amphibious force. Also called ATF. (JP 1-02. SOURCE: JP 3-02)

amphibious transport dock. A ship designed to transport and land troops, equipment, and supplies by means of embarked landing craft, amphibious vehicles, and helicopters. Designated as LPD. (JP 1-02. SOURCE: JP 3-02)

amphibious transport group. A subdivision of an amphibious task force composed primarily of transport ships. The size of the transport group will depend upon the scope of the operation. Ships of the transport group will be combat-loaded to support the landing force scheme of maneuver ashore. A transport unit will usually be formed to embark troops and equipment to be landed over a designated beach or to embark all helicopter-borne troops and equipment. (JP 1-02. SOURCE: JP 3-02)

amphibious vehicle. A wheeled or tracked vehicle capable of operating on both land and water. (JP 1-02. SOURCE: JP 3-02)

amphibious vehicle availability table. A tabulation of the type and number of amphibious vehicles available primarily for assault landings and for support of other elements of the operation. (JP 1-02. SOURCE: JP 3-02)

amphibious vehicle employment plan. A plan showing in tabular form the planned employment of amphibious vehicles in landing operations, including their employment after the initial movement to the beach. (JP 1-02. SOURCE: JP 3-02)

amphibious vehicle launching area. An area, in the vicinity of and to seaward of the line of departure, to which landing ships proceed and launch amphibious vehicles. (JP 1-02. SOURCE: JP 3-02)

amphibious withdrawal. A type of amphibious operation involving the extraction of forces by sea in ships or craft from a hostile or potentially hostile shore. (JP 1-02. SOURCE: JP 3-02)

approach schedule. In amphibious operations, this schedule indicates, for each scheduled wave, the time of departure from the rendezvous area, from the line of departure, and from other control points and the time of arrival at the beach. (This term and its definition modify the existing term and its definition and are approved for inclusion in JP 1-02.)

area air defense commander. Within a unified command, subordinate unified command, or joint task force, the commander will assign overall responsibility for air defense to a single commander. Normally, this will be the component commander with the preponderance of air defense capability and the command, control, and communications capability to plan and execute integrated air defense operations. Representation from the other components involved will be provided, as appropriate, to the area air defense commander's headquarters. Also called AADC. (JP 1-02. SOURCE: JP 3-52)

area of operations. An operational area defined by the joint force commander for land and maritime forces. Areas of operation do not typically encompass the entire operational area of the joint force commander, but should be large enough for component commanders to accomplish their missions and protect their forces. Also called AO. (JP 1-02. SOURCE: JP 3-0)

assault. 1. The climax of an attack, closing with the enemy in hand-to-hand fighting. 2. In an amphibious operation, the period of time between the arrival of the major assault forces of the amphibious task force in the objective area and the accomplishment of the amphibious task force mission. (JP 1-02. SOURCE: JP 3-02). 3. To make a short, violent, but well-ordered attack against a local objective, such as a gun emplacement, a fort, or a machine gun nest. 4. A phase of an airborne operation beginning with delivery by air of the assault echelon of the force into the objective area and extending through attack of assault objectives and consolidation of the initial airhead. (JP 1-02. SOURCE: JP 3-18)

assault area. None. (Approved for removal from JP 1-02.)

assault area diagram. None. (Approved for removal from JP 1-02.)

assault breaching. A part of amphibious breaching in support of an amphibious assault involving a fire support mission using precision guided munitions to neutralize mines and obstacles in the surf zone and on the beach. (Approved for inclusion in JP 1-02.)

assault craft. A landing craft or amphibious vehicle primarily employed for landing troops and equipment in the assault waves of an amphibious operation. (JP 1-02. SOURCE: JP 3-02)

assault craft unit. A permanently commissioned naval organization, subordinate to the commander, naval beach group, that contains landing craft and crews necessary to provide lighterage required in an amphibious operation. Also called ACU. (JP 1-02. SOURCE: JP 3-02)

assault echelon. In amphibious operations, the element of a force comprised of tailored units and aircraft assigned to conduct the initial assault on the operational area. Also called AE. (JP 1-02. SOURCE: JP 3-02)

assault follow-on echelon. In amphibious operations, that echelon of the assault troops, vehicles, aircraft, equipment, and supplies that, though not needed to initiate the assault, is required to support and sustain the assault. In order to accomplish its purpose, it is normally required in the objective area no later than five days after commencement of the assault landing. Also called AFOE. (JP 1-02. SOURCE: JP 3-02)

assault phase. In an airborne operation, a phase beginning with delivery by air of the assault echelon of the force into the objective area and extending through attack of assault objectives and consolidation of the initial airhead. (This term and its definition modify the existing term and its definition and are approved for inclusion in JP 1-02 and sourced to JP 3-18.)

assault schedule. In amphibious operations, this schedule provides the formation, composition, and timing of waves landing over the beach. (This term and its definition modify the existing term and its definition and are approved for inclusion in JP 1-02.)

assault shipping. Shipping assigned to the amphibious task force and utilized for transporting assault troops, vehicles, equipment, and supplies to the objective area. (JP 1-02. SOURCE: JP 3-02)

attack group. A subordinate task organization of the Navy forces of an amphibious task force. It is composed of assault shipping and supporting naval units designated to transport, protect, land, and initially support a landing group. (This term and its definition modify the existing term and its definition and are approved for inclusion in JP 1-02.)

battalion landing team. In an amphibious operation, an infantry battalion normally reinforced by necessary combat and service elements; the basic unit for planning an assault landing. Also called BLT. (JP 1-02. SOURCE: JP 3-02)

beach. 1. The area extending from the shoreline inland to a marked change in physiographic form or material, or to the line of permanent vegetation (coastline). 2. In amphibious operations, that portion of the shoreline designated for landing of a tactical organization. (JP 1-02. SOURCE: JP 3-02)

beachhead. A designated area on a hostile or potentially hostile shore that, when seized and held, ensures the continuous landing of troops and materiel, and provides maneuver space requisite for subsequent projected operations ashore. (JP 1-02. SOURCE: JP 3-02)

beach minefield. None. (Approved for removal from JP 1-02.)

beach organization. None. (Approved for removal from JP 1-02.)

beach party. The Navy component of the landing force support party under the tactical control of the landing force support party commander. (This term and its definition modify the existing term and its definition and are approved for inclusion in JP 1-02.)

beach reserves. None. (Approved for removal from JP 1-02.)

beach support area. In amphibious operations, the area to the rear of a landing force or elements thereof, established and operated by shore party units, which contains the facilities for the unloading of troops and materiel and the support of the forces ashore; it includes facilities for the evacuation of wounded, enemy prisoners of war, and captured materiel. Also called BSA. (JP 1-02. SOURCE: JP 3-02)

boat diagram. None. (Approved for removal from JP 1-02.)

boat group. The basic organization of landing craft. One boat group is organized for each battalion landing team (or equivalent) to be landed in the first trip of landing craft or amphibious vehicles. (JP 1-02. SOURCE: JP 3-02)

boat lane. A lane for amphibious assault landing craft, which extends from the line of departure to the beach. (This term and its definition modify the existing term and its definition and are approved for inclusion in JP 1-02.)

boat space. The space and weight factor used to determine the capacity of boats, landing craft, and amphibious vehicles. With respect to landing craft and amphibious vehicles, it is based on the requirements of one person with individual equipment. The person is assumed to weigh 224 pounds and to occupy 13.5 cubic feet of space. (JP 1-02. SOURCE: JP 3-02)

carrier strike group. A standing naval task group consisting of a carrier, embarked airwing, surface combatants, and submarines as assigned in direct support, operating in mutual support with the task of destroying hostile submarine, surface, and air forces within the group's assigned operational area and striking at targets along hostile shore lines or projecting power inland. Also called CSG. (This term and its definition modify the existing term "carrier battle group" and its definition and are approved for inclusion in JP 1-02.)

casualty receiving and treatment ship. In amphibious operations, a ship designated to receive, provide treatment for, and transfer casualties. (JP 1-02. SOURCE: JP 3-02)

causeway launching area. An area located near the line of departure but clear of the approach lanes to an area located in the inner transport area. (This term and its definition modify the existing term and its definition and are approved for inclusion in JP 1-02.)

center of gravity. The source of power that provides moral or physical strength, freedom of action, or will to act. Also called COG. (JP 1-02. SOURCE: JP 3-0)

central control officer. The officer designated by the amphibious task force commander for the overall coordination of the waterborne ship-to-shore movement. The central control officer is embarked in the central control ship. Also called CCO. (JP 1-02. SOURCE: JP 3-02)

close support area. Those parts of the ocean operating areas nearest to, but not necessarily in, the objective area. They are assigned to naval support carrier strike groups, surface action groups, surface action units, and certain logistic combat service support elements. (This term and its definition modify the existing term and its definition and are approved for inclusion in JP 1-02.)

colored beach. That portion of usable coastline sufficient for the assault landing of a regimental landing team or similar sized unit. In the event that the landing force consists of a single battalion landing team, a colored beach will be used and no further subdivision of the beach is required. (JP 1-02. SOURCE: JP 3-02)

combat loading. The arrangement of personnel and the stowage of equipment and supplies in a manner designed to conform to the anticipated tactical operation of the organization embarked. Each individual item is stowed so that it can be unloaded at the required time. (JP 1-02. SOURCE: JP 3-02)

combat service support area. An area ashore that is organized to contain the necessary supplies, equipment, installations, and elements to provide the landing force with combat service support throughout the operation. Also called CSSA. (JP 1-02. SOURCE: JP 3-02)

command element. The core element of a Marine air-ground task force that is the headquarters. The command element is composed of the commander, general or executive and special staff sections, headquarters section, and requisite communications support, intelligence, and reconnaissance forces necessary to accomplish the mission. The command element provides command and control, intelligence, and other support essential for effective planning and execution of operations by the other elements of the Marine air-ground task force. The command element varies in size and composition. Also called CE. (This term and its definition modify the existing term and its definition and are approved for inclusion in JP 1-02.)

commander, amphibious task force. The Navy officer designated in the initiating directive as the commander of the amphibious task force. Also called CATF. (This term and its definition modify the existing term and its definition and are approved for inclusion in JP 1-02.)

commander, landing force. The officer designated in the initiating directive as the commander of the landing force for an amphibious operation. Also called CLF. (This term and its definition modify the existing term and its definition and are approved for inclusion in JP 1-02.)

commanding officer of troops. On a ship that has embarked units, a designated officer (usually the senior embarking unit commander) who is responsible for the administration, discipline, and training of all embarked units. Also called COT. (JP 1-02. SOURCE: JP 3-02)

composite warfare commander. An officer to whom the officer in tactical command of a naval task organization may delegate authority to conduct some or all of the offensive and defensive functions of the force. Also called CWC. (This term and its definition modify the existing term and its definition and are approved for inclusion in JP 1-02.)

consecutive voyage charter. None. (Approved for removal from JP 1-02.)

control group. Personnel, ships, and craft designated to control the waterborne ship-to-shore movement. (JP 1-02. SOURCE: JP 3-02)

covering fire. 1. Fire used to protect troops when they are within range of enemy small arms. 2. In amphibious usage, fire delivered prior to the landing to cover preparatory operations such as underwater demolition or mine countermeasures. (This term and its definition modify the existing term and its definition and are approved for inclusion in JP 1-02.)

D-day. See times. (JP 1-02. SOURCE: JP 3-02)

departure point. 1. A navigational check point used by aircraft as a marker for setting course. (JP 1-02. SOURCE: JP 3-17) 2. In amphibious operations, an air control point at the seaward end of the helicopter approach lane system from which helicopter waves are dispatched along the selected helicopter approach lane to the initial point. (JP 1-02. SOURCE: JP 3-02)

deployment diagram. None. (Approved for removal from JP 1-02.)

distant retirement area. In amphibious operations, the sea area located to seaward of the landing area. This area is divided into a number of operating areas to which assault ships may retire and operate in the event of adverse weather or to prevent concentration of ships in the landing area. (This term and its definition modify the existing term and its definition and are approved for inclusion in JP 1-02.)

distant support area. None. (Approved for removal from JP 1-02.)

dock landing ship. A ship designed to transport and launch loaded amphibious craft and/or amphibian vehicles with their crews and embarked personnel and/or equipment and to render limited docking and repair services to small ships and craft. Also called LSD. (This term and its definition modify the existing term "landing ship dock" and its definition and are approved for inclusion in JP 1-02.)

embarkation phase. In amphibious operations, the phase that encompasses the orderly assembly of personnel and materiel and their subsequent loading aboard ships and/or aircraft in a sequence designed to meet the requirements of the landing force concept of operations ashore. (JP 1-02. SOURCE: JP 3-02.1)

embarkation plans. The plans prepared by the landing force and appropriate subordinate commanders containing instructions and information concerning the organization for embarkation, assignment to shipping, supplies and equipment to be embarked, location and assignment of embarkation areas, control and communication arrangements, movement schedules and embarkation sequence, and additional pertinent instructions relating to the embarkation of the landing force. (JP 1-02. SOURCE: JP 3-02)

establishing directive. An order issued to specify the purpose of the support relationship. (Approved for inclusion in JP 1-02.)

evacuation control ship. None. (Approved for removal from JP 1-02.)

fire support area. An appropriate maneuver area assigned to fire support ships by the naval force commander from which they can deliver gunfire support to an amphibious operation. Also called FSA. (JP 1-02. SOURCE: JP 3-09)

fire support station. An exact location at sea within a fire support area from which a fire support ship delivers fire. (JP 1-02. SOURCE: JP 3-02)

floating dump. Emergency supplies preloaded in landing craft, amphibious vehicles, or in landing ships. Floating dumps are located in the vicinity of the appropriate control officer, who directs their landing as requested by the troop commander concerned. (JP 1-02. SOURCE: JP 3-02)

floating reserve. None. (Approved for removal from JP 1-02.)

follow-up. In amphibious operations, the reinforcements and stores carried on transport ships and aircraft (not originally part of the amphibious force) that are offloaded after the assault and assault follow-on echelons have been landed. (JP 1-02. SOURCE: JP 3-02)

follow-up shipping. Ships not originally a part of the amphibious task force but which deliver troops and supplies to the objective area after the action phase has begun. (This term and its definition modify the existing term and its definition and are approved for inclusion in JP 1-02.)

force protection. Preventive measures taken to mitigate hostile actions against Department of Defense personnel (to include family members), resources, facilities, and critical information. Force protection does not include actions to defeat the enemy or protect against accidents, weather, or disease. Also called FP. (JP 1-02. SOURCE: JP 3-0)

general unloading period. In amphibious operations, that part of the ship-to-shore movement in which unloading is primarily logistic in character, and emphasizes speed and volume of unloading operations. It encompasses the unloading of units and cargo from the ships as rapidly as facilities on the beach permit. It proceeds without regard to class, type, or priority of cargo, as permitted by cargo handling facilities ashore. (JP 1-02. SOURCE: JP 3-02)

go no-go. The condition or state of operability of a component or system: "go," functioning properly; or "no-go," not functioning properly. Alternatively, a critical point at which a decision to proceed or not must be made. (JP 1-02)

helicopter coordination section. The section within the Navy tactical air control center that coordinates rotary-wing air operations with all helicopter direction centers and air traffic control center(s) in the amphibious force. Also called HCS. (Approved for inclusion in JP 1-02.)

helicopter direction center. In amphibious operations, the primary direct control agency for the helicopter group/unit commander operating under the overall control of the tactical air control center. Also called HDC. (JP 1-02. SOURCE: JP 3-02)

helicopter transport area. Areas to the seaward and on the flanks of the outer transport and landing ship areas, but preferably inside the area screen, used for launching and/or recovering helicopters. (JP 1-02. SOURCE: JP 3-02)

H-hour. See times. (JP 1-02. SOURCE: JP 3-02)

high-density airspace control zone. Airspace designated in an airspace control plan or airspace control order, in which there is a concentrated employment of numerous and varied weapons and airspace users. A high-density airspace control zone has defined dimensions which usually coincide with geographical features or navigational aids. Access to a high-density airspace control zone is normally controlled by the maneuver commander. The maneuver commander can also direct a more restrictive weapons status within the high-density airspace control zone. Also called HIDACZ. (JP 1-02. SOURCE: JP 3-52)

horizon. None. (Approved for removal from JP 1-02.)

hydrographic reconnaissance. Reconnaissance of an area of water to determine depths, beach gradients, the nature of the bottom, and the location of coral reefs, rocks, shoals, and man-made obstacles. (This term and its definition modify the existing term and its definition and are approved for inclusion in JP 1-02.)

initial reserves. None. (Approved for removal from JP 1-02.)

initial unloading period. In amphibious operations, that part of the ship-to-shore movement in which unloading is primarily tactical in character and must be instantly responsive to landing force requirements. All elements intended to land during this period are serialized. (JP 1-02. SOURCE: JP 3-02)

initiating directive. An order to a subordinate commander to conduct military operations as directed. It is issued by the unified commander, subunified commander, Service component commander, or joint force commander delegated overall responsibility for the operation. (JP 1-02. SOURCE: JP 3-18)

inner transport area. In amphibious operations, an area as close to the landing beach as depth of water, navigational hazards, boat traffic, and enemy action permit, to which transports may move to expedite unloading. (JP 1-02. SOURCE: JP 3-02)

integrated planning. In amphibious operations, the planning accomplished by commanders and staffs of corresponding echelons from parallel chains of command within the amphibious task force. (JP 1-02. SOURCE: JP 3-02)

joint amphibious operation. None. (Approved for removal from JP 1-02.)

joint amphibious task force. None. (Approved for removal from JP 1-02.)

joint logistics over-the-shore operations. Operations in which Navy and Army logistics over-the-shore forces conduct logistics over-the-shore operations together under a joint force commander. Also called JLOTS operations. (JP 1-02. SOURCE: JP 4-01.2)

joint terminal attack controller. A qualified (certified) Service member who, from a forward position, directs the action of combat aircraft engaged in close air support and other offensive air operations. A qualified and current joint terminal attack controller will be recognized across the Department of Defense as capable and authorized to perform terminal attack control. Also called JTAC. (JP 1-02. SOURCE: JP 3-09.3)

landing area. 1. That part of the operational area within which are conducted the landing operations of an amphibious force. It includes the beach, the approaches to the beach, the transport areas, the fire support areas, the airspace above it, and the land included in the advance inland to the initial objective. 2. (Airborne) The general area used for landing troops and materiel either by airdrop or air landing. This area includes one or more drop zones or landing strips. 3. Any specially prepared or selected surface of land, water, or deck designated or used for takeoff and landing of aircraft. (This term and its definition modify the existing term and its definition and are approved for inclusion in JP 1-02.)

landing area diagram. A graphic means of showing, for amphibious operations, the beach designations, boat lanes, organization of the line of departure, scheduled waves, landing ship area, transport areas, and the fire support areas in the immediate vicinity of the boat lanes. (This term and its definition modify the existing term "assault area diagram" and its definition and are approved for inclusion in JP 1-02.)

landing attack. None. (Approved for removal from JP 1-02.)

landing beach. That portion of a shoreline usually required for the landing of a battalion landing team. However, it may also be that portion of a shoreline constituting a tactical locality (such as the shore of a bay) over which a force larger or smaller than a battalion landing team may be landed. (JP 1-02. SOURCE: JP 3-02)

landing craft. A craft employed in amphibious operations, specifically designed for carrying troops and their equipment and for beaching, unloading, and retracting. It is also used for resupply operations. (JP 1-02. SOURCE: JP 3-02)

landing craft and amphibious vehicle assignment table. A table showing the assignment of personnel and materiel to each landing craft and amphibious vehicle and the assignment of the landing craft and amphibious vehicles to waves for the ship-to-shore movement. (JP 1-02. SOURCE: JP 3-02)

landing craft availability table. A tabulation of the type and number of landing craft that will be available from each ship of the transport group. The table is the basis for the assignment of landing craft to the boat groups for the ship-to-shore movement. (JP 1-02. SOURCE: JP 3-02)

landing diagram. A graphic means of illustrating the plan for the ship-to-shore movement. (JP 1-02. SOURCE: JP 3-02)

landing force. A Marine Corps or Army task organization formed to conduct amphibious operations. The landing force, together with the amphibious task force and other forces, constitute the amphibious force. Also called LF. (JP 1-02. SOURCE: JP 3-02)

landing force supplies. None. (Approved for removal from JP 1-02.)

landing force support party. A temporary landing force organization composed of Navy and landing force elements, that facilitates the ship-to-shore movement and provides initial combat support and combat service support to the landing force. The landing force support party is brought into existence by a formal activation order issued by the commander, landing force. Also called LFSP. (JP 1-02. SOURCE: JP 3-02)

landing group. In amphibious operations, a subordinate task organization of the landing force capable of conducting landing operations, under a single tactical command, against a position or group of positions. (JP 1-02. SOURCE: JP 3-02)

landing group commander. In amphibious operations, the officer designated by the commander, landing force as the single tactical commander of a subordinate task organization capable of conducting landing operations against a position or group of positions. (JP 1-02. SOURCE: JP 3-02)

landing plan. In amphibious operations, a collective term referring to all individually prepared naval and landing force documents that, taken together, present in detail all instructions for execution of the ship-to-shore movement. (This term and its definition modify the existing term and definition and are approved for inclusion in the next edition of JP 1-02 and sourced to JP 3-02.)

landing schedule. None. (Approved for removal from JP 1-02.)

landing sequence table. A document that incorporates the detailed plans for ship-to-shore movement of nonscheduled units. (JP 1-02. SOURCE: JP 3-02)

landing ship. An assault ship which is designed for long sea voyages and for rapid unloading over and on to a beach. (JP 1-02. SOURCE: JP 3-02)

landing site. 1. A site within a landing zone containing one or more landing points. 2. In amphibious operations, a continuous segment of coastline over which troops, equipment and supplies can be landed by surface means. (JP 1-02. SOURCE: JP 3-02)

L-hour. See times. (JP 1-02. SOURCE: JP 3-02)

lighterage. The process in which small craft are used to transport cargo or personnel from ship to shore. Lighterage may be performed using amphibians, landing craft, discharge lighters, causeways, and barges. (JP 1-02. SOURCE: JP 4-01.6)

line of departure. 1. In land warfare, a line designated to coordinate the departure of attack elements. Also called LD. (JP 1-02. SOURCE: JP 3-31) 2. In amphibious warfare, a suitably marked offshore coordinating line to assist assault craft to land on designated beaches at scheduled times the seaward end of a boat lane. Also called LOD. (JP 1-02. SOURCE: JP 3-02) (This term and its definition modify the existing term and its definition and are approved for inclusion in JP 1-02.)

logistics over-the-shore operations. The loading and unloading of ships without the benefit of deep draft-capable, fixed port facilities; or as a means of moving forces closer to tactical assembly areas dependent on threat force capabilities. Also called LOTS operations. (JP 1-02. SOURCE: JP 4-01.6)

maritime pre-positioning force operation. A rapid deployment and assembly of a Marine expeditionary force in a secure area using a combination of intertheater airlift and forward-deployed maritime pre-positioning ships. (JP 1-02. SOURCE: JP 4-01.6)

marker ship. None. (Approved for removal from JP 1-02.)

massed fire. 1. The fire of the batteries of two or more ships directed against a single target. 2. Fire from a number of weapons directed at a single target point or small area. (JP 1-02. SOURCE: JP 3-02)

Military Sealift Command. A major command of the US Navy reporting to Commander Fleet Forces Command, and the US Transportation Command's component command responsible for designated common-user sealift transportation services to deploy, employ, sustain, and redeploy US forces on a global basis. Also called MSC. (JP 1-02. SOURCE: JP 4-01.2)

Military Sealift Command-controlled ships. None. (Approved for removal from JP 1-02.)

movement group. Those ships and embarked units that load out and proceed to rendezvous in the objective area. (JP 1-02. SOURCE: JP 3-02)

movement phase. In amphibious operations, the period during which various elements of the amphibious force move from points of embarkation to the operational area. This move may be via rehearsal, staging, or rendezvous areas. The movement phase is completed when the various elements of the amphibious force arrive at their assigned positions in the operational area. (JP 1-02. SOURCE: JP 3-02)

movement plan. In amphibious operations, the naval plan providing for the movement of the amphibious task force to the objective area. It includes information and instructions concerning departure of ships from embarkation points, the passage at sea, and the approach to and arrival in assigned positions in the objective area. (JP 1-02. SOURCE: JP 3-02)

naval beach group. A permanently organized naval command within an amphibious force composed of a commander and staff, a beachmaster unit, an amphibious construction battalion, and assault craft units, designed to provide an administrative group from which required naval tactical components may be made available to the attack force commander and to the amphibious landing force commander. Also called NBG. (This term and its definition modify the existing term and its definition and are approved for inclusion in JP 1-02.)

naval support area. None. (Approved for removal from JP 1-02.)

naval surface fire support. Fire provided by Navy surface gun and missile systems in support of a unit or units. Also called NSFS. (JP 1-02. SOURCE: JP 3-09.3)

nonscheduled units. Units of the landing force held in readiness for landing during the initial unloading period, but not included in either scheduled or on-call waves. This category usually includes certain of the combat support units and most of the combat service support units with higher echelon (division and above) reserve units of the landing force. Their landing is directed when the need ashore can be predicted with a reasonable degree of accuracy. (JP 1-02. SOURCE: JP 3-02)

numbered beach. In amphibious operations, a subdivision of a colored beach, designated for the assault landing of a battalion landing team or similarly sized unit, when landed as part of a larger force. (JP 1-02. SOURCE: JP 3-02)

operational control. Command authority that may be exercised by commanders at any echelon at or below the level of combatant command. Operational control is inherent in combatant command (command authority) and may be delegated within the command. Operational control is the authority to perform those functions of command over subordinate forces involving organizing and employing commands and forces, assigning tasks, designating objectives, and giving authoritative direction necessary to accomplish the mission. Operational control includes authoritative direction over all aspects of military operations and joint training necessary to accomplish missions assigned to the command. Operational control should be exercised through the commanders of subordinate organizations. Normally this authority is exercised through subordinate joint force commanders and Service and/or functional component commanders. Operational control normally provides full authority to organize commands and forces and to employ those forces as the commander in operational control considers necessary to accomplish assigned missions; it does not, in and of itself, include authoritative direction for logistics or matters of administration, discipline, internal organization, or unit training. Also called OPCON. (JP 1-02. SOURCE: JP 1)

organization for combat. In amphibious operations, task organization of landing force units for combat, involving combinations of command, ground and aviation combat, combat support, and combat service support units for accomplishment of missions ashore. (JP 1-02. SOURCE: JP 3-02)

organization for embarkation. In amphibious operations, the organization for embarkation consisting of temporary landing force task organizations established by the commander, landing force and a temporary organization of Navy forces established by the commander, amphibious task force for the purpose of simplifying planning and facilitating the execution of embarkation. (JP 1-02. SOURCE: JP 3-02)

organization for landing. In amphibious operations, the specific tactical grouping of the landing force for the assault. (JP 1-02. SOURCE: JP 3-02)

outer landing ship areas. None. (Approved for removal from JP 1-02.)

outer transport area. In amphibious operations, an area inside the antisubmarine screen to which assault transports proceed initially after arrival in the objective area. (JP 1-02. SOURCE: JP 3-02)

over-the-horizon amphibious operations. An operational initiative launched from beyond visual and radar range of the shoreline. (JP 1-02. SOURCE: JP 3-02)

parallel chains of command. In amphibious operations, a parallel system of command, responding to the interrelationship of Navy, landing force, Air Force, and other major forces assigned, wherein corresponding commanders are established at each subordinate level of all components to facilitate coordinated planning for, and execution of, the amphibious operation. (JP 1-02. SOURCE: JP 3-02)

plan for landing. In amphibious operations, a collective term referring to all individually prepared naval and landing force documents which, taken together, present in detail all instructions for execution of the ship-to-shore movement. (JP 1-02. SOURCE: JP 3-02)

planning directive. In amphibious operations, the plan issued by the designated commander, following receipt of the initiating directive, to ensure that the planning process and interdependent plans developed by the amphibious force will be coordinated, completed in the time allowed, and important aspects not overlooked. (This term and its definition modify the existing term and its definition and are approved for inclusion in JP 1-02.)

planning phase. In amphibious operations, the phase normally denoted by the period extending from the issuance of the initiating directive up to the embarkation phase. The planning phase may occur during movement or at any other time upon receipt of a new mission or change in the operational situation. (This term and its definition modify the existing term and its definition and are approved for inclusion in JP 1-02.)

preassault operations. Operations conducted by the amphibious force upon its arrival in the operational area and prior to H-hour and/or L-hour. (This term and its definition modify the existing term "preassault operation" and its definition and are approved for inclusion in JP 1-02.)

prelanding operations. None. (Approved for removal from JP 1-02.)

primary control officer. In amphibious operations, the officer embarked in a primary control ship assigned to control the movement of landing craft, amphibious vehicles, and landing ships to and from a colored beach. Also called PCO. (JP 1-02. SOURCE: JP 3-02)

primary control ship. In amphibious operations, a ship of the task force designated to provide support for the primary control officer and a combat information center control team for a colored beach. Also called PCS. (JP 1-02. SOURCE: JP 3-02)

regimental landing team. A task organization for landing composed of an infantry regiment reinforced by those elements that are required for initiation of its combat function ashore. (This term and its definition modify the existing term and its definition and are approved for inclusion in JP 1-02.)

regulating point. An anchorage, port, or ocean area to which assault and assault follow-on echelons and follow-up shipping proceed on a schedule, and at which they are normally controlled by the commander, amphibious task force, until needed in the transport area for unloading. (JP 1-02. SOURCE: JP 3-02)

rehearsal phase. In amphibious operations, the period during which the prospective operation is practiced for the purpose of: (1) testing adequacy of plans, the timing of detailed operations, and the combat readiness of participating forces; (2) ensuring that all echelons are familiar with plans; and (3) testing communications-information systems. (JP 1-02. SOURCE: JP 3-02)

rendezvous area. In an amphibious operation, the area in which the landing craft and amphibious vehicles rendezvous to form waves after being loaded, and prior to movement to the line of departure. (JP 1-02. SOURCE: JP 3-02)

salvage group. None. (Approved for removal from JP 1-02.)

screening group. None. (Approved for removal from JP 1-02.)

sea areas. Areas in the amphibious objective area designated for the stationing of amphibious task force ships. Sea areas include inner transport area, sea echelon area, fire support area, etc. (JP 1-02. SOURCE: JP 3-02)

seabasing. The deployment, assembly, command, projection, reconstitution, and re-employment of joint power from the sea without reliance on land bases within the operational area. (This term and its definition modify the existing term and its definition and are approved for inclusion in JP 1-02.)

sea echelon. A portion of the assault shipping which withdraws from or remains out of the transport area during an amphibious landing and operates in designated areas to seaward in an on-call or unscheduled status. (JP 1-02. SOURCE: JP 3-02)

sea echelon area. In amphibious operations, an area to seaward of a transport area from which assault shipping is phased into the transport area, and to which assault shipping withdraws from the transport area. (JP 1-02. SOURCE: JP 3-02)

sea echelon plan. In amphibious operations, the distribution plan for amphibious shipping in the transport area to minimize losses due to enemy attack by weapons of mass destruction and to reduce the area to be swept of mines. (JP 1-02. SOURCE: JP 3-02)

selective unloading. In an amphibious operation, the controlled unloading from assault shipping, and movement ashore, of specific items of cargo at the request of the landing force commander. Normally, selective unloading parallels the landing of nonscheduled units during the initial unloading period of the ship-to-shore movement. (JP 1-02. SOURCE: JP 3-02)

serial. 1. An element or a group of elements within a series which is given a numerical or alphabetical designation for convenience in planning, scheduling, and control. 2. A serial can be a group of people, vehicles, equipment, or supplies and is used in airborne, air assault, amphibious operations, and convoys. (JP 1-02. SOURCE: JP 3-02)

serial assignment table. A table that is used in amphibious operations and shows the serial number, the title of the unit, the approximate number of personnel; the material, vehicles, or equipment in the serial; the number and type of landing craft and/or amphibious vehicles required to boat the serial; and the ship on which the serial is embarked. (JP 1-02. SOURCE: JP 3-02)

ship-to-shore movement. That portion of the action phase of an amphibious operation which includes the deployment of the landing force from the assault shipping to designated landing areas. (This term and its definition modify the existing term and its definition and are approved for inclusion in JP 1-02.)

shore party. A task organization of the landing force, formed for the purpose of facilitating the landing and movement off the beaches of troops, equipment, and supplies; for the evacuation from the beaches of casualties and enemy prisoners of war; and for facilitating the beaching, retraction, and salvaging of landing ships and craft. It comprises elements of both the naval and landing forces. Also called beach group. (JP 1-02. SOURCE: JP 3-02)

staging area. 1. Amphibious or airborne – A general locality between the mounting area and the objective of an amphibious or airborne expedition, through which the expedition or parts thereof pass after mounting, for refueling, regrouping of ships, and/or exercise, inspection, and redistribution of troops. 2. Other movements – A general locality established for the concentration of troop units and transient personnel between movements over the lines of communications. Also called SA. (JP 1-02. SOURCE: JP 3-35)

stowage. The method of placing cargo into a single hold or compartment of a ship to prevent damage, shifting, etc. (JP 1-02. SOURCE: JP 3-02)

subsidiary landing. In an amphibious operation, a landing usually made outside the designated landing area, the purpose of which is to support the main landing. (JP 1-02. SOURCE: JP 3-02)

support. 1. The action of a force that aids, protects, complements, or sustains another force in accordance with a directive requiring such action. 2. A unit that helps another unit in battle. 3. An element of a command that assists, protects, or supplies other forces in combat. (JP 1-02. SOURCE: JP 1)

supported commander. 1. The commander having primary responsibility for all aspects of a task assigned by the Joint Strategic Capabilities Plan or other joint operation planning authority. In the context of joint operation planning, this term refers to the commander who prepares operation plans or operation orders in response to requirements of the Chairman of the Joint Chiefs of Staff. 2. In the context of a support command relationship, the commander who receives assistance from another commander's force or capabilities, and who is responsible for ensuring that the supporting commander understands the assistance required. (JP 1-02. SOURCE: JP 3-0)

supporting aircraft. None. (Approved for removal from JP 1-02.)

supporting arms. Weapons and weapons systems of all types employed to support forces by indirect or direct fire. (JP 1-02. SOURCE: JP 3-02)

supporting arms coordination center. A single location on board an amphibious command ship in which all communication facilities incident to the coordination of fire support of the artillery, air, and naval gunfire are centralized. This is the naval counterpart to the fire support coordination center utilized by the landing force. Also called SACC. (JP 1-02. SOURCE: JP 3-02)

supporting commander. 1. A commander who provides augmentation forces or other support to a supported commander or who develops a supporting plan. This includes the designated combatant commands and Department of Defense agencies as appropriate. 2. In the context of a support command relationship, the commander who aids, protects, complements, or sustains another commander's force, and who is responsible for providing the assistance required by the supported commander. (JP 1-02. SOURCE: JP 3-0)

supporting operations. In amphibious operations, those operations conducted by forces other than those conducted by the amphibious force. (JP 1-02. SOURCE: JP 3-02)

surface action group. A temporary or standing organization of combatant ships, other than carriers, tailored for a specific tactical mission. Also called SAG. (JP 1-02. SOURCE: JP 3-02)

survey, liaison, and reconnaissance party. None. (Approved for removal from JP 1-02.)

tactical air commander (ashore). None. (Approved for removal from JP 1-02.)

tactical air control party. A subordinate operational component of a tactical air control system designed to provide air liaison to land forces and for the control of aircraft. Also called TACP. (JP 1-02. SOURCE: JP 3-09.3)

tactical air coordinator (airborne). An officer who coordinates, from an aircraft, the actions of other aircraft engaged in air support of ground or sea forces. Also called TAC(A). (JP 1-02. SOURCE: JP 3-09.3)

tactical air direction center. An air operations installation under the overall control of the Navy tactical air control center or the Marine Corps tactical air command center, from which aircraft and air warning service functions of tactical air operations in support of amphibious operations are directed. Also called TADC. (JP 1-02. SOURCE: JP 3-09.3)

tactical air groups (shore-based). None. (Approved for removal from JP 1-02.)

tactical air officer (afloat). The officer (aviator) under the amphibious task force commander who coordinates planning of all phases of air participation of the amphibious operation and air operations of supporting forces en route to and in the objective area. Until control is passed ashore, this officer exercises control over all operations of the tactical air control center (afloat) and is charged with the following: a. control of all aircraft in the objective area assigned for tactical air operations, including offensive and defensive air; b. control of all other aircraft entering or passing through the objective area; and c. control of all air warning facilities in the objective area. (JP 1-02. SOURCE: JP 3-02)

tactical air operation. None. (Approved for removal from JP 1-02.)

tactical control. Command authority over assigned or attached forces or commands, or military capability or forces made available for tasking, that is limited to the detailed direction and control of movements or maneuvers within the operational area necessary to accomplish missions or tasks assigned. Tactical control is inherent in operational control. Tactical control may be delegated to, and exercised at any level at or below the level of combatant command. Tactical control provides sufficient authority for controlling and directing the application of force or tactical use of combat support assets within the assigned mission or task. Also called TACON. (JP 1-02. SOURCE: JP 1)

tactical deception group. None. (Approved for removal from JP 1-02.)

tactical-logistical group. Representatives designated by troop commanders to assist Navy control officers aboard control ships in the ship-to-shore movement of troops, equipment, and supplies. Also called TACLOG group. (JP 1-02. SOURCE: JP 3-02)

target classification. None. (Approved for removal from JP 1-02.)

target information center. The agency or activity responsible for collecting, displaying, evaluating, and disseminating information pertaining to potential targets. Also called TIC. (This term and its definition modify the existing term and its definition and are approved for inclusion in JP 1-02.)

task element. A component of a naval task unit organized by the commander of a task unit or higher authority. (JP 1-02. SOURCE: JP 3-02)

task group. A component of naval task force organized by the commander of a task force or higher authority. Also called TG. (JP 1-02. SOURCE: JP 3-02)

task unit. A component of a naval task group organized by the commander of a task group or higher authority. (JP 1-02. SOURCE: JP 3-02)

times. (C-, D-, M-days end at 2400 hours Universal Time (Zulu time) and are assumed to be 24 hours long for planning.) The Chairman of the Joint Chiefs of Staff normally coordinates the proposed date with the commanders of the appropriate unified and specified commands, as well as any recommended changes to C-day. L-hour will be established per plan, crisis, or theater of operations and will apply to both air and surface movements. Normally, L-hour will be established to allow C-day to be a 24-hour day. a. **C-day.** The unnamed day on which a deployment operation commences or is to commence. The deployment may be movement of troops, cargo, weapon systems, or a combination of these elements using any or all types of transport. The letter "C" will be the only one used to denote the above. The highest command or headquarters responsible for coordinating the planning will specify the exact meaning of C-day within the aforementioned definition. The command or headquarters directly responsible for the execution of the operation, if other than the one coordinating the planning, will do so in light of the meaning specified by the highest command or headquarters coordinating the planning. b. **D-day.** The unnamed day on which a particular operation commences or is to commence. (JP 3-02) c. **F-hour.** The effective time of announcement by the Secretary of Defense to the Military Departments of a decision to mobilize Reserve units. d. **H-hour.** The specific hour on D-day at which a particular operation commences. e. **H-hour (amphibious operations).** For amphibious operations, the time the first assault elements are scheduled to touch down on the beach, or a landing zone, and in some cases the commencement of countermine breaching operations. (JP 3-02) f. **L-hour.** The specific hour on C-day at which a deployment operation commences or is to commence. g. **L-hour (amphibious operations).** In amphibious operations, the time at which the first helicopter of the helicopter-borne assault wave touches down in the landing zone. (JP 3-02) h. **M-day.** The term used to designate the unnamed day on which full mobilization commences or is due to commence. i. **N-day.** The unnamed day an active duty unit is notified for deployment or redeployment. j. **R-day.** Redeployment day. The day on which redeployment of major combat, combat support, and combat service support forces begins in an operation. k. **S-day.** The day the President authorizes Selective Reserve callup (not more than 200,000). l. **T-day.** The effective day coincident with Presidential declaration of national emergency and authorization of partial mobilization (not more than 1,000,000 personnel exclusive of the 200,000 callup). m. **W-day.** Declared by the President, W-day is associated with an adversary decision to prepare for war (unambiguous strategic warning). (This term and its definition modify the existing term and its definition and are approved for inclusion in JP 1-02.)

transport area. In amphibious operations, an area assigned to a transport organization for the purpose of debarking troops and equipment. (JP 1-02. SOURCE: JP 3-02)

transport group. An element that directly deploys and supports the landing of the landing force, and is functionally designated as a transport group in the amphibious task force organization. A transport group provides for the embarkation, movement to the objective, landing, and logistic support of the landing force. Transport groups comprise all sealift and airlift in which the landing force is embarked. They are categorized as follows: a. airlifted groups; b. Navy amphibious ship transport groups; and c. strategic sealift shipping groups. (This term and its definition modify the existing term and its definition and are approved for inclusion in JP 1-02.)

vertical landing zone. A specified ground area for landing vertical takeoff and landing aircraft to embark or disembark troops and/or cargo. A landing zone may contain one or more landing sites. Also called VLZ. (JP 1-02. SOURCE: JP 3-02)

vertical takeoff and landing aircraft. Fixed-wing aircraft and helicopters capable of taking off or landing vertically. Also called VTOL aircraft. (JP 1-02. SOURCE: JP 3-02)

vertical takeoff and landing aircraft transport area. None. (Approved for removal from JP 1-02.)

wave. A formation of forces, including ships, craft, amphibious vehicles or aircraft, required to beach or land about the same time. Waves can be classified by function: scheduled, on-call, or non-scheduled. Waves can also be classified by type of craft, e.g., assault, helicopter, or landing craft. (This term and its definition modify the existing term and its definition and are approved for inclusion in JP 1-02.)

JOINT DOCTRINE PUBLICATIONS HIERARCHY

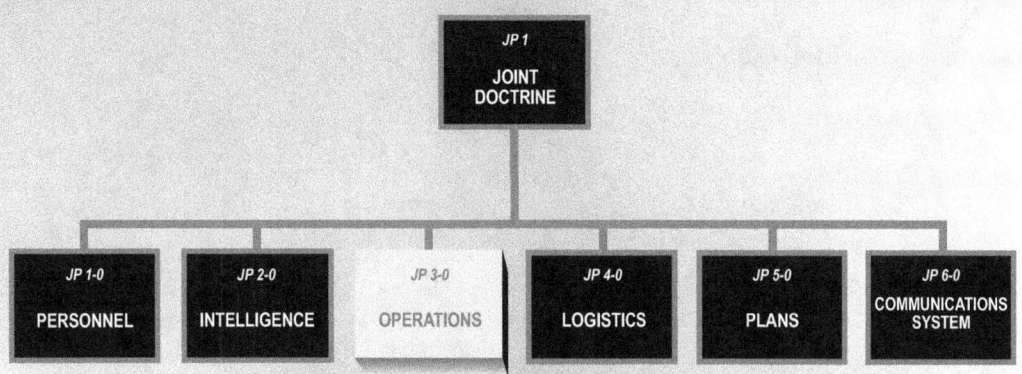

All joint publications are organized into a comprehensive hierarchy as shown in the chart above. **Joint Publication (JP) 3-02** is in the **Operations** series of joint doctrine publications. The diagram below illustrates an overview of the development process:

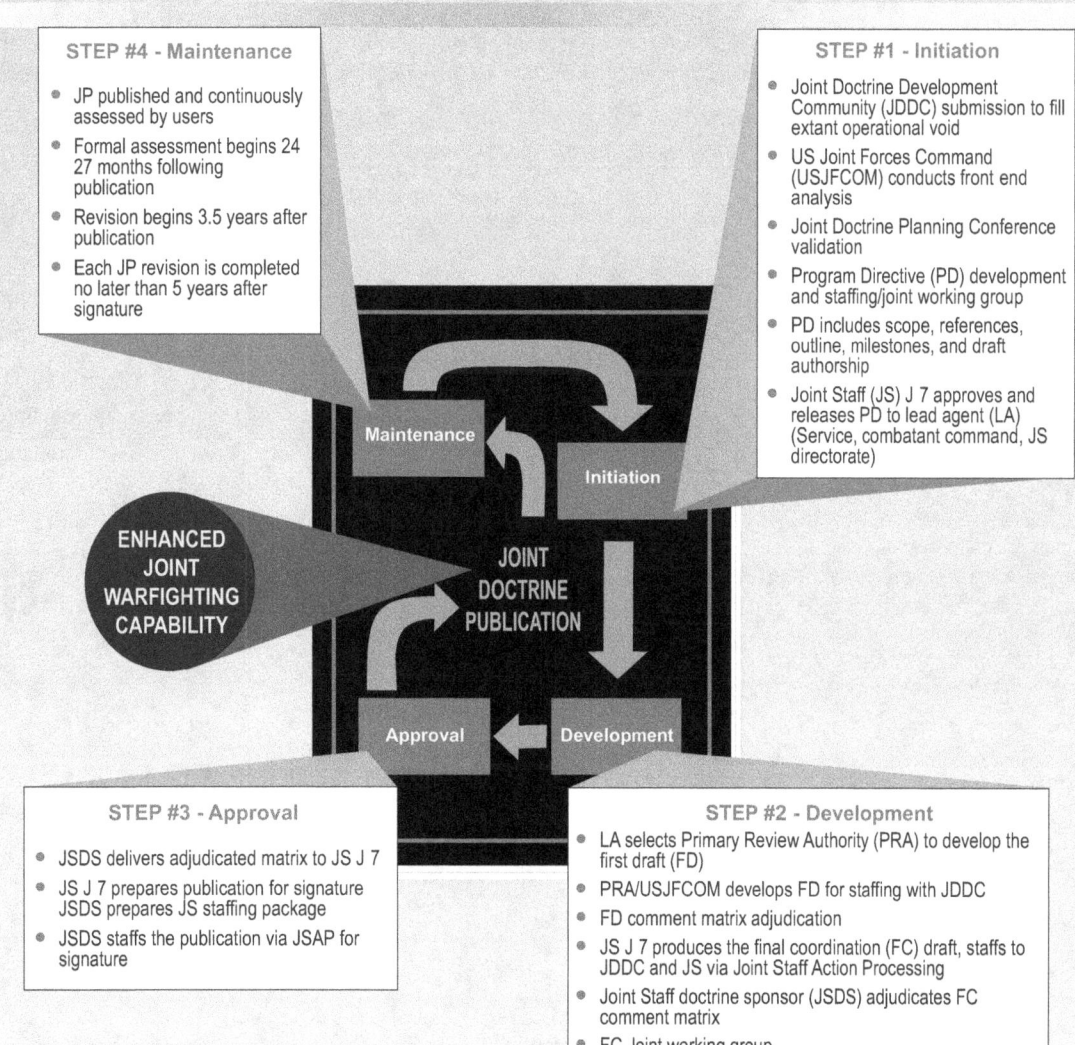

STEP #4 - Maintenance

- JP published and continuously assessed by users
- Formal assessment begins 24 27 months following publication
- Revision begins 3.5 years after publication
- Each JP revision is completed no later than 5 years after signature

STEP #1 - Initiation

- Joint Doctrine Development Community (JDDC) submission to fill extant operational void
- US Joint Forces Command (USJFCOM) conducts front end analysis
- Joint Doctrine Planning Conference validation
- Program Directive (PD) development and staffing/joint working group
- PD includes scope, references, outline, milestones, and draft authorship
- Joint Staff (JS) J 7 approves and releases PD to lead agent (LA) (Service, combatant command, JS directorate)

STEP #3 - Approval

- JSDS delivers adjudicated matrix to JS J 7
- JS J 7 prepares publication for signature JSDS prepares JS staffing package
- JSDS staffs the publication via JSAP for signature

STEP #2 - Development

- LA selects Primary Review Authority (PRA) to develop the first draft (FD)
- PRA/USJFCOM develops FD for staffing with JDDC
- FD comment matrix adjudication
- JS J 7 produces the final coordination (FC) draft, staffs to JDDC and JS via Joint Staff Action Processing
- Joint Staff doctrine sponsor (JSDS) adjudicates FC comment matrix
- FC Joint working group